Thank you for your
continued support!

The Global War on Your Guns

Inside the U.N. Plan to
Destroy the Bill of Rights

Wayne LaPierre

NELSON CURRENT

A Subsidiary of Thomas Nelson, Inc.

Published in Nashville, Tennessee, by Nelson Current, a division of a wholly-owned subsidiary (Nelson Communications, Inc.) of Thomas Nelson, Inc.

Nelson Current books may be purchased in bulk for educational, business, fundraising, or
sales promotional use. For information, please e-mail SpecialMarkets@ThomasNelson.com.

Library of Congress Cataloging-in-Publication data on file with the Library of Congress.

ISBN 1-59555-041-0

Printed in the United States of America

06 06 07 08 09 10 QW 5 4 3 2 1

Acknowledgments

For a decade, I have been warning American gun owners about the threats to our Second Amendment rights posed by gun-ban bureaucrats at the United Nations. Over that time, it has been increasingly clear to me that, as one who loves our country and the freedom for which it stands, I needed to sound the alarm with great clarity and intensity. The result is this book chronicling U.N. hypocrisy, corruption, and its blatant contempt for freedom, human rights, and self-defense for ordinary citizens worldwide. It could not have seen the light of day without the expertise of David B. Kopel who, as a preeminent scholar and writer, has been skillfully tracking the international gun ban crusade even longer than I. In sections of this work, you will see David's exhaustive research and insights unfold, since his findings are so powerful as to demand inclusion along with my own first-hand observations. As a researcher, David takes a backseat to no one when it comes to documenting the indictments contained herein with facts crucial to this debate.

To four million fellow members of the National Rifle Association,
whose unyielding allegiance and selfless activism have thus far
safeguarded American freedom from the
global offensive of the United Nations

Contents

Acknowledgments: iii

Introduction:
The U.N. Gun Ban Treaty vii

Chapter 1:
Global Repression: The International Gun Control Movement 1

Chapter 2:
U.N. Disarmament Agenda: Looking Back, Looking Forward 19

Chapter 3:
Demonizing Lawful Gun Owners 39

Chapter 4:
Choking off the Second Amendment in the United States 53

Chapter 5:
*Congress and the Second Amendment: Views of the
Popular Branch* 61

Chapter 6:
U.N. Gun Prohibition: One Country at a Time 91

Chapter 7:
United Nations Corruption 105

Chapter 8:
United Nations and Genocide: A Historical Perspective 125

CONTENTS

Chapter 9:
More Gun Control for Genocide Victims 151

Chapter 10:
The U.N. and Terrorism: A Blood and Money Trail 161

Chapter 11:
Don't Trust Direct Democracy 187

Chapter 12:
U.N. and the Internet 207

Epilogue 223

Notes 227

Index 269

INTRODUCTION

The U.N. Gun Ban Treaty

It was 1996, in the dark days of the Clinton administration, when I first began to sound the alarm to the unsuspecting gun owners of our nation. The gun-ban lobby, having been forced to a standstill in Congress, was looking for new avenues on which to attack our Second Amendment rights. At the same time, the vast apparatus of the United Nations and its associated non-governmental organizations was fresh off a global campaign to ban land mines and looking for a new rallying cry. It was 1997 when a U.N. panel of "government experts on small arms" delivered a formal recommendation for a global conference to be held in the near future. The goal? A global treaty to restrict "small arms and light weapons."

The U.N. had plunged headlong into the gun-ban business.

Upping the ante in 1999, the U.N. issued another demand for a small arms conference to be held in 2001. They were making a high-stakes bet on the outcome of the 2000 presidential election. They were counting on Al Gore to not only take the Oval Office, but also encourage the creation of the global gun-ban manifesto as the next natural step of the relentless Clinton-Gore drive to destroy Americans' Second Amendment rights. And so the conference was slated for July 2001, to make sure that the newly elected Gore would have enough time to install the antigun lobby's operatives into key positions with authority over the United States' negotiating positions. Self-appointed social engineers all over the world were silently cheering for the Gore campaign, and the major funders of the global gun-ban movement poured their resources into shadowy political operations intended to ensure a Gore victory.

The plan was simple, and the bets were laid. But the silk-stocking set forgot to account for a single, major political force that would come to play a pivotal role in the presidential election—the National Rifle Association, and more importantly, its base of grassroots supporters.

NRA president Charlton Heston and I went on the road for weeks leading up the presidential election. In every city we visited, our message was simple: our gun rights could not survive another four years of Clinton-Gore assaults. We took our message to the heartland and to the battleground states. Just before the elections, we held our last rallies in Tennessee and Arkansas—just to make sure that the voters who had first elected Clinton and Gore would know exactly how far their favored son had strayed from their home state's political values. At every venue, capacity crowds jammed shoulder-to-shoulder to hear our message and to join our battle cry in unison—to "Vote Freedom First" and elect George W. Bush to the U.S. presidency.

The outcome is now well-charted in history. Against the backdrop of the agonizing weeks spent on the Florida recounts, analysts were musing over results that indicated vast departures from past voting history. Against all odds and predictions, George W. Bush had won Arkansas, Tennessee, and three other states, states that Bill Clinton himself credited the NRA with helping President Bush to win.[1] Once the Supreme Court put an end to the partisanship in Florida, the victor was declared.

We were all exhausted for weeks. It had taken every penny we could muster to pay for the advertising, direct mail, phone banks, and political rallies. It had taken every ounce of personal energy to keep up the breakneck pace of weeks of political rallies, some of them held in three different cities per day. And it had taken every last vote we could summon from the nation's sportsmen to Vote Freedom First, defeat Al Gore, and protect our rights from another four years of withering assault in the nation's capital.

But the U.N. was another story entirely.

It was too late for the U.N. puppet-masters to beat a strategic retreat. The plan for the gun-ban conference and treaty continued right on pace. The global gun-ban forces planned to avenge their defeated champion Al Gore. They knew that the Bush administration would not let them run roughshod over the constitutionally guaranteed freedoms of American citizens, so they were going to turn the event into a media circus.

And then they made another bet. The demands issuing from the conference would include another conference in 2006, for another bite of the apple after the 2004 presidential elections. And here we are—about to witness the U.N.'s second concerted effort to strip the Second Amendment from our Constitution. This time, however, we don't have to worry about the drafting of a wide-ranging treaty to demand that our rights be sacrificed on the altar of global political correctness.

Because this time, the treaty is already in place. It has been for five years.

In July 2001, the conference stage was set, and I traveled to New York City just to observe the spectacle. The official title of the meeting was "United Nations Conference on the Illicit Trade in Small Arms and Light Weapons in All its Aspects"—not the first or last time the U.N. crowd would demonstrate its passion for long, ambiguous phrases to describe the proceedings.

You see, there really are no definitions at the U.N. Specific meanings for terms of discussion would force the diplomats to abandon their rambling rhetoric. Diplomacy as practiced at the U.N. includes intentional vagueness, apparently intended to spare the diplomats from being forced to make concrete decisions over agreed-upon terms. There are no definitions, and there are no votes. The only progress made by the body as a whole would come in the celebrated process of "consensus." Consensus, to my observation, meant wearing down your opponents with media ambushes and other confrontations designed purely to reduce resistance.

But it was immediately clear to me what the terms "small arms and light weapons" meant to the U.N. delegates. As I climbed the steps to the U.N. building on that morning, I came across the single most prominent statue on the plaza. It shows a revolver with its barrel twisted into a pretzel. And when I stepped in the doors, I saw another special piece of "artwork" commissioned specifically for the conference. It consisted of more than 7,000 rifles, pistols, and shotguns crushed into the shape of a cube. Over the cube shined a single light from above, "epitomizing hope for change in the future." Other themed artworks designed to inspire the conference included murals entitled "Guns 'R Us" and the "Mural of Pain," the latter showing photos and drawings of "victims of gun violence."

There were no pictures of mortars, shoulder-fired rockets, heavy crew-served machine guns, or anything else you and I might consider to be "small arms and light weapons." There was no criticism of rogue military forces or genocidal governments. The conference and its artwork focused only on the "scourge of small arms" and the "flood of weaponry," with all fingers pointed to the United States and our "lax gun laws" as their source.

No, the target of the conference was revolvers, pistols, shotguns, and rifles. Your guns. And your rights.

The day before the conference opened, the spectacle was fully underway. And what a show! Remember, the staff and diplomats at the U.N. are outnumbered many fold by the representatives of non-governmental organizations, or NGOs. Thousands of these groups are accredited at the U.N. and make a full-time living from pressing their demands before the body. The largest and most influential NGOs serve as puppet-masters for delegates who support their extremist agendas. With supreme arrogance, the NGOs refer to themselves and their pet delegates at the U.N. as "civil society."

Media grandstanding is part and parcel of their program. Even before the conference was officially underway, supporters took to the streets with giant protest puppets, most depicting the newly elected President Bush in a less-than-flattering light. The U.N. itself made its plaza available for a day-long series of speeches, exhibits, displays, posters, and video-loop "documentaries." The crowning touch was a page from the U.S. antigun lobby playbook, the so-called Silent March, where thousands of shoes were arranged on a red carpet. There were candles and incense, singing, and much holding of hands. It had all the hallmarks of protest marches in the nation's capital, complete with hundreds of barefoot NGO activists, except here the protesters were also the professionals. The next day, they would move into the U.N. building in force, and play a major role in the outcome of the negotiations.

Let's talk about what happens during a U.N. conference. Most folks probably envision the typical shot of the U.N. chamber, with delegates plugged into headphones offering translation to their native tongue. This scene did play out during the conference, but it is only the smallest part of the proceedings.

The bulk of the theater takes place outside the U.N. building, with staged events and media productions built around themes assigned to different days of discussion. The first day of the gun-ban conference was called "Small Arms Destruction Day," complete with a U.N.-issued handbook "to aid those in charge of such destruction." Countries around the world were encouraged to destroy "confiscated, collected, seized, or surplus" firearms and to invite the local media for maximum exposure.

Other themes to play out during the conference included "Children's Day" and "Women's Day," as well as Africa, Asia, and Latin America Day. And the U.N. helpfully published a daily "Disarmament Times" newspaper to help keep activists up to speed on the day's events. A total of 119 of the approved 177 NGOs registered for the conference, dispatching 380 representatives. Some of those NGOs were umbrella groups, such as the International Action Network on Small Arms (IANSA), which in turn includes more than 500 other NGOs. That made for plenty of street theater during the conference.

Back in the U.N. headquarters building, the discussions proceeded at several levels. The only visible evidence of the conference came in the form of regular speeches offered by delegates of participating countries. These vague, rambling speeches touched on various issues within the negotiations, occasionally offering a nation's perspective but still couched in blurred, equivocal rhetoric that seemed essentially meaningless. The U.N. also allowed the NGOs to make their own presentations to the delegates, a process that reminded me of the frequent sight on Capitol Hill of a lone congressman speaking to an empty chamber.

The real action went on in dozens of conference rooms deep in the bowels of the building. That's where hundreds of staff-level negotiators from the major participating nations hammered out specific language to propose to their country's delegates upstairs. The United States had representatives present from its headquarters, U.N. staff, the Department of State, the Department of Defense, and dozens of smaller agencies. But it's impossible to know what's going on in these discussions, as they are closed to the public and to NGOs as well. In fact, the entire two final days of the conference were conducted in closed session, when the major nations finally began to negotiate in earnest over the final document.

It struck me as more than mildly ironic that the U.N., an institution purportedly striving for democracy and representative government all over the globe, would conduct its business behind an unyielding façade of official silence. *Where was the outrage?* My professional lifetime has been devoted to affecting the policy decisions of elected lawmakers. In the fifty state legislatures and U.S. Congress, not even our fiercest enemies ever tried to deprive us of the opportunity to witness debate and affect the outcome of votes. Here, there would be no voting. There would be no opportunity to witness the real debate over the provisions of the treaty. And there was certainly no way to lobby the delegates for or against anything in particular, if by chance you could find out what was really under debate behind closed doors.

The process needed a central focus, a starting point from which to draw our battle lines. And that's when Undersecretary of State John Bolton showed up.

Undersecretary Bolton was then fairly new to the job. Appointed by President George W. Bush, Bolton had a reputation as a hard-liner in foreign policy, one that was well-deserved. Bolton was once asked, under questioning from a congressman, to explain his approach to negotiating foreign policy with other nations. The congressman suggested to Bolton that perhaps a carrot-and-stick approach would be more fruitful than a hard-line position. Bolton cut him off, saying curtly, "I don't do carrots."

But he brought his stick to the U.N., appearing before the delegates on July 9, 2001. He began his address with the typical flourishes of the U.N. idiom, addressing the audience as "Excellencies and distinguished colleagues." But diplomacy stopped there, and Bolton went directly to the heart of the matter, first attempting to force some definitions into the process.

"Small arms and light weapons, in our understanding, are the strictly military arms—automatic rifles, machine guns, shoulder-fired missile and rocket systems, light mortars," he said. "We separate these military arms from firearms such as hunting rifles and pistols, which are commonly owned and used by citizens in many countries."

Bolton went on: "As U.S. Attorney General John Ashcroft has said, 'just as the First and Fourth Amendments secure individual rights of speech and security respectively, the Second Amendment protects and individual right to keep and bear arms.' We therefore do not begin with the presumption that all small arms and light weapons are the same, or that they are problematic."

Bolton then outlined the opposition of the United States to many of the treaty's proposed elements, saying, "We do not support measures that would constrain legal trade and legal manufacturing of small arms and light weapons. . . . We do not support the promotion of international advocacy activity by international or non-governmental organizations, particularly when those political or policy views advocated are not consistent with the views of all member states. . . . We do not support measures that prohibit the civilian possession of small arms [and] the United States will not join consensus on a final document that contains measures contrary to our Constitutional right to bear arms."

He closed by calling the opposition's bet on a 2006 conference, saying, "The United States also will not support a mandatory Review Conference, which serves only to institutionalize and bureaucratize this process. . . . Neither will we commit to begin negotiations and reach agreement on any legally binding instruments, the feasibility and necessity of which may be in question and in need of review over time."[2]

Timid applause greeted the end of his remarks, but many of the delegates were silently fuming. Bolton had just slammed the door on U.S. participation in the holy grail of the conference—a legally binding global treaty, designed and intended to restrict the rights of American citizens.

But again, the U.N. would not be so easily defeated. The forces behind the gun-ban treaty retreated overnight to recalculate their strategy. By the next morning, their tactic was clear: proceed under the framework established by Bolton's comments, continue negotiations over treaty language considered "politically binding" but not legally binding, and wear down the United States until it surrendered.

Bolton returned to D.C. but left behind his enormous team of negotiators from the various U.S. agencies. The United States also appointed three "public" members of the official delegation, all of whom understood the political implications of the proposed treaty: Congressman Bob Barr of Georgia, former Congressman Chip Pashayan of California, and former U.S. ambassador to Switzerland Faith Whittlesey.

Still, the next ten days played out as a David and Goliath metaphor, with the United States alone in the position of fighting off the biased media, antigun delegations from countries such as Japan and Canada, and the relentless fervor of the hundreds of antigun NGOs represented at the conference.

Other nations that opposed elements of the treaty were content to sit back and let the United States take the heat, knowing from Bolton's speech that the U.S. position was firm, and that they wouldn't have to get their own hands dirty. The central talking point of the global gun-ban elite was to claim that the United States had isolated itself against a global consensus to restrict firearms in a U.N. treaty. On Main Street, USA, this is a claim to glory. But in the hallways of the U.N. building, isolation was considered a major offense against the very concept of the U.N. itself.

Chip Pashayan later told NewsMax.com, "It was magnificent to see the U.S. stand up against these forces and not buckle under to what was international political pressure, which was very formidable notwithstanding the fact that the U.S. is the big boy on the block."[3]

Second Amendment scholar David Kopel, who monitored the discussions, later wrote in *National Review*: "The U.S. delegation consistently rejected efforts at 'compromise,' which would have kept some antigun language in the treaty but made it softer and more ambiguous. An American delegation that was terrified of being 'isolated' would have accepted the ambiguous language—on the theory that the Americans could later apply a pro-rights interpretation to the ambiguities. The Bush delegation was wiser: It recognized that, at the U.N., a conference final document is just the starting point. From there, U.N. bureaucrats will 'monitor' how a country 'complies' with such documents, and the bureaucrats resolving the ambiguities will favor their own radical agendas."[4]

The antigun delegates were befuddled. In the past, they had successfully worked together to wear down the United States in negotiating the specifics of other treaties. The U.S. negotiators were conditioned to moving their positions incrementally in the process, and checking back frequently with their bosses in Washington to see what they could live with. In his NewsMax interview, Pashayan noted, "The people from the State Department would have been more inclined to compromise to produce an agreement, that's their business. But they were prepared to follow the directions coming from above to stick with the 'redlines' and not go along with watered-down language."[5]

Going completely against the grain of the soft and fuzzy consensus process, Bolton's speech had drawn a line in the sand. The United States team had no intention of allowing that line to be crossed, despite the relentless and growing pressure.

The standoff would last beyond the scheduled closing of the conference, forcing negotiators to go into an all-night bargaining session on the final night.

————————————

Delegates were huddled in Conference Room 4 of the U.N. General Assembly building. It was Friday, July 20—slated as the final day of the conference. Tense negotiations had gone on late into the night on Thursday. The major bones of contention had boiled down to two of the "redlines" established in Bolton's speech.

The U.S. team refused to budge on language to prohibit small arms exports to "non-state actors," an artful term coined by the diplomatic set to describe anyone who was not an official government recognized by the U.N. The American team rightly refused this language outright, noting that it would prohibit support for freedom fighters, people resisting tyrannical governments (such as our colonial minutemen at Lexington and Concord) or even long-time allies like Taiwan that are not formally recognized by the U.N. as a state.

The other redline was drawn over language to "seriously consider legal restrictions on unrestricted trade in and ownership of small arms and light weapons." In the alarmingly vague U.N. vernacular, this language amounted to a direct attack on the civilian ownership of firearms of any kind.

African nations were insisting on the "non-state actor" language, due in no small part to their desire to solidify and consolidate power behind their current governments, and strip opposition forces of the means to challenge their authority.

Antigun delegates moved to preserve some shred of the language prohibiting civilian ownership. Conference president Camillo Reyes of Colombia attempted to mediate, proposing a compromise in which the language would be moved to the preamble of the document, where it would be perceived as having less force. At every impasse, Reyes complained about the Americans' stubborn refusal to entertain compromise and ordered the conference to finish debate over some other, unresolved language irrelevant to the core negotiations.

It was by then Saturday morning, about 4 a.m., and the core dispute could be avoided no longer. Canadian negotiators introduced another watered-down version of the "non-state actor" language, which would say only that a nation "has to bear special responsibility when it would send arms to non-state actors." Canada dangled a package deal; if the U.S. would accept this vague statement, it would agree to deletion of the language on civilian ownership. Negotiators fell into silence as they realized that Canada had decided to push the United States to the edge of the envelope.

We said no.

Reyes again criticized the United States and ordered a break. Pashayan told NewsMax that some exhausted members of the negotiating team wanted to accept the Canadian compromise, although it, too, could hamper a future U.S. president in foreign policy. Drawing on more than a decade's experience as a congressman, Pashayan counseled a steady hand, suggesting that the U.S. simply refuse the deal and see what happened next.

Pashayan's counsel was correct. When the conference reconvened, the African nations dropped their demands. Following their lead, the developed nations opposing the U.S. position said they would follow the Africans' lead. As the sun rose over Manhattan, the final document was readied for consideration while the negotiators got a few hours sleep.

The document was consolidated into a single draft and headed with the title "Programme of Action." It would be considered "politically binding," meaning that it lacked legal authority but nonetheless represented the consensus of participating nations. It did not violate any of the American's stated redlines, at least not technically, and it allowed the opposition to salvage some "face" for the time and effort spent on negotiations. In sum, it was the perfect *political* deal—no one was particularly happy with it, it meant essentially nothing in terms of binding law, but it nonetheless allowed everyone involved to say they had "done something" about the problem, whether real or imagined.

U.S. negotiators were not pleased, however, that the final draft still contained a call for a follow-up conference in 2006. But it was too late for more discussions. Reyes quickly brought the final document up for consideration and pronounced it passed by consensus. The delegates then proceeded to deliver a lengthy series of speeches congratulating Reyes for garnering approval, but expressing disappointment that the Americans had prevailed in negotiations.

Pashayan summed up the experience for NewsMax: "This is not the end. This is the beginning skirmish of a war. . . . All of this has to be understood as part of a process leading ultimately to a treaty that will give an international body power over our domestic laws. That is why we must make sure that there is nothing, express or implied, that would give even the appearance of infringing on our Bill of Rights, which includes the Second Amendment."[6]

Now the U.N. is gearing up for the second conference. The Programme of Action is just the starting point for this next round of discussions. Countries will gather to evaluate the effectiveness of the document, and to assess the efforts of participating nations to fulfill its provisions. Not surprisingly, the document has had no effect on containing or preventing global conflict. So the next natural step is to accuse nations of noncompliance, demand far more restrictive language, and insist that the next conference produce a document that is legally binding.

Translation: All fingers will be pointed at America, and all of their demands will once again be focused on your gun collection.

The Programme of Action will be the starting point of the 2006 conference. Our opponents may decide, in the face of stiff U.S. resistance, to not seek changes but simply attempt to make the treaty legally binding. So if there are no changes in the document itself, what impact could the existing document have on our rights?

The answer is—plenty. The language is vague and sweeping, and it doesn't take much imagination to see how the gun-ban crowd could insist on the most extreme reading of its elements. Here's a rundown of the major existing provisions agreed to by consensus in 2001, quoted directly from the document.[7]

INTRODUCTION

To put in place, where they do not exist, adequate laws, regulations and administrative procedures to exercise effective control over the production of SALW (small arms and light weapons) within their areas of jurisdiction, and over the export, import, transit or retransfer of such weapons.

Read it again, and remember, there is no definition of "small arms and light weapons." Not to mention adequate laws, effective control, and transit or retransfer. Who decides what is adequate? Who defines "effective control"? I do know the meaning of transit and retransfer, and these terms encompass merely traveling with firearms and/or giving or selling firearms to friends, family, or at a gun show.

Ensure that comprehensive and accurate records are kept for as long as possible on the manufacture, holding and transfer of SALW.

Comprehensive and accurate records, kept as long as possible. The United States already does that for the manufacturing of firearms, but "holding and transfer" means possession and purchase. Taken in sum, this provision is code for a massive, international gun registration database, a deep pond for unlimited fishing expeditions by U.N. bureaucrats and investigators.

Develop adequate national legislation or administrative procedures regulating the activities of those who engage in SALW brokering.

What is a gun dealer if not a broker between the manufacturer and customer? And here again, what exactly is "adequate"? As the U.S. team realized during negotiations, the answers to these questions will come not from a dictionary or neutral party, but from U.N. bureaucrats who are already on record opposing our constitutional freedoms.

Ensure confiscated, seized or collected SALW are destroyed.

Any Americans who aren't worried about firearms being confiscated have their heads in the sand. In 2005 we saw authorities going house to house in

New Orleans after the Hurricane Katrina disaster, pounding on doors and illegally confiscating firearms. The National Rifle Association stopped them in court, and the judge ordered the confiscated guns returned, but if the U.N. has its way there would be nothing to return but scraps of metal and heaps of ashes.

> *Develop and implement, where possible, effective disarmament, demobilization, and reintegration programmes.*

So after we are disarmed, the U.N. wants us demobilized and reintegrated. I can hear it now: "Step right this way for your reprogramming, sir. Once we confiscate your guns, we can demobilize your aggressive instincts and reintegrate you into civil society."

No thanks.

> *Encourage regional negotiations with the aim of concluding relevant legally binding instruments aimed at preventing, combating and eradicating the illicit trade, and where they do exist to ratify and fully implement them.*

The antigun forces are encouraging countries to use other multinational groups, such as the Organization of American States or the European Union, to negotiate stricter treaties, make them binding, and push them through to ratification. It's intended to open up other fronts of attack, and it has been successful, as you will learn.

> *Encourage the strengthening of moratoria or similar initiatives in affected regions or subregions on the transfer and manufacture of SALW.*

This one is simple. "Moratoria" is the plural of moratorium, a fancy word for ban.

Finally, the real whopper:

> *Promote a dialogue and a culture of peace by encouraging education and public awareness programmes on the problems of the illicit trade in SALW.*

Let's connect the dots here. SALW means our guns. Illicit trade, to many U.N. delegates, means any civilian trade whatsoever. So the "culture of peace" means no guns in civilian hands—a monopoly of force held by the state.

We don't need a dialogue about that concept; our Founding Fathers had a vigorous dialogue when they crafted the Bill of Rights to the U.S. Constitution. They expressly rejected a monopoly of force held by the state, and for good reason. But if the U.N. has its way, our cherished constitutional freedoms will be obliterated to reach the naïve fantasy of a "culture of peace."

I can hear some readers now, "Oh, Wayne's just overreacting. That's not what these people really want."

It is. And you don't have to take my word for it.

In 2004, I traveled to London to publicly debate Rebecca Peters, head of the International Action Network on Small Arms (IANSA). She is the chief of an umbrella group of NGOs, more than 500 of them, who are all working together toward a global gun ban. Debating before an audience at King's College, I was amazed at how openly Ms. Peters was willing to admit the long-term goals of their movement.[8]

Peters quoted U.N. head Kofi Annan as saying, "The easy availability of small arms has contributed to violence and political insecurity, and have [sic] imperiled human security in every way." She told the audience that, "Guns are involved in human rights abuses . . . guns obstruct peacekeeping activities . . . guns hinder development, investment, and tourism."

That's a long indictment! But she was just getting started.

"Guns don't respect borders," she continued, citing the same argument of our national gun-ban groups when they complain about "lax" gun laws in our rural states causing crime in major cities. "There is a patchwork of laws globally," she started, echoing another canard of our domestic debate. And she grabbed one last arrow from the rhetorical quiver of the U.S. gun-ban lobby, claiming that increased crime rates in Britain were due not to their gun bans, but the "loophole" of failing to ban airguns and replicas. And then she told the group that the Programme of Action represented only "moderate measures" to "reform" gun laws globally. She stated that the

U.N.'s efforts to pass a gun-ban treaty represented "civil society saying stop!" to the United States.

It became clear that in Peters's view, our guns were equivalent to military ordnance and weapons of mass destruction. "Treaties are how we deal with nuclear, chemical and biological weapons," she said, "only guns are exempt." She vented her wrath on the United States, saying, "The U.S. should recognize it's not exempt from the world, contributes disproportionately to world problems, and should cooperate."

An audience member pointed out that the U.S. Constitution prevented her vision of "cooperation" with the gun-ban treaty, but she persisted, complaining that the U.S. position represented the attitude that American citizens are "more equal than others."

Peters detailed the starting point of the "moderate reforms" she wanted the U.N. to ram down the throat of America's law-abiding citizens: "owner licensing, registration, certain categories of guns should not be available, and limits on the number of guns civilians can own. Her goal, she claimed, was to "keep guns out of the hands of people who are irresponsible." When asked who that might be, she shrugged, saying that "good people sometimes do bad things" and that lawful self-defense "only happens in the movies."

I told the audience that if Peters and the U.N. couldn't tell the bad people from the good, we were all going to be in a lot of trouble. The audience pressed Peters for more detail on what type of firearms Americans should be allowed to own.

Peters responded, "I think American citizens shouldn't be exempt from the rules that apply to the rest of the world.... Americans should have only guns suitable for purposes they can prove."

An audience member told Peters his target shooting guns had been confiscated, and asked if this disturbed her in any way. She responded, "Countries change, laws change, why are firearms exempt? The definition of sporting activity is always under pressure. Target shooting is not a legitimate sport! If you miss your sport, take up another!"

Now the audience was riled, and Peters was flustered when she delivered her closing remarks, saying: "Guns cause enormous suffering in the world at large. So much for guns and freedom. The U.S. is the country with the largest proportion of its population in prison . . . we should be talking about prevention. People have a right to live free from fear. Wayne has been watching too many movies. Common sense dictates that guns do not make people or societies safer."

The audience had grown skeptical, and I tried to put her words in a larger perspective. I told the crowd that we saw the IANSA mission for what it was—the reemergence of the same old socialist fantasies of the twentieth century—fantasies that prey on citizens who fall for the false promise of social engineering. I described the global gun-ban forces as elitists who think they know better than us how to live our lives, spend our money, educate our children, and protect our homes. They are people who believe that if they could just be in charge, they could make our lives perfect. Their basic premise now is that if you will surrender your right to own a firearm to the whims of a new global bureaucracy, you will be safe. But I counseled the audience to study the history of nations where the social engineers have had their way, and suggested they should think twice about the bargain.

Americans simply won't fall for it, I explained. We are the freest nation in the world, and the false promise of the social engineers is precisely the bargain rejected by our forefathers.

I explained why Peters's vision was so frightening to Americans. Her vision is sweeping international police powers, offensive to every notion of our Bill of Rights. I told the audience to look at her own words, papers, and testimony, and they would find endless demands for recordkeeping, oversight, inspections, supervision, tracking, tracing, surveillance, marking, verification, paper trails, and databases.

And I pointed out that—no matter Peters's lofty words and noble rhetoric—nowhere in her documents would you find any provision by which oppressed people would be liberated or freed from dictatorship. Nowhere in her work is there a thought about respecting the right to self-defense, privacy, property, due process, or political freedom of any kind.

I closed by asking the audience to join the fight for freedom—because these competing visions will now clash again, in 2006 on the debate floors of the U.N. in New York City.

––––––––––––

The U.N. conference is not the only battlefield, it's just the largest. The global gun-ban forces have spent the years since the first conference opening new fronts for the clash of competing visions, and each one poses a unique threat to our freedoms. Each is also intended to add to the growing global clamor for the U.S. to surrender its principled stand on the private ownership of firearms.

Just in October 2005, two other major international groups pushed forward for new restrictions on small arms. At an October 3 meeting in Luxembourg, foreign ministers of the European Union "backed demands for a new international treaty on the arms trade to outlaw trafficking in small arms," according to an article in *Defense News*.[9] Proposed by Great Britain's foreign secretary Jack Straw, the statement was greeted gleefully by global gun-ban groups. Simon Grey, the arms control campaign manager at NGO Oxfam, "hailed the decision as a 'massive step toward stricter' controls on firearms." A hemisphere away, in our own nation's capital, the Organization of American States (OAS) held a two-day meeting "aimed at developing steps to prevent and combat illicit arms trafficking in the Western Hemisphere," according to a press release from our very own Department of State.[10] The assistant secretary-general of the OAS called the arms trade a "transnational scourge," and said its effect on society "ranks among the most disastrous criminal activities against humankind." The meeting was led by a delegate from Colombia and held in accordance with the OAS "Inter-American Convention Against the Illicit Manufacturing and Trafficking in Firearms, Ammunition, Explosives, and Other Related Materials." In the press release, the Colombian delegate called the convention "'groundbreaking and unique' as it is the first binding legal agreement on this issue."

Wait a minute. Isn't this the same "legally binding" concept we're fighting at the U.N.? And why did you never hear about the Senate approving this treaty?

Because it never has. The OAS treaty was first proposed in 1998, during the Clinton years. Since then, the career State Department bureaucrats have pushed for Senate ratification of the proposed OAS treaty, but the Foreign Relations Committee has never taken it up.

But instead of stopping the process, the Senate's considerable delay only inspired the bureaucrats to seek an avenue of less resistance. They recast the proposed treaty as a mere "convention," not requiring Senate approval.

The bureaucrats are surely proud of their work. In the press release, they stated that "the entry into force in 1998 of the Inter-American convention against illicit arms trafficking made the OAS a leader in multilateral efforts to address the problem of illicit weapons trafficking."[11] How did the "entry into force" happen without Senate approval? The press release states, "The United States is a signatory to the convention and supports efforts to 'aggressively' implement its provisions."

So now we have treaties that don't require Senate ratification, by merely making the United States a "signatory" to a "convention" instead.

So much for checks and balances.

————————————

The clash of competing visions is not limited to the United States versus the global gun-ban groups. In the midst are career bureaucrats, both here and abroad, whose jobs depend on negotiating agreements, not making principled stands. They are pushing forward on multiple fronts, out of the public eye, and seemingly without supervision.

This is their business, and we are newcomers to the process, vastly outnumbered by their legions. They are operating in venues that didn't even exist a few short years ago. They are supported by the global media and reinforced by the work of thousands of paid NGO staffers who are dedicated solely to moving a global gun ban forward. We are vastly underfunded compared to the billions of dollars received by NGOs in "international aid and development" grants, some of which originate in our very own tax coffers. There are times when I wonder whether it's even possible to beat them at their own game.

But then I am reminded that this debate is not about process, policy, or global politics. At its core, this debate is about people, and the value we place on freedom.

Another development in October 2005 reminded me of freedom's enduring appeal. Social engineers in Brazil placed a binding gun-ban question on the national ballot for the October 23 elections. With majority support, the ballot question would completely outlaw the sale of firearms and ammunition to private citizens. Rebecca Peters awaited the results of the vote on the edge of her seat, telling *The Nation*, "If it passes, the referendum will show other countries that the gun lobby can be beaten. If that happens, we believe campaigns will arise in other countries, in Latin American and elsewhere, for a moratorium, or for serious restrictions, on the proliferation of guns."[12] There's their favorite word for ban again, "moratorium." And now she's talking about "serious" restrictions, not just the "moderate" ones she outlined in our debate. No wonder she was so excited at the prospect of a national vote in Brazil to ban guns.

On the day of the vote, voters stood in long lines to cast their ballots— voting is mandatory in Brazil, punishable by a fine. Political observers predicted the ban would pass by a landslide. And at the end of the day, however, the referendum was rejected by a vote of nearly 65 percent. Freedom's enduring appeal had triumphed again.

But not for long.

Despite all the pundits who said the referendum would set a global precedent, Brazil's gun-ban groups vowed to try again. The vaunted "will of the people" only seems to count when the people agree with the gun-ban agenda. "This closes the issue now, but maybe the next generation will be able to have this discussion again," said a local leader of the gun-ban campaign. "I hope the whole world will be able to deal with this again."[13]

The whole world will certainly deal with it again—ironically just as Americans celebrate Independence Day on July 4th—when it convenes at the U.N. in the summer of 2006. And freedom will face its fiercest challenge yet, from the concerted forces of the global gun-ban corps who have spent the years since 2001 gearing up for their second bite at the apple—a second attempt to destroy the freedoms that are as American as apple pie.

The chapters that follow will confirm the stakes of this epic battle. And they will illustrate how critical it is for every freedom-loving American to join this battle, and work together to ensure that freedom prevails again.

The U.N., which recently celebrated its sixtieth anniversary, was founded with the highest hopes to promote peace among the world's nations and human rights for the world's peoples. Yet when it comes to both its peacekeeping and human rights missions, the U.N. has proven itself utterly bankrupt. *The Economist* recently brought this manifest failure into sharp relief in an editorial focusing on the U.N.'s disgraceful fifty-three-member Commission on Human Rights. *The Economist* pointed out that the Commission "is packed with members who are themselves serial abusers of human rights." It called Zimbabwe, Sudan, China, Cuba, Saudi Arabia, Nepal, and Russia "a veritable roll call of the worst offenders."[14]

Add to this the almost daily recordings in the media of U.N. corruption, including what can only be described as a "culture of rape" among U.N. peacekeepers around the world. Decent men and women, not only in America but worldwide, must vigorously oppose U.N. attempts to disarm civilian populations—especially those in dire need of the tools for self-defense.

Not long after the United Nations was founded, Sir Winston Churchill offered the following about the new world body: "We must make sure that its work is fruitful, that it is a reality and not a sham, that it is a true temple of peace in which the shields of many nations can some day be hung up, and not merely a cockpit in a Tower of Babel."[15]

When this great leader said "we," he was really speaking of you and me. What would he say today?

Chapter 1

Global Repression: The International Gun Control Movement

Stymied by the outcome of elections in the United States—solidifying pro-Second Amendment majorities in the U.S. House and Senate—the gun-prohibition lobby turned to the courts, filing meritless suits against gun manufacturers with the hope of imposing prohibition through industry bankruptcy. As the lawsuit strategy fell apart, gun-prohibition groups sought victory through international law. Under their new strategy, the further the locus of decision-making moved from democratic, American control, the better the chances for success in achieving universal disarmament through an international, U.N.-backed treaty.

REBECCA PETERS

Billionaire George Soros's protégé, Rebecca Peters, runs the International Action Network on Small Arms (IANSA), which coordinates the gun prohibition efforts of groups around the world, including the Brady Campaign in America. IASNA claims at least 500 accomplices worldwide and is funded with countless millions from governments, international foundations, and billionaires like Soros. In spreading its dangerous doctrine of civil disarmament, IANSA receives the patronage of the same governments that push gun prohibition at the U.N. In effect, IANSA is the cutting-edge public relations arm of the U.N.'s gun prohibition campaign.

When I debated Peters at King's College in London on October 12, 2004, she was very forthright in saying that the gun prohibition movement was aimed squarely at Americans: "Americans are people like everyone else on Earth. They should abide by the same rules as everyone else."[1]

Peters would deny firearms, the proven means of self-defense to resist tyrants and genocide, to good citizens worldwide: "It's not going to be up to each individual person to be like a hero in a movie defending against this threat to freedom."[2]

At the debate, I reminded the audience of NRA's public awareness campaign, which asked: "Would you shoot a rapist before he slit your throat?" She responded by denying even rape victims the right to defend themselves against violent attack:

> Women need to be protected by police forces, by judiciaries, by criminal justice systems. People who have guns for self-defense are not safer than people who don't . . . having a gun in that situation escalates the problem.[3]

When Peters claimed that all she wanted was "moderate" gun control, I repeated her mantra, in which she advocates banning every hunting rifle and works toward eliminating firearms of any kind:

> Your definition of "moderate" is the most extreme definition imaginable. From your own words, here you are in a CNN interview in October 2003. You want to ban every rifle that can shoot over 100 meters. That's basically a football field for people back in the U.S. That's every hunting rifle in the United States. The founding document of IANSA, your very own organization says, and I quote, "Reduce the availability of weapons to civilians in all societies." Duck hunters . . . in Australia. Taking away their pump shotguns. Here's your ad, and I can give you all these NGOs you work with. Pamphlet after pamphlet after pamphlet, I can stack them to the ceiling, where you call for no [right] to individual armament. So let's be honest. You want to take guns away from all people, a global bureaucracy to do it. We're not going to let it happen.[4]

The moderator asked her, "So is that true?" She answered honestly:

> We want to see a drastic reduction in gun ownership across the world. Yes. We want to see much lower proliferation of guns among the civil-

ian population, and also among governments. . . . Yeah, we want to reduce the number of guns in circulation around the world.[5]

Her "moderate" gun-ban plan includes more than just banning every hunting rifle. She wants to ban every semiautomatic shotgun, every semiautomatic rifle, and every single handgun:

> Moderator: Do you believe, as you said in the past, that semiautomatic rifles and shotguns have no legitimate role in civilian hands?
>
> Rebecca Peters: Yes, I do. Semiautomatic weapons are designed to kill large numbers of people. They were designed for military use. Many people have bought them for other purposes, for example, for hunting because they've been available. But there's no justification for semiautomatic weapons to be owned by members of the civilian population. Yes, I believe that semiautomatic rifles and shotguns have no legitimate role in civilian hands. And not only that, handguns have no legitimate role in civilian hands....[6]

Her long-term objective is a worldwide gun ban, which would be enforced against the U.S. In her generosity, she would allow selected Americans to prove that they need a single-shot rifle—with a range of less than 100 meters—for hunting:

> I think American citizens should not be exempt from the rules that apply to the rest of the world. At the moment there are no rules applying to the rest of the world. That's what we're working for. American citizens should have guns that are suitable for the legitimate purposes that they can prove. I think that eventually Americans will realize that their obsession with arming themselves in fear, in a paranoid belief that they're going to be able to stave off the ills of the world through owning guns, through turning every house into an arsenal, eventually Americans will go away from that. I think Americans who hunt—and who prove that they can hunt—should have single-shot rifles suitable for hunting whatever they're hunting. I mean American citizens should be like any other citizens of the world.[7]

Peters extolled a decree she would impose on the U.S., already in effect in the Australia and Great Britain: prohibition of defensive gun ownership. In those countries, she proclaims, "You were not allowed to have guns for self-defense. If you had a gun for self-defense you were breaking the law."[8]

Peters shares that worldview with Neil Arya, who heads Physicians for Global Survival in Canada. He told the U.N. in 2001 that physicians do not care whether firearms are involved in incidents where the shooter was a gangster, a soldier, or a law-abiding gun owner. In this perverse view, no distinction exists between an armed criminal murdering a robbery victim, an innocent victim saving her life by shooting the violent felon, a Nazi soldier shooting a Jew, or an American soldier shooting a Nazi soldier.[9]

Yet it's a view espoused by the U.N., run by dictatorships that facilitate genocide, rape, kidnapping, and slavery around the world. And this is the bankrupt organization that Peters believes should impose its "culture" on the U.S. During our debate, when the question was posed: "Why do you place such unquestioning trust in governments and the United Nations, when you clearly do not trust individuals for the best way to protect themselves and their families?" she replied:

> It's called civilization. Individuals come together. They form societies. They form governments. That's part of the contract that we make. It's a long time gone now since Thomas Hobbes described society as being characterised by a continual fear and danger of violent death and the life of man is solitary, poor, nasty, brutish and short. I have confidence that people coming together into countries are going to operate better than a whole lot of individuals making up their own rules, taking the law into their own hands.[10]

In other words, the dictatorial governments of Iran, North Korea, Cuba, Syria, and China should be empowered to mandate whether peaceful citizens may defend themselves against violence. Exercising the God-given right to protect oneself would no longer exist.

To fully understand the danger the global enemies of freedom pose to our Second Amendment, Americans must understand the ever-shifting vocabulary and bizarre legal theories masking the endgame of the international gun-ban movement.

For the true, sinister meaning of benign-sounding phrases such as "gun control," or "gun law reform," or "sensible firearms regulation," or "violence prevention"—the phony, deceptive vocabulary of the international gun-ban crowd—look no further than the mind of Rebecca Peters and her allies. Their ideology—wherever it is applied—is deadly to freedom.

With Peters, there are no words or phrases that mean what average world citizens might naturally construe. She lives in the murky sea of newspeak of her own invention—Peters-speak, if you will.

Peters's doctrine is based on a concept of collective punishment, or a kind of neo-Marxist redistribution—where guilt is transferred from evildoers, criminals, or mass killers, to be assigned to the innocent masses—law-abiding gun owners. In applying this twisted view on a global scale, her goal is to implement total civil disarmament through the U.N., either by an overriding binding treaty or piecemeal, one country at a time, outlawing and confiscating whole classes of firearms.

To understand what Peters is pushing for on the world scale—what she would do to firearms owners in every nation—those working to protect freedom must study her past to define her words and actions today. The nightmare for peaceable gun owners in Australia is a glimpse into the future for those who are not vigilant and strong.

As the proclaimed architect of the 1996–97 long-gun confiscation in Australia,[11] Peters saw law-abiding firearms owners forfeit more than 700,000 rifles and shotguns for destruction under the guise of what she and the government called a "buyback."[12] The forfeiture scheme, which Peters says "is the world's biggest,"[13] is the seminal example of gun control. And gun control shouldn't be about punishing criminals—"there is in America," she sniffs, "a very entrenched idea that the purpose of gun laws is to punish bad guys."[14]

Australia, Peters has often said, is the standard for the rest of what she calls "civil society"—meaning, a society without gun ownership. She always refers to the 700,000 confiscated and destroyed rifles and shotguns banned in Australia as "inherently dangerous," "weapons of war," as "battlefield weapons," or "military style-weapons," and the media always obliges by adopting her Peters-speak. [15]

But the semiauto and pump shotguns and the self-loading rifles she marks as being "inherently dangerous" were almost all ordinary sporting arms. The official government forfeiture list included all semiauto .22s, including the Ruger 10/22, Winchester Model 1905, and Remington Nylon 66. As for shotguns and center-fire rifles, the list included the Winchester Model 12, Remington 870, Mossberg 500, Browning Auto 5, Remington 1100 and 11-87, Remington 740 and 7400, and the Winchester Model 100.[16] Think of any semiauto sporting long gun and any pump shotgun—whatever the make—those firearms became contraband under Peters's "weapons of war" big lie.

The collected words of Rebecca Peters resemble a Shakespearean aside, she says one thing to the other actors on the stage, then something else past the back of her hand to be heard by her agreeable global partners. For example, at our King's College debate, Peters mocked the use of the term "gun confiscation." She claimed "the gun lobby has very much overstated . . . confiscation, which seems to be the preoccupation of the gun lobby. There has [sic] not been mass confiscation programs."[17]

Nailing Peters down as to her real worldview is simple. Don't believe what she might say to sound moderate—perhaps before an American audience—but bank on what she says when she's pushed into a corner.

Again in the King's College debate—broadcast to a worldwide audience—she characterized her international plan for global gun control through the U.N. as "very, very moderate."[18] Then she defined "moderate" by describing what any American gun owner would recognize as the oppressive nature of what she foisted on her fellow Australians.

> We're not talking about banning *all* guns . . . but "moderate gun control" means people who own guns should have a license. Guns should be registered. It means ensuring that certain categories of guns are not available to private citizens . . . for example, high-powered, rapid-fire ones like the ones we banned in Australia. And there should be a limit on the number of guns civilians can own.[19]

The public outcry that Peters and her fellow gun haters managed and the media hysteria that they manipulated to create Australia's long-gun ban came as a result of a mass killing in the Tasmanian resort town of Port Arthur on April 28, 1996. A lone gunman—a violent sociopath who had repeatedly been brought to the attention of police and mental health authorities to no avail—killed thirty-five people using two semiautomatic rifles, which he had stolen from a licensed collector, after murdering the man and his wife.[20] Port Arthur came weeks after a mass murder of children in Dunblane, Scotland, by a depraved killer wielding a handgun. Britain reacted with a ban on all registered handguns; Australia went after all semiauto rifles and shotguns and all pump shotguns in private hands.

Punishing gun owners in those two formerly free nations made no sense—except when Rebecca Peters's extremist theories were applied. She spelled them out very clearly in Australia, where her concepts for gun control remained out of sight and her goals unachieved until Port Arthur. Then she was everywhere, managing the media, spoon-feeding Australia's prime minister and gun-ban legislative politicians in the states and territories, and pressing them to embrace her model legislation.

One of her international sisters in the global gun-ban movement, Adele Kirsten, a founding member and later director of Gun Free South Africa, wrote a lengthy paper comparing various ban efforts around the world. She shed light on the Australian experience:

> The Australian campaign was not just the result of public outrage to the Port Arthur massacre. A group of social activists had been working on the issue for several years prior to the events. . . . They were surprised when the national media outlets said: "we need uniform gun laws, we need registration of all guns, and we need to ban all semiautomatics."[21]

She quotes Peters here, saying, "We thought we were still trying to establish this as the norm, but in fact what happened is that *it had become so established that these newspapers and TV thought this was their opinion . . .*" Kirsten said it this way: "A defining moment doesn't just happen—it is constructed by social actors."[22] In other words, the media were willing gun-ban allies.

Peters's notions of gun control were like a long-dormant pathenogen incubating. Her ideas—accepted blithely by the media and government as an answer to dealing with a crazed mass murderer—never had anything to do with Port Arthur, or with real crime. They had—and always will have— only one intent: disarming innocent people. For Peters, the Australian gun ban is the global model. She says it over and over. The absolute key element is registration and licensing—which she calls "moderate" and "common sense."

As a reward for her gun-ban success in Australia, Peters received a grant from George Soros's Justice Foundation to "research gun violence and gun control laws internationally, so that countries considering the reform of their gun laws can be informed by the experience elsewhere." Under that arrangement, she became a fellow at the Center for Gun Policy and Research at the Johns Hopkins Bloomberg School of Public Health.[23]

From there, Peters was elevated by her sugar daddy to Programme Director for the Funders' Collaborative for Gun Violence Prevention at Soros' Open Society Institute in New York. With Soros' funds, Peters bankrolled the most notorious punitive lawsuits to destroy the U.S. firearms industry, and then began making demands as a self-styled citizen of the world on all free nations.

In a paper designed to give credence to her new demand for a handgun ban in Australia, Peters and Roland Browne, her former cochair at the National Coalition for Gun Control, laid out a manifesto—the basis for everything she now does on the world stage. The roadmap is titled "Australia's New Gun Control Philosophy: Public Health is Paramount."[24]

In that seminal November 2000 declaration, Peters expanded her theory that if guns were taken from society, all the ills associated with firearms misuse would be curtailed. It is what she believes today as head of IASNA. Of Port Arthur, she said:

> [T]hose killings also propelled Australia to the forefront of the global movement for rational gun laws. The regulatory scheme created by our Police Ministers in 1996 exemplified the new approach to gun policy: treating gun violence as a public health issue, rather than simply as a crime.[25]

She suggests that without private firearms ownership by all ordinary citizens, victims of other violence would be better off:

Likewise a gun law based on the public health approach seeks to reduce the likelihood of threats, assaults and suicide attempts, but especially to improve the victims' chances of survival if those events do occur. An assault with a machete is preferable to one with a gun, because fewer people are likely to be injured and they are more likely to survive their injuries.[26]

Possibly she should try to peddle that curious notion in Rwanda.

As part of her transferal of guilt to innocent gun owners, she offers what has become a common theme in her global gun-ban aspirations:

Regulation based on the public health approach recognizes that most illegal guns are simply legal guns that have been stolen or sold second-hand. Since the supply source for the illegal market is legal owners, imposing greater accountability on legal owners will cut down the flow to the illegal market.[27]

And "greater accountability on legal owners" means that they must forfeit their legal property to prevent it from falling into illegal use. Peters, moreover, ridicules what she says is the downside of the gratuitous punishment she would inflict upon innocent gun owners—loss of their property, loss of their rights, loss of their dignity as human beings by the unjust transfer of public guilt:

From a narrow political perspective, the public health model comes at an electoral price. It involves an obvious encroachment on (perceived by some) rights, being the "right" to own or possess a firearm. The supposed encroachment on this perceived right is heightened in the minds of some gun owners, because, they would say, they have "done nothing wrong."[28]

Those few words sum up the insanity, the injustice of the Peters-Soros worldview, where honest, decent, and above all *innocent* people are punished on a massive scale under their twisted gun-ban dogma. Indeed, in their world the very act of owning guns, exercising a right is doing something wrong.

Although Rebecca Peters has clearly sketched out the long-term goal of a worldwide gun ban, the international gun-prohibition movement is perfectly content with proceeding one step at a time. In recognition of the practical difficulty in disarming every civilian in the world at once, a 2002 U.N. book offers a model national law to require licensing and registration of all gun owners, with no gun owner allowed to possess more than a single handgun, or five guns of any type. Periodic "competency testing" would be required for all gun owners.[29]

Before the 2001 U.N. antigun conference, Peters and her allies released a public letter equating guns with terrorists, calling them "a new source of terror: the glut of small arms and 'civilian' weapons that are seeping from many industrialized nations, through channels both legal and illegal, to virtually all four corners of the globe." Note that the very idea of civilians owning firearms was highlighted by quotation marks.

Of course if a gun-hating government, like the one in South Africa, wants to make gun ownership impossible, it merely has to impose a licensing and testing requirement, and then make it nearly impossible to take the test, and to ensure that the licensing system imposes such extreme delays as to make it impossible to acquire to a license to own or sell firearms.[30]

INTERNATIONAL GUN-CONTROL GROUPS

The number and extent of international gun-control groups is mind-boggling, and, unlike our homegrown radicals, they do not usually maintain a high public profile. They don't have to—they are not particularly interested in affecting the opinions of voters, members of Congress or state legislators. The people they are trying to influence are the decision makers in the international arena who are generally somewhat removed from domestic political pressures—officials in foreign ministries.

These international gun banners work quietly and behind the scenes. Most American gun owners have neither heard of them or have any idea of the resources at their disposal. It is this vast government and foundation money that has enabled these groups to grow at a frightening rate and influence policy all over the world. Let's examine this international web.

INTERNATIONAL ACTION NETWORK
ON SMALL ARMS (IANSA)

The group was started in 1998 and grew out of the relationship between academics/consultants and the U.N. Department for Disarmament Affairs. In 1998, IANSA was an association of thirty-three NGOs from ten countries, but by 2005 it had over five hundred member associations from one hundred countries. It is the leading antigun NGO and coordinates the attendance and participation of its member associations at the various U.N. workshops and conferences. IANSA has a permanent staff and maintains a headquarters in London.

Funding IANSA are the governments of the United Kingdom, the Netherlands, Belgium, Sweden, and Norway.[31] It also receives funding from a broad collection of left-wing foundations, including the Ford Foundation, Rockefeller Foundation, Compton Foundation, Ploughshares Fund, John D. and Catherine T. MacArthur Foundation, and the Samuel Rubin Foundation.[32]

The namesake of the Samuel Rubin Foundation, not coincidentally, was a member of the Communist Party U.S.A. Rubin's daughter, Cora Weiss, now runs the foundation, which is headquartered on United Nations Plaza in New York City. The Foundation funds a variety of far-left and antigun groups,[33] and Cora Weiss is famous for her December 1969 trip to North Vietnam, after which she claimed that American POWs were comfortable in their "immaculate" facilities, and that two released POWs who challenged her claims were "war criminals."[34]

One of IANSA's members is Barbara Frye, a University of Minnesota law professor who is the U.N.'s Special Rapporteur on "the Prevention of Human Rights Violations Committed with Small Arms and Light Weapons." Notice that her very title precludes any consideration of the use of firearms to prevent human rights violations, including genocide.

IANSA's Web site routinely carries features on U.S. domestic gun-control issues such as the end of the so-called assault weapons ban and opposition to the passage of the "Protection of Lawful Commerce in Arms Act," which rightfully shielded firearms manufacturers from lawsuits designed to bankrupt the industry. The involvement of such an NGO, financed by foreign government money, in U.S. domestic political issues is totally improper and unacceptable.[35]

In addition to its member organizations, IANSA has spawned regional affiliates all over the world including, the Southern Africa Action Network on Small Arms (SAANSA), the Nigeria Action Network on Small Arms (NANSA), the Congolese Action Network on Small Arms (RECAAL), the Argentina national network (Red Argentina para el Desarme), the Japan Action Network on Small Arms (JANSA), the Cameroon Action Network on Small Arms (CANSA), the Liberian Action Network on Small Arms (LANSA), the Togo national network, *La Coalition de la Société Civile Togolaise de Lutte Contre la Prolifération des Arms Légères et pour La Paix* and the Serbian national network, *Mreza za Mirovnu politiku* (Network for Peace Politics).

THE SMALL ARMS SURVEY

The Small Arms Survey (SAS) is probably one of the most unique and dangerous antigun organizations in the world.[36] Basically a research institute specializing in small arms issues, it is housed at the Graduate Institute for International Studies in Geneva, Switzerland. The SAS authors a yearly *Small Arms Survey,* published by the Oxford University Press. It also prepares numerous reports looked upon by many governments as objective sources of information on small arms, and does substantial consulting work for the U.N.

The SAS is a large organization with full-time employees and consultants. It is funded by grants from the governments of Australia, Belgium, Canada, Finland, Denmark, France, the Netherlands, New Zealand, Norway, Sweden, Switzerland, and the U.K. Given its resources, credibility, and relationship to the U.N., the SAS is a formidable foe.

CENTRE FOR HUMANITARIAN DIALOGUE

Also operating out of Geneva is the Centre for Humanitarian Dialogue or CHD.[37] It has twenty-one full-time staff, although not all are devoted to small arms issues. The Centre is funded by foundation money and grants from the governments of Australia, Canada, Denmark, Japan, the Netherlands, Norway, Sweden, Switzerland, the U.K., and the U.S.

The CHD has made opposition to civilian possession of firearms its own particular cause. From March 16–18, 2005, CHD hosted a major workshop in Rio de Janeiro, Brazil, entitled "Regulating Civilian Ownership of Weapons."[38] Though there was a request to include representatives of the hundreds of millions of legal firearm owners in the meeting, it was specifically rejected. The conclusions of the workshop were the usual gun control panaceas, bans, registration, and the like.[39]

OTHER INTERNATIONAL ANTIGUN GROUPS: WHO AND WHAT GUN OWNERS FACE

While IANSA works with American gun-ban groups, most of the active international antigun NGOs are not from the U.S. and, with the possible exception of Amnesty International, are not well known in this country. They make up a frightening network of activists:

- Amnesty International

- BASIC (British American Security Information Council): Its main focus is on nuclear issues, but it has been active on the "small arms issue" for ten years.

- Bonn International Center for Conversation: a German disarmament think tank.

- GRIP (*Groupe de recherche et d'information sur la paix et la sécurité*), Brussels: One of the most active international antigun NGOs, it has produced numerous reports on firearms marking, tracing, and brokering.

- ISS (Institute for Security Studies): a South African think tank.

- OXFAM: a U.K.-based peace and disarmament NGO.

- Ploughshares: a major Canadian "peace" NGO, extremely active in the small arms issue from the very start.

- Saferworld: major U.K. peace organization.

- SIPRI (Stockholm International Peace Research Institute), Sweden: also active in the small arms issue for almost ten years.

These individuals are leaders of the international gun-ban movement:

Philip Alpers, New Zealand: Former television producer, now a "gun control" researcher

Ilhan Berkol, Belgium: GRIP

Loretta Bondi, U.S.: Johns Hopkins University

Cate Buchanan, Switzerland: Centre for Humanitarian Dialogue

Wendy Cukier, Canada: Ryerson University

Owen Greene, U.K.: Bradford University

Adele Kirsten, South Africa: Gun Free South Africa

Edward Laurence, U.S.: Monterey Institute of International Studies

Lora Lumpe, Norway: Norwegian Initiative on Small Arms Transfers

Sarah Meek, South Africa: Institute for Security Studies,

Rebecca Peters, Australia: IANSA

Overall there are fifty full-time paid NGO activists working on the gun-ban issue, with total budgets between $5–10 million a year. Remember this is an effort aimed at a small, select group of international decision makers and not fifty legislatures and the U.S. Congress. Given the size of the target audience, this international gun-ban effort represents a large, well-financed movement.

Here is a list of materials international gun control groups distributed to delegates at the 2005 Biennial Meeting of the States on Small Arms that occurred at U.N. Headquarters during July 11-15. These items were given out by the hundreds.

- 4 different books
- 13 different book size reports

- 4 DVDs or software packages on CDs

- 20 different posters

- 6 different T-shirts

- 40 different brochures

- 30 different position papers

- 5 different bumper stickers

- 3 miscellaneous items (folding guides on small arms, etc.)

REGIONAL INTERNATIONAL ORGANIZATIONS

As the U.N. pushes for international gun control, there are also numerous regional efforts. Here is just a very brief overview.

- European Union[40]: The E.U. has been extremely active in the small arms field, issuing proposals to the U.N. and developing its own comprehensive policy.

- Economic Community of Western African States (ECOWAS)[41]: This African regional organization adopted a moratorium on the import and manufacture of small arms in 1997.

- Nairobi Small Arms Protocol[42]: Similar to ECOWAS, these African countries in the Kenya regional adopted their own protocol in 2003.

- Organization of American States[43]: The OAS adopted a Firearms Protocol in 1997. The U.S. has not ratified this instrument.

- Organization for Security and Cooperation in Europe (OSCE)[44]: Most Americans have never heard of the OSCE, a European regional group founded to address security issues. Regardless, it has been very active in the small arms issue, especially the destruction of surplus arms from Eastern Europe.

- South African Development Community[45]: SADC is a regional group and has adopted its own firearms protocol.

FIREARMS OWNERS RESPOND

The National Rifle Association has been defending gun owner rights on the international stage since the mid-1990s and has reached out to hunting and sport shooting groups all over the world to establish a common front against this threat.[46]

In 1997, NRA and several other groups formed the World Forum on the Future of Sport Shooting Activities—the WFSA.[47] The WFSA now has more than forty different groups, including associations from Australia, Austria, Canada, Denmark, Finland, France, Germany, Italy, Ireland, Italy, Japan, Malta, Spain, South Africa, Switzerland, and the U.K. In 1999, the WFSA became an official U.N. Non-Governmental Organization (NGO).

International gun control has been institutionalized at the U.N. It is on the U.N.'s permanent agenda. It is not going to go away. If there is one thing the U.N. does well, it is that it stubbornly stays with a cause year after year. American gun owners have to be at the ready year after year, and we must unify every hunter, sport shooter, and firearms owner in the world if we are to succeed in quashing the fashionable hysteria peddled by gun banners.

It may be tempting to dismiss the threat. Who really takes the United Nations seriously? As international analyst Stefan Halper observed, "After more than a half century, the verdict on the United Nations is in. The data on reform or lack thereof are available for all to see—and they are not a pretty picture. There is abundant evidence that waste, fraud, and abuse are rampant throughout the U.N. system."[48]

Yet the enemies of the right to bear arms are both determined and patient. As is often the case in politics, a small number of activists, with ample funding and sympathetic media coverage, can create the illusion of a consensus—in this case, one for a global gun ban. They see the U.S. Constitution as but a small barrier to their global ambitions. International activists have undertaken a more insidious strategy as well, working to change not only the public perception that Americans have a right to own a firearm, but the legal understanding that the Constitution guarantees the right to gun ownership.

One report contends "there is no evidence of a general right to un-restricted civilian access to arms under any International Human Rights instrument. Even within the United States, where constitutional claims of the civilian right to bear arms are often invoked, courts repeatedly and unanimously have maintained that the U.S. Constitution does not guarantee individuals the right to possess or carry guns."[49]

The U.N. and its many conferences seem far removed from most Americans. But its actions have real consequences, and it is intent on eliminating the right of self-defense for every man and woman on earth. In this way, the gun banners will destroy freedom, for the freedom of self-defense underlies all other liberties.

The governments pushing for a global gun ban recognize this. After all, the vast majority of the nations pushing the arms treaty don't allow their citizens the individual freedoms guaranteed to Americans under the Bill of Rights. It's not just that other governments aren't concerned about liberty, believing that it's not very important. Most actively oppose individual rights. These governments desire to expand their own authority, and gun owner rights stand in the way.

Anyone can look around the world and see how most governments use excessive power. Some honest gun-control activists acknowledge that citizens often purchase firearms because their governments do not protect them.[50] One report even admitted "some make the argument that where democratic institutions are weak, curtailing civilian possession may simply be a means of strengthening the control of authoritarian regimes."[51]

What the advocates of a global gun ban never acknowledge is that virtually all firearm atrocities and massacres around the world aren't committed by individual criminals. Instead, the vast majority of wanton killings around the globe are committed by governments—the members of the U. N. themselves. The same governments that now want to extinguish the right to self-defense in America and every other nation so that only governments will have guns.

Most discussions at the United Nations are deservedly obscure, but the debate over guns really matters. It's about firearm ownership. But not only gun ownership—it's also a fight for individual liberty and national sovereignty. It's a battle for America's soul.

CHAPTER 2

U.N. Disarmament Agenda: Looking Back, Looking Forward

One would think that the end of the Cold War would have little to do with the U.N. global gun-ban movement, but its impact was enormous. The most compelling, dramatic issue of the Cold War involved the possibility of nuclear conflict between the United States and the Soviet Union, spawning what could be called the "disarmament establishment."

The disarmament establishment comprises U.N. disarmament agencies, disarmament bureaucrats, agencies in the various foreign ministries, foreign policy think tanks, academics, and non-governmental organizations (NGOs)—a formidable institution in the truest sense of the word. And, like all institutions, it has institutional survival at the top of its agenda, no matter its public rhetoric.

Notwithstanding the fact that President Ronald Reagan's steadfastness did more to end the Cold War than any arms treaty, disarmament per se continues as an article of faith in the U.N.'s mind-set. That is, arms themselves are bad; they cause wars and cause violence in and of themselves. Once the Cold War ended, the disarmament establishment literally needed a mission, and it wasn't much of a leap for the disarmament crowd to see small arms as its next target. They needed the work and willingly focused on small arms prohibition in a world beset with terrorism, nuclear proliferation, and government-sponsored genocide.

SOWING THE SEEDS

Where both U.N. and U.S. policy-making are political processes, the U.N. disarmament movement has its roots in and depends in large measure on academic conferences, where contacts are made and strategies formulated.

That convergence occurred on February 24–25, 1994, at a conference entitled International Trade in Light Weapons, held in Cambridge, Massachussetts, by the American Academy of Arts and Sciences. The list of thirty-nine participants reads like a Who's Who of the international gun control movement. Participants from the U.S. government were present, as was Jody Williams, the American who would later win the 1997 Nobel Peace Prize for her work to ban land mines.

The academics gathered in Cambridge that winter and mapped out a gun-ban strategy that is still being pursued more than ten years later:

> As can be seen in the long debate on gun control in the United States, nothing happens as long as the "recipients" (gun owners!) can make the argument that possession of such weapons is defensive in nature and adds to stability. [We] would submit that the legislation outlawing semiautomatic weapons in the United States only passed when a majority of the public concluded that it was the *guns themselves* that were a major factor in killings taking place in their cities and neighborhoods. In regard to international transfers of light weapons, this may be difficult to achieve even at the national level, although many states have well-established norms against the possession and trade in these kinds of weapons. But, as noted above, the surfeit (oversupply) of such weapons in the wake of the end of the Cold War makes the problem at a minimum regional or international in nature.
>
> The campaign initiated by human rights and development NGOs to ban antipersonnel land mines serves as an excellent example of what can be done to establish such a norm. In this age of the Internet and CNN, much more could be done to change world opinion regarding the negative consequences of the light weapons trade. . . .[1]

These academics were, and are, the intellectual foot soldiers of the international gun-ban movement. What we have accomplished intellectually in the domestic gun control debate, with scholars such as David Kopel, Don Kates, Steve Halbrook, and others of national repute, has yet to penetrate the international arena where in the past ten years the other side has put out more than thirty books arguing its case for global disarmament.[2]

THE LAND MINE TREATY

In 1997, a watershed event in the history of international relations occurred: the adoption of the international treaty banning land mines, known as the Ottawa Treaty. Significantly, NGOs were its driving force. The effort was unique: NGOs were involved in the actual negotiations of the treaty, and the work was done outside of the U.N. system itself, with Britain's Princess Diana the iconic symbol for the movement.

The adoption of the land mine treaty inspired and empowered the NGO movement. NGOs had been the prime sponsors of the treaty and had, in effect, arranged an alliance with like-minded governments, which made the treaty possible. The second effect was to motivate governments to get ahead of the process and not let NGOs take too much of a leadership role. Another effect was to dangle the ultimate reward in international relations, the Nobel Peace Prize, before the eyes of U.N. gun-ban advocates. A Nobel Prize means (in addition to the cash) a place in history, celebrity status, credibility on just about any issue you want to discuss, and a lifetime of lucrative honorariums and social events.

The thinking, after the successful land mine treaty, was intoxicatingly simple: ban small arms and win the Nobel Peace Prize again.

The litany of heinous gun-related events in Montreal, Dunblane, Port Arthur, and Columbine allowed unscrupulous politicians to ban and confiscate firearms in Canada, the U.K., and Australia. The Montreal incident occurred in 1989, Dunblane and Port Arthur occurred in 1996, and Columbine in 1999. While the U.S. successfully resisted the gun-ban hysteria, these tragic events energized gun-ban movements throughout the world. Antigunners from Canada,[3] Australia, and South Africa[4] formed the leadership cadre of the international gun-ban movement. The U.N., although ostensibly concerned with international matters, also found it convenient to cite these tragedies as justification for its own gun-ban agenda.[5]

Disarmament has always been a priority at the U.N. The Conventional Arms Register came into operation in 1992, and various academics sought to expand it to small arms. The issue was first raised by then U.N. Secretary-General Boutros Boutros-Ghali in a Supplement to an Agenda for Peace in January 1995.[6] It was here a new term, *micro-disarmament*, was used—a concept pushed by the grand dame of the U.N. Department for Disarmament Affairs, Swadesh Rana, a high caste Indian woman and ubiquitous U.N official whose job was to lecture the world on how to behave properly.[7] That year, two parallel U.N. attacks on firearms began.

One came out of the U.N. Department for Disarmament Affairs at its New York headquarters, while the other emerged from the U.N. Office on Drugs and Crime located in Vienna, Austria.[8] Here is the basic chronology:

- In 1995, the U.N. Department for Disarmament Affairs began a series of studies, which led to the U.N. Conference on Small Arms in 2001. The 2001 Conference generated the Programme of Action against small arms that continues to this day to be focal point of much of the international gun-ban effort.

- The U.N. Office on Drugs and Crime began its own formal study of firearms, which would lead to the U.N. Firearms Protocol in 2001. Efforts under the Protocol continue today.

These are extensive, well-financed efforts involving hundreds of U.N. personnel, national government officials, NGO members, and academics. Walk into one of the many conferences on small arms conducted at U.N. headquarters in New York, and you would be awestruck by the size of the conference, the numbers of people involved, and the extensiveness of the program: 500-plus diplomats, U.N. officials, and NGO gun banners all gathered to do one thing—take guns away from every law-abiding citizen in the world. Then, you realize how serious the threat is.

POLITICS IN THE "GLOBAL VILLAGE"

On October 18, 1992, a sixteen-year-old Japanese exchange student, Yoshihiro Hattori, misread an address on the way to a Halloween party and tried to enter a homeowner's garage in Baton Rouge, Louisiana. The owner tragically mistook Hattori for a burglar and shot him. Hattori died and though the homeowner was charged, he was eventually found not guilty. This incident, however, laid the foundations for Japanese efforts at international gun control. The tragedy received major attention in the Japanese media, and Hattori's parents gathered 1.7 million signatures on a gun-control petition, which was presented to President Bill Clinton.[9]

The Clinton administration was sympathetic to the Japanese, and in a speech in 1996 the U.S. ambassador to Japan, Walter Mondale, adopted the theme,

> Our ability to lead in Asia will be largely colored by what we do at home. . . . Many look at violence in America, especially the wanton availability of guns and argue that our emphasis on the individual really means personal license at the expense of social stability.
>
> The importance of this issue has been brought home to me by the number of Japanese citizens who have been killed in America since I have been Ambassador. I have met loving parents who sent young and innocent students to the United States only to have them lose their lives. . . . Failure to deal with violence in America, failure to restrict the use of guns as weapons of wanton bloodshed, is no longer just a domestic issue. It is costing us terribly as world leaders. . . .[10]

Clearly, Walter Mondale was willing to sacrifice American gun owners' Second Amendment rights for Japanese goodwill. And this would prove to be just the opening salvo.

Since the mid-1990s, Japan, which profits from its significant sporting firearms industry (it claims that it doesn't produce small arms, because only military firearms are small arms), has seen to it that gun control stays atop of the U.N. disarmament agenda.

On December 12, 1995, the U.N. General Assembly passed the first of many resolutions on small arms (A/RES/50/70 B). [11]It called for a panel of government experts that was appointed in April 1996, chaired by Ambassador Mitsuro Donowaki of Japan.[12] The effort was staffed by the previously mentioned Swadesh Rana, and the U.N. hired as its consultant Dr. Edward J. Lawrence from the Monterey Institute for International Studies in Monterey, California. Lawrence[13] had been doing consulting work for the U.N. Department for Disarmament Affairs since 1992. More importantly, he was also one of the academics who met in Cambridge in 1994,[14] typifying the incestuous relationship between the disarmament lobby and the U.N. It is a source of funding for the academics, and the U.N. receives the benefits of the spadework of these advocates. Tracing money in the arcane U.N. system is a difficult task, but it was common knowledge that Japan was paying for a substantial part of all of these efforts.[15]

In 1997, the panel of experts issued its report, A/52/298. An early draft was inadvertently circulated, and it contained recommendations for strong limits on civilian possession of small arms. After protests from America, these recommendations were toned down, but the report still contained twenty-four recommendations, not the least of which was that the U.N. hold an international conference on small arms. The report defined what was included in the category of "small arms," with five definitions that cumulatively covered virtually every firearm possible.[16]

In response to the 1997 report, the U.N. General Assembly passed another resolution (A/52/38 J), which called for the appointment of a group of government experts to continue the work on small arms prohibition. The group was appointed in April 1999, and was again chaired by Ambassador Donowaki and staffed by Swadesh Rana. The consultant this time was another disarmament advocate, Dr. Owen Greene, from the University of Bradford in the U.K.

The group submitted its report in August 1999, and among its recommendations was an international conference to be convened no later than 2001 on "the illicit arms trade in all its aspects."[17] The last three words in that phrase were to cause the most trouble for the eventual conference. The advocates of international gun control resemble the old Tammany Hall politician: "I seen my opportunities and I took them!" Their opportunity was to use all of the factors we have discussed to hijack the existing mechanisms and institutions for disarmament between states and use them for good old-fashioned "gun control."

Since America opposes illicit trafficking in small arms—just as on the domestic front we remain opposed to the criminal misuse of firearms—we tried to steer U.N. efforts toward illicit trafficking. International gun-control advocates, however, were determined to expand the focus and thus the addition of the key words *in all its aspects.*

The theme throughout all of these international conferences remained constant: to control illicit small arms, the number of legal arms owned must be reduced. This is why the phrase *in all its aspects* was the opening gun banners sought.

Three formal preparatory committee meetings and innumerable workshops were held prior to the 2001 Conference. This process produced a draft Programme of Action (POA) that the conference was supposed to adopt as its product. This was not to be a treaty, but a commitment on behalf of the agreeing states to continue the U.N. small arms program for at least a five-year period.

The draft POA[18] considered by the 2001 Conference was highly objectionable, written using "U.N. language"[19] and filled with references to humanitarian and development issues. There were no references to the rights of firearms owners, hunting, or sport shooting. The tone was exceedingly antifirearm and internationalist. Many of the issues were totally inappropriate for the U.N. even to be considering. Here are just a few of the provisions found objectionable by the firearms community:

- Article II Paragraph 2[20]—A reduction in the number of small arms (i.e., firearms included).

- II/4—Increased control.

- II/7 and II/10—Record keeping over transfers, which amounted to massive gun registration requirements.

- II/13—A prohibition of transfer of arms to "non-state actors," meaning the U.S. could never arm any insurgent group no matter how oppressive the regime.

- II/16—"Stockpile" control (again, gun registration)

- II/17—Destruction of all surplus arms, destroying the surplus market and making the U.S. Civilian Marksmanship Program illegal.

- II/19—Arms destruction to be public, essentially institutionalizing antifirearms propaganda.

- II/20—A ban on civilian possession of military weapons.

- II/23—"Public awareness" programs (i.e., more propaganda).

- II/24—Regional moratoria on manufacturing, export, and so on.

- II/35—An international instrument of tracing, involving firearms marking or an international registration scheme.

- II/38—Working with "Civil Society" (i.e., institutionalization of the role of NGOs).

- II/39—The promotion of a "Culture of Peace" (i.e., antigun propaganda).

- III/6—More state legislation.

- III/8—The U.N. to get permanently involved in "stockpile management."

- III/18—Funding of advocacy programs.

- IV/1/a—A review conference in the year 2006.

- IV/1/c—A treaty on "tracing."

- IV/1/d—A treaty on restricting manufacturing.

These provisions were being strongly advocated by Japan, Canada, numerous African countries, and most of South America. The U.S., on the other hand, was strongly opposed to most of these proposals. America let it be known that there were certain "red line" items, which, if adopted, would cause the U.S. to reject the conference outcome completely. These included:

- Any limitation on civilian possession.

- Any restrictions on manufacture.

- Any attempt to ban transfers to "non-state actors."

- Any attempt to commit the U.S. to negotiate legally binding treaties on "marking," "tracing," or "brokering."

The stage was set when the conference opened July 9, 2001. Nearly all of the U.N. member states were represented by 500 delegates, and 177 NGOs were also approved to attend. Twelve of the 177 NGOs were from the firearms community.[21] Ambassador Camilo Reyes, of Columbia, was selected as president of the conference. These conferences are huge events that include not only regular "plenary sessions" where states, NGOs and others speak, but innumerable side shows, literature tables, demonstrations, video presentations, and press conferences. A house-trailer-sized sculpture of crushed guns adorned the main U.N. lobby, while the infamous sculpture of a revolver with a knotted barrel stood outside.

On July 16, 2001, the NGOs made their presentations. Thirty antigun NGOs and all twelve pro-freedom groups spoke, among them the National Rifle Association (NRA). Although significantly outnumbered, the firearms community NGOs were given an hour to speak, one-third of the three-hour plenary session for NGO presentations. The difference between the two groups was striking. In short, respectful presentations, gun owners' representatives emphasized civil rights, the heritage of hunting and sport shooting, and the necessity to find real solutions to the issue of violence worldwide. The antigun groups' presentations were an emotional litany of recycled clichés—guns are bad, guns cause violence, and so forth.

Theoretically, decisions are made at most international conferences by consensus. This essentially means that everybody has to agree. It is not that a vote, such as in Congress or the legislatures, cannot be held, but this is usually avoided at all costs. Further, some countries are more equal than other countries. Countries are pressured into agreements at a conference, and diplomats are genetically programmed to compromise and not fight.

To the chagrin of the international gun banners, this was not to be the case at the 2001 conference. On the opening day, Undersecretary of State for Disarmament Affairs John R. Bolton categorically and unequivocally stated the U.S. positions. In the strongest possible terms, Bolton laid down America's position. Here are excerpts from his remarks:

> Excellencies and distinguished colleagues, it is my honor and privilege to present United States views at this United Nations Conference on the Illicit Trade in Small Arms and Light Weapons in All its Aspects.

> The abstract goals and objectives of this Conference are laudable. Attacking the global illicit trade in small arms and light weapons (SA/LW) is an important initiative which the international community should, indeed must, address because of its wide ranging effects.

The illicit trade in SA/LW can be used to exacerbate conflict, threaten civilian populations in regions of conflict, endanger the work of peacekeeping forces and humanitarian aid workers, and greatly complicate the hard work of economically and politically rebuilding war-torn societies. Alleviating these problems is in all of our interest.

Small arms and light weapons, in our understanding, are the strictly military arms—automatic rifles, machine guns, shoulder-fired missile and rocket systems, light mortars—that are contributing to continued violence and suffering in regions of conflict around the world. *We separate these military arms from firearms such as hunting rifles and pistols, which are commonly owned and used by citizens in many countries. As U.S. Attorney General John Ashcroft has said, "just as the First and Fourth Amendments secure individual rights of speech and security respectively, the Second Amendment protects an individual right to keep and bear arms." The United States believes that the responsible use of firearms is a legitimate aspect of national life.* Like many countries, the United States has a cultural tradition of hunting and sport shooting. We, therefore, do not begin with the presumption that all small arms and light weapons are the same or that they are all problematic. It is the illicit trade in military small arms and light weapons that we are gathered here to address and that should properly concern us. (Emphasis added.)

Believing that it is in our interest to stem the illicit trade in military arms, the United States has avidly promoted and supported such international activities as the Wassenaar Arrangement and the U.N. Register of Conventional Arms. Bilaterally, we offer our financial and technical assistance all over the world to mitigate the illicit trade in SA/LW. We have worked with countries to develop national legislation to regulate exports and imports of arms, and to better enforce their laws. We have provided training, technical assistance, and funds to improve border security and curb arms smuggling in many areas of the world where this problem is rampant. And in the past year, we have instituted a program to assist countries in conflict-prone regions to secure or destroy excess and illicit stocks of small arms and light weapons.

[W]e strongly support measures in the draft Programme of Action calling for effective export and import controls, restraint in trade to regions of conflict, observance and enforcement of UNSC embargoes, strict regulation of arms brokers, transparency in exports, and improving security of arms stockpiles and destruction of excess. These measures, taken together, form the core of a regime that, if accepted by all countries, would greatly mitigate the problems we all have gathered here to address.

There are, however, aspects of the draft Programme of Action that we cannot support. Some activities inscribed in the Program are beyond the scope of what is appropriate for international action and should remain issues for national lawmakers in member states. Other proposals divert our attention from practical, effective measures to attack the problem of the illicit trade in SA/LW where it is most needed. This diffusion of focus is, indeed, the Program's chief defect, mixing together as it does legitimate areas for international cooperation and action and areas that are properly left to decisions made through the exercise of popular sovereignty by participating governments.

We do not support measures that would constrain legal trade and legal manufacturing of small arms and light weapons. The vast majority of arms transfers in the world are routine and not problematic. Each member state of the United Nations has the right to manufacture and export arms for purposes of national defense. Diversions of the legal arms trade that become "illicit" are best dealt with through effective export controls. To label all manufacturing and trade as "part of the problem" is inaccurate and counterproductive. Accordingly, we would ask that language in Section II, paragraph 4 be changed to establish the principle of legitimacy of the legal trade, manufacturing and possession of small arms and light weapons, and acknowledge countries that already have in place adequate laws, regulations and procedures over the manufacture, stockpiling, transfer and possession of small arms and light weapons.

We do not support the promotion of international advocacy activity by international or non-governmental organizations, particularly when those political or policy views advocated are not consistent with the views of all member states. What individual governments do in this regard is for them to decide, but we do not regard the international governmental support of particular political viewpoints to be consistent with democratic principles. Accordingly, the provisions of the draft Program that contemplate such activity should be modified or eliminated.

We do not support measures that prohibit civilian possession of small arms. This is outside the mandate for this Conference set forth in UNGA Resolution 54/54V. We agree with the recommendation of the 1999 U.N. Panel of Governmental Experts that laws and procedures governing the possession of small arms by civilians are properly left to individual member states. *The United States will not join consensus on a final document that contains measures abrogating the Constitutional right to bear arms.* We request that Section II, paragraph 20, which refers to restrictions on the civilian possession of arms, to be eliminated from the Program of Action, and that other provisions which purport to require national regulation of the lawful possession of firearms such as Section II, paragraphs 7 and 10 be modified to confine their reach to illicit international activities. (Emphasis added.)

We do not support measures limiting trade in SA/LW solely to governments. This proposal, we believe, is both conceptually and practically flawed. It is so broad that in the absence of a clear definition of small arms and light weapons, it could be construed as outlawing legitimate international trade in all firearms. Violent non-state groups at whom this proposal is presumably aimed are unlikely to obtain arms through authorized channels. Many of them continue to receive arms despite being subject to legally binding UNSC embargoes. Perhaps most important, this proposal would preclude assistance to an oppressed non-state group defending itself from a genocidal government. Distinctions between governments and non-governments are irrelevant in determining responsible and irresponsible end users of arms.

The United States also will not support a mandatory Review Conference, as outlined in Section IV, which serves only to institutionalize and bureaucratize this process. We would prefer that meetings to review progress on the implementation of the Program of Action be decided by member states as needed, responding not to an arbitrary timetable, but specific problems faced in addressing the illicit trade in small arms and light weapons. Neither will we, at this time, commit to begin negotiations and reach agreement on any legally binding instruments, the feasibility and necessity of which may be in question and in need of review over time.

Through its national practices, laws, and assistance programs, through its diplomatic engagement in all regions of the world, the United States has demonstrated its commitment to countering the illicit trade in small arms and light weapons. During the next two weeks, we will work cooperatively with all member states to develop a final document which is legitimate, practical, effective, and which can be accepted by all nations. As we work toward this goal over the next two weeks, we must keep in mind those suffering in the regions of the world where help is most desperately needed and for whom the success of this Conference is most crucial.

Almost two weeks later, when the conference closed in the early morning hours of June 21, 2001, the U.S. had prevailed on every point but one—a review conference in 2006. The Americans had taken one of the toughest stances ever at an international conference. On the final night, pressured by the Europeans, the Japanese, the Canadians and the Africans, the U.S. steadfastly refused to budge on key issues. The other side blinked. The U.S.'s four red lines had not been crossed!

Gun control advocates at the conference were incensed, and antigun NGOs predictably blamed NRA. Typical was Aaron Karp, writing in *The Brown Journal of World Affairs*:

> As activists mobilized in recent years to support efforts to control the spread of small arms, they triggered a response from gun advocates. In a twist of Newtonian physics that should surprise no one, the reaction was opposite and overpowering.
>
> The immediate catalyst was the U.N. Conference which compelled the gun advocates—led by the National Rifle Association—to take the defensive. *The contradictory result of the U.N. Conference was*

leading the NRA to become internationally active for the first time. Even if America's final position at the event had been assembled under President Al Gore, the immense clout of one of the country's most effective single-issue lobbies would still have been felt. As it was under the George W. Bush administration, the impact was just plain huge. *At the Conference itself, the NRA emerged as a greater force than all the 180 other NGOs there combined,* dominating the American delegation to a degree few had previously imagined possible. (Emphasis added.)[22]

John Bolton, of course, is now U.S. Ambassador to the U.N. and one of the strongest defenders of American interests to serve in that role in years. Antigunners never seem to realize that some public officials support the Second Amendment, not because of the power of NRA, but because they truly, sincerely, and personally support that inalienable right. And, much to the dismay of the international crowd, there are public officials in other countries who support the concept behind the Second Amendment—the basic human right to defend oneself from tyranny.

Regardless of this outcome, U.N. efforts to ban firearms continue with numerous small arms projects funded by the U.N. national governments and foundations. Each country is supposed to have a "national point of contact" on small arms and file reports with the U.N. on its activities. Sweden alone reports that it has spent $50 million on small arms projects, and the process internationally has no end in sight.

OPENING SHOTS: THE UNITED NATIONS FIREARMS PROTOCOL

The U.N. office on Drugs and Crime in Vienna launched its efforts at the Ninth U.N. Congress on the Prevention of Crime and the Treatment of Offenders in Cairo, Egypt, April 29 to May 8, 1995. There, Japan introduced its first resolution for international gun control.[23] The Japanese developed the basic theme and concept of international gun control that remains today, i.e., international gun control means domestic gun control in all of the U.N. member states. The background paper supporting the resolution recommended universal registration, bans of civilian possession of military weapons, and a whole series of other onerous measures.[24]

The Japanese media picked up the drumbeat: "Strict gun control is a major contributing factor to the safe society we are proud of [and] Japan must become a leader in gun control in international society."[25]

This was the first international event where NRA had a presence. An NRA member attending the Congress on another matter offered to monitor the Japanese effort. We gratefully accepted his offer, and NRA's very presence had an effect on the meeting. The Cairo meeting started a series of events. An international study of firearms regulation in the various U.N. jurisdictions was authorized.[26] The study was supervised by Canadian James Hayes and paid for by Japan, Canada, and Australia.[27]

A series of four regional workshops on firearms regulations were scheduled: Ljubljana, Slovenia, September 22–26, 1997; Arusha, Tanzania, November 3–7, 1997; Sao Paulo, Brazil, December 8–12, 1997; and New Delhi, India, January 27–31, 1998. The workshops would reach absurd recommendations: paying taxes before being allowed to own a firearm; a limit of one firearm per person; a medical exam; upper and lower age limits; smooth bore firearms only; and no collecting of firearms except by museums.[28] Both NRA and antigun groups were present at these workshops, but there was a systematic exclusion of these private groups from many of the meetings on the grounds that sensitive "law enforcement matters" were being discussed.

In 1998, a resolution was adopted accepting the international firearms study and starting the process of drafting an "international instrument to combat the illicit manufacturing of and trafficking in firearms, their parts and component and ammunition." The actual form of this instrument was that of an attachment, or "protocol," to an international "convention" against transnational organized crime that was being drafted at the same time. A "convention" is nothing more than a broad treaty signed by more than two states.

THE UNITED NATIONS FIREARMS PROTOCOL: AN EXERCISE IN HYPOCRISY

The effort to draft what became known as the firearms protocol proceeded until March 2, 2001, when it was adopted as one of the four protocols attached to the U.N. Transnational Organized Convention. The firearms protocol was modeled on the Organization of American States Firearms Protocol which went into effect in July 3, 2005 without ratification by the U.S.

The U.N. firearms protocol does not contain any of the more radical proposals mentioned earlier, but it serves as an excuse for states that sign it to pass more and more harassing firearms legislation. The most objectionable aspects of the firearms protocol are what it does not do.

Throughout the drafting of the protocol, and the parallel effort on the disarmament side, there did emerge a very limited consensus on a few things that might actually impact illegal trafficking of firearms. One of these was that all firearms should be marked with a unique serial number. This of course is long-standing U.S. law. It was on this point that real hypocrisy of U.N. gun-ban efforts emerged.

Although there is a requirement, under the protocol, that all firearms be marked with the name of the manufacturer and a unique serial number, there are two exceptions to this rule. One exception is galling and the other is a scandal.

The basic marking requirement reads:

Article 8—Marking of firearms
At the time of manufacture of each firearm, either require unique marking providing the name of the manufacturer, the country or place of manufacture and the serial number . . .[29]

The first exception is found in Article 4 of the Protocol:

Article 4—Scope of application
2. This Protocol shall not apply to state-to-state transfers or to state transfers in cases where the application of the Protocol would prejudice the right of a State Party to take action in the interest of national security consistent with the Charter of the United Nations.[30]

In other words, a state can transfer arms that do not have serial numbers to another state. In addition, if a state decides that "in the interest of national security"[31] it wants to manufacture and transfer small arms without serial numbers, it can. This is astounding considering that these types of transfers are the root of much of the perceived problems with small arms. If these transfers are the cause of problems the U.N. says it is concerned with, why exempt them from the marking requirement?

The answer is simple: it is a lot easier to regulate legal firearms owners than it is to control rogue states dumping arms across borders. It is the same hypocrisy we find with domestic gun control efforts, writ large—it is easier to take guns away from law-abiding citizens than it is to take them away from criminals. If this example of U.N. hypocrisy were not bad enough, the second exception to the marking requirement is an outrage.

THE UNITED NATIONS FIREARMS PROTOCOL: THE CHINESE OUTRAGE

Like the beasts in George Orwell's *Animal Farm*, all nations in the U.N. are equal, but some are more equal than others. The U.S. may be the only superpower in the world, but China is the emerging "number two," and everybody at the U.N. knows it. While players at the U.N. love to criticize the U.S., they willingly to defer to China.[32] This is what happened with the U.N. Firearms Protocol. Earlier I quoted the first part of the protocol marking requirement. Here is the rest:

> *Article 8—Marking of firearms*
> At the time of manufacture of each firearm, either require unique marking providing the name of the manufacturer, the country or place of manufacture and the serial number, *or maintain any alternate unique user-friendly marking with simple geometric symbols in combination with numeric and or alphanumeric code, permitting the ready identification by all States of the country of manufacturer . . .*[33]
> (Emphasis added.)

As our academic friends say, let's "deconstruct" this. The phrase starts with "or." In other words, there are two marking requirements found in the article. You can mark firearms with the name of the manufacturer, country/place of manufacture, and a serial number, *or* you can meet the alternative requirement. And what does this alternative require? Well, first, it says "or *maintain*"—meaning countries have to be doing this already. What country is using "simple geometric symbols"? That would be China. This discloses "the country of manufacture," but it does not provide a unique serial number. The bottom line is that there is a special exception in the marking requirement for China, which only places sufficient information on the firearm to allow one to tell that it is from China. This makes a mockery of the whole protocol. Every country in the world that agrees to the protocol must place unique serial numbers on the firearms it manufactures—except China.

How did this happen? The drafting of the protocol in Vienna went until late into the evening of March 2, 2001. At about 10:00 p.m., the translators were far beyond their usual overtime and 200–300 officials attending the meeting were faced with the possibility there would be no agreement because time was running out. That's when the Chinese made their bid to insert special language into the marking article. The head of the U.S. delegation met privately with the Chinese in a closed session without her advisors who usually dealt with firearms matters. Elizabeth Verille was a human rights specialist from the U.S. Department of State and not all that familiar with firearms issues. Verille, like so many State Department regulars, could not face the idea of leaving Vienna without an agreement. She might not have even understood what the language meant. Regardless, she agreed to the Chinese exemption.

The new language was read on the floor and there were immediate objections from those who understood the Chinese proposal. Attorneys attached to the U.S. delegation and experts from the E.U. explained to their delegations the effect of the language. Both the U.S. and the E.U. then tried to amend the Chinese language to include a requirement for an individual serial number. The proposals were rejected.[34]

The Chinese exception is not only in the firearms protocol but also in the POA, as well as other U.N. instruments. So all the pious talk about "marking and tracing" as a tool to save lives in the Third World amounts to a bunch of hokum. Legitimate manufacturers in the U.S. and Europe now face additional paperwork and regulatory burdens in their sales to law-abiding exporters. Meanwhile, the Chinese government is explicitly allowed to feather its nest by continuing the corrupt sale of unmarked guns to evil-doers.

Shocking though this special treatment of a totalitarian state may be, it is hardly surprising. As we shall see beyond all doubt, cozy deals and political corruption are a way of life at the U.N.

CHAPTER 3

Demonizing Lawful Gun Owners

T his is not the end. This is the opening skirmish of a war," announced retired Rep. Charles Pashayan (R-CA, 1979–91), a U.S. delegate to the July 2001 U.N. Small Arms Conference. Pashayan warned that issues of restricting private ownership of firearms and of banning gun sales to persons not authorized by a government (e.g., freedom fighters) would return, even though they were defeated at the conference. As he explained, "All of this has to be understood as part of a process leading ultimately to a treaty that will give an international body power over our domestic laws."

U.S. Sen. Dianne Feinstein (D-CA) agreed: "[T]he Conference is the first step, not the last, in the international community's efforts to control the spread of small arms and light weapons."

As July 2001 approached, Americans sent the U.N. e-mails, protesting the upcoming small arms conference. The U.N. adopted a two-fold scheme to deal with them. First, it turned many of the e-mails over to its security office, apparently under the theory that those citizens holding strong opinions on Second Amendment rights must be dangerous—even though not one of the letters made a threat.[1]

Second, it cranked out a press release claiming that the conference posed no threat to law-abiding gun owners.[2] The last claim was a patent falsehood, although many in the American media took the U.N.'s public relations arm at its word and failed to observe the massive evidence that restricting domestic gun ownership was clearly the intended purpose of the conference.

The U.N. Conference on Small Arms was held in a room where a large poster proclaimed: SMALL ARMS KILL WOMEN & CHILDREN. The two-week conference was the result of General Assembly Resolution 54/54, adopted December 15, 1999. According to the U.N., the conference "was convened to address the increasing threat to human security from the spread of small arms and light weapons and their illegal trade." Note that illegal trade was only part of the threat; the spread of small arms (and that includes every firearm in your gun cabinet) was considered a threat in itself.

At the conference, speaker after speaker made it clear that "excessive" quantities of guns (i.e., any guns in civilian hands) was a problem in itself, separate from the issue of illegal trade. Rey Pagtakhan, the Canadian secretary of state, condemned the "excessive and destabilizing accumulation and uncontrolled spread of small arms."

Ireland's U.N. delegate declared, "States must stop exporting of small arms and light weapons to all except other governments. All states must suppress private ownership of small arms and light weapons."

Yemen's Abdalla Saleh Al-Ashtal explained, "The goal is to prevent any further increase in the traffic in small arms. It is a problem which relates not only to the illicit trade, but to all issues connected with the legal trade." He touted the situation in Yemen, where "individuals voluntarily surrender their weapons. The media is used to convince people to hand over their weapons."

Burchell Whiteman, Jamaica's minister of education, youth and culture, called guns and drugs "a double-barreled force of evil and mayhem." Since the imposition of Jamaican gun prohibition in the 1970s, the Jamaican government has used gun and drug prohibition as justifications for eliminating almost all privacy and due-process elements of the common-law legal tradition.[3] "The time has come," Jamaica's minister continued, "for the international community, particularly states which manufacture arms, to consider the implementation of measures that would limit the production of such weapons to levels that meet the needs for defense and national security." In other words, Jamaica's ban on gun possession by citizens should spread worldwide.

Proposed language required signatory governments to "seriously consider" banning civilian ownership of small arms "designed for military purposes"—a proposal that would outlaw the M1 carbine, M1 Garand (designed for World War II), many antique firearms (designed for the Civil War), and scores of bolt-action rifles (designed for World War I). Since almost all guns are derivative of military designs, the language would have been a wedge for near-total gun prohibition. The U.N.'s January 9, 2001, Draft Programme of Action mandated that "[w]here appropriate, moratoria on the production, export and import of small arms and light weapons will be developed and implemented on a regional and subregional basis."[4]

The opening of the conference was marked by the unveiling of *The Art of Peacemaking*, a five-ton sculpture created by Canadians Sandra Bromley and Wallis Kendal with a subsidy from the Canadian War Museum. The sculpture consists of 7,000 firearms welded together into a giant cube, designed to remind viewers of a tomb or a prison.[5] This sculpture perfectly symbolized the U.N. philosophy of guns: violence comes not from the human heart, but from "bad" objects, and the duty of the U.N. is to destroy those objects.

The American media blazed with fury that the National Rifle Association was impeding U.N. efforts to control rocket launchers. But the U.N. definition of small arms plainly did include ordinary firearms, and encompassed revolvers, self-loading pistols, ordinary rifles, semiauto rifles and fully automatic firearms. The light weapons category included heavy machine guns, mortars, hand grenades, grenade launchers, portable anti-aircraft or antitank guns, and portable missile launchers.

Notably, Small Arms Destruction Day and the *Art of Peacemaking* sculpture were not about grenades or rocket launchers; they celebrated the destruction of firearms.

The U.N.'s draft protocol for the conference called for "tighter control over their [firearms and ammunition] legal transfer," for "strengthening current laws and regulation . . . concerning their use and civilian possession," and for "enhancing accountability, transparency and the exchange of information at the national, regional and global levels." This latter goal (a euphemism for universal gun registration in U.N.-run databases) was to be achieved by "systematic tracking of firearms and, where possible, their parts and components and ammunition from manufacturer to purchaser." Government-owned firearms were to be explicitly exempted from these controls.[6]

The European Institute called for "obligatory liability insurance" for gun owners, plus an "ammunition tax" and "firearm recycling deposit"— whose proposed benefits including making guns less affordable. Further, ammunition calibers "5.56 (.223), 7.62 (.308), and 9mm would be reserved for the military and police." So, the thinking went, "In a period of less than 10 years compulsory changes of the calibers of weapons in private possession could be implemented." An ammunition ban "should be acceptable to all nations because it does not directly interfere with national regulations of private ownership of guns."[7]

Likewise pushing for severe domestic restrictions was the euphemistic Eminent Persons Group, consisting of twenty-three antigun politicians[8] including U.S. Senator Dianne Feinstein and Robert McNamara. McNamara followed his tenure as U.S. Defense Secretary during the Vietnam War with an even more destructive tenure as president of the World Bank, through which he shoveled aid and loans to third-world kleptocracies that used the money to oppress their subject peoples. The indigenous victims of the World Bank/kleptocracy alliance are the very people whom the Eminent Persons Group would disarm.

Formally, the conference was intended to adopt a nonbinding protocol, but gun prohibitionists insisted that even a nonbinding document must lead to a mandatory review of national responses.

In short, the U.N.'s protestations that the conference had nothing to do with American gun possession were true only in a hypertechnical sense; the goal was to create long-term international pressure for severe restrictions on American's Second Amendment rights, even though the conference itself would not directly impose those restrictions.

The United States was denounced by the Toronto *Globe & Mail* on July 12, 2001, when it asserted that "the purpose of the U.N. initiative is not to take hunting rifles away from American good old boys. It is to stop the international trafficking of machine guns, rocket launchers and other lethal weapons."

But, of course, the U.N. definition of small arms specifically included: "revolvers and self-loading pistols, rifles and carbines, assault rifles, submachine guns and light machine guns."[9] This definition was created in a report whose page one heading was "General and Complete Disarmament: Small Arms."

Simply because shotguns were not specifically named did not mean that they were excluded from the definition. Certainly the international gun prohibition movement never claimed that shotguns were not among its targets.

The U.N. Conference conveniently ignored data from the *Small Arms Survey 2001*, published by the Graduate Institute of International Studies,[10] which reported that almost all small arms killing of civilians is perpetrated by organized crime, pirates/bandits, and rebel groups. Collectively, these groups possess about 900,000 guns—only two-tenths of 1 percent of all the small arms in the world. Fifty-six percent of the world's 551 million small arms are held by private citizens, 41 percent by armies, and 3 percent by police forces.

In other words, in the world as in the U.S., more than 99 percent of firearms are possessed by decent citizens or issued to military and law enforcement agencies. Firearms misuse is perpetrated almost exclusively by criminals who own a fraction of 1 percent of all the guns.

If the real objective were to reduce misuse, then nations would follow the lead of the U.S., which has extremely strict laws on the export of small arms, including firearms. All firearms made or sold in the U.S. must have registration marks, allowing for tracing. The American export controls are far more rigorous than the controls of the hypocritical nations like the U.K. and Sweden, which impose near-prohibition on their own people, while often turning a blind eye toward exports to terrorists and gangsters.

And as in the U.S., the misuse of two-tenths of 1 percent is a pretext for prohibitionists to outlaw every lawfully possessed firearm.

GLOBAL GUN REGISTRATION:
THE EXPLICIT FIRST STEP TO CONFISCATION

At the 2001 Small Arms Conference, one of the buzzwords of gun-prohibition advocates was the need for "transparency" in small arms. This was shorthand for saying that there should be no privacy regarding gun ownership and government authorities should have a list of every gun owner and every gun in the country. Registration has been used over the years to facilitate gun confiscation in Canada, the United Kingdom, Australia, Jamaica, California, New York City, Nazi-occupied Europe, Soviet-occupied Europe, the Philippines, Bermuda, and many other places. Registration is a critical step to total gun prohibition. U.N. disarmament staff have explicitly stated the advantage of registration as a preparatory step toward confiscation.[11]

A U.N. press release touted mandatory gun registration for every (non-government) firearm anywhere in the world, but said that a U.N.-controlled registry was "premature"—not that a U.N. registry was a bad idea, just premature in light of current political realities. [12]

The Canadian government, having sunk over two billion dollars into its domestic gun registry, and having used gun registration for gun confiscation, pushed hard for international registration mandates. Apparently the Canadian government's failed registration scheme would look less foolish if other governments followed suit.

"Transparency for thee, but not for me" could be the U.N. motto. While trying to abolish privacy for gun owners, the U.N. barred the press from the debate and deliberation on the official Programme of Action. Americans would be appalled if Congress threw the press out of the Capitol while debating a gun law, but that is precisely what the U.N. did.

To the extent that gun "transparency" can actually help track down how criminals and terrorists obtain firearms, the world's responsible firearms manufacturers already provide it.

Since the Gun Control Act of 1968, all guns manufactured in or imported into the U.S. must have serial numbers and markings indicating the identity of the manufacturer and place of manufacture. In conjunction with the U.N. Conference, the world's firearms manufacturers, working through their World Forum on the Future of Sport Shooting Activities, signed an agreement with the Eminent Persons Group to provide similar markings on all their firearms. Such identification has never been objectionable to the manufacturers. At a previous international conference, the only reason that a binding agreement on markings was not achieved was that China objected. Later, the "Protocol against the Illicit Manufacturing of and Trafficking in Firearms" specifically exempted China—even though the hugely corrupt Chinese military is an enormous source of arms for warlords, criminal gangs, and despots throughout the Third World.

The U.S. has not signed the Protocol, but the Canadian government has. Canada's former ruling Liberal Party used the Protocol as a pretext to require that all firearms imported into Canada undergo a special marking and stamping process that will add about $200 to the cost of each gun. The Protocol does require marking, but not the extreme process recently imposed by the Canadian government. Abuse of the law in Canada shows how any international gun control treaty, if ratified by the U.S., could easily be twisted by an antigun U.S. administration to impose severe restrictions on law-abiding gun sales and ownership.

At the 2001 U.N. Small Arms Conference, the U.S. again supported firearms identification—provided that the language clearly did not open the door for registration of gun owners. That's good enough for legitimate investigations—but not good enough for the prohibition groups that planned to use the trade in illicit arms as a pretext for destroying the privacy of every (non-government) gun owner in the world.

Another component of the U.N.'s gun prohibition program is ammunition control, supported by falsehoods from the gun prohibition lobbies. For example, a May 2005 report titled "Biting the Bullet" claims that ammunition is terribly dangerous, because it spontaneously explodes.[13] Rules against "stockpiling" ammunition (that is, owning a few hundred rounds) and against home reloading are clearly in the works.

U.N.-SPONSORED GUN-BURNING FESTIVALS AND THE DEMONIZATION OF GUN OWNERS

The U.N. is fiercely determined to eradicate "the gun culture." The beginning of the conference on July 9, 2001, was commemorated with the celebration of the U.N.'s Small Arms and Light Weapons Destruction Day. Around the world, governments made huge piles of firearms—not firearms owned by the government, but rather firearms seized by the government from citizens.[14] Of course, guns meant for destruction could be crushed— but mere crushing would not excite the special symbolism of destruction by burning.

July 9 was not the first time that governments had lit bonfires to destroy resistance to the power of the government. Germany's Josef Goebbels ordered all Jewish books to be burned in public on May 10, 1933. University towns were centers of Jewish Books Destruction Day.

As the *Völkischer Beobachter* ("Populist Observer") reported on May 12, 1933, "The German student body of the Berlin universities assembled yesterday for a torchlight procession on Hegel Platz. They formed up, accompanied by a truckload of 25,000 books and writings harmful to the people. The procession ended at Opera Platz, where as a symbolic act, these Un-German writings were set aflame on a pile of logs."

The burning of Jewish and un-German books was followed within a few years by the burning of Jews and other un-German people. Jewish Books Destruction Day helped change popular consciousness so as to pave the way for genocide. Likewise paving the way for genocide was the systematic disarmament of Jews and all other opposition elements, in Nazi Germany itself and in conquered territories.

How long until a U.N.-declared official day of hate is celebrated with governments actually killing people?

That day has already come. The U.N.'s Office on Drugs and Crime has declared that every June 26 shall be celebrated as U.N.s' International Day Against Drug Abuse and Illicit Drug Trafficking. June 26 is the anniversary of the signing of the declaration at the 1987 International Conference on Drug Abuse and Illicit Trafficking. The declaration is the basis for the U.N.'s 1988 Convention Against the Illicit Traffic in Narcotic Drugs and Psychoactive Substances. This treaty commits its signatories, including the U.S., to maintaining a policy of domestic prohibition.

The long-term objective of many at the Small Arms Conference was to replicate the success of their predecessors at the Drugs and Psychoactive Substances Conference—creating an international regime of prohibition, enforced not only by individual governments, but by transnational power—and explicitly designed to destroy the freedom of individual governments to choose to change their prohibition laws in the future.

China celebrates U.N. "drug hate day" by executing drug criminals. Although the Chinese Communist government asserts that all the executed are "drug traffickers," Amnesty International has shown otherwise. In one case, a young woman was returning to her home province from her honeymoon in January 1996. An acquaintance offered to pay her to carry a package for him, as is common in China. On the train, she became suspicious, and attempted to open the package, but could not. A ticket checker noticed her agitation and notified the police. The Guangxi High People's Court sentenced her to death on June 26, 1996, in honor of the U.N. antidrug day.[15]

At a 2001 press conference, U.N. deputy spokesman Manoel de Almeida e Silva was asked about China's execution festival. While acknowledging that "as far as I am aware the convention does not provide for the application of the death penalty," the U.N. spokesman would not criticize the Chinese executions.

According to Harry Wu's Laogai Research Foundation, Chinese doctors are required to promptly harvest organs whenever a group of antidrug executions is scheduled. Kidneys, other organs, and even skin are sold for as much as $15,000.[16]

What does the future hold as "Small Arms and Light Weapons Destruction Day" on July 9 works its way onto the U.N. holiday calendar? Will the mass burning of firearms help set the stage for mass executions of gun traffickers? Will the U.N. sponsor events around the world designed to reinforce fears about small arms, and to forestall dissent about small arms prohibition? Regardless of whether one likes or dislikes the U.N. antidrug program, it provides the tested blueprint for a long-term U.N. program against guns.

Already, the public relations effort to equate guns and drugs has begun. The U.N. Development Program announced that drugs are the largest illicit business in the world, and arms trafficking is second. At the Small Arms Conference, Durga P. Bhattarai of Nepal expressed the commonly held view that (non-government) guns were as pernicious as drugs, as he asserted that guns turn children into "addicted killers."

The European Institute for Crime Prevention and Control, which is affiliated with the U.N., was more explicit:

> Bringing the diffusion of firearms under control is not merely a legal act, it requires to overcome the latent gun culture whose 'virus' is more firmly established in some societies than in others. Unfortunately the propagation of the gun culture is presently well entrenched in the global electronic media. Some non-governmental organisations like the US-based National Rifle Association strategically sponsor the gun culture.[17]

Kofi Annan has equated small arms to nuclear weapons or chemical warfare weapons—thus demonizing them and implying that they should never be in civilian hands.[18] He said that small arms are "'weapons of mass destruction' in terms of the carnage they cause."[19]

Annan further claimed that firearms "exacerbate conflict, spark refugee flows, undermine the rule of law, and spawn a culture of violence and impunity. In short, small arms are a threat to peace and development, to democracy and human rights."[20] It would be more accurate to say that Kofi Annan and the corrupt U.N. exacerbate conflict, spark refugee flows, undermine the rule of law, and spawn a culture of violence and impunity, and are a threat to peace and development, to democracy and human rights.

Back in the U.S., Second Amendment activists declared July 9 to be National Firearms Purchase Day, urging citizens to buy small arms or small-arms ammunition.[21]

The litany of disinformation produced by the U.N. and its various organs is staggering. For example, the U.N. and its gun prohibition allies claim that civilian possession of defensive arms impedes economic development. To the contrary, arms possession by law-abiding citizens helps promote the rule of law, and hence promotes economic development. The major cause of economic underdevelopment is corrupt government, a problem that the U.N. abets. Also harming economic development in the Third World are the malaria and AIDS epidemics, both of which are worsened by the U.N.'s war against DDT, and by its funneling of anti-AIDS money to governments that steal much of the aid.[22]

STOPPING RESISTANCE TO TYRANNY

At the 2001 U.N. Small Arms Conference, Iran took the lead in promoting a ban on arms supplied to "non-state actors." The "non-state actors" clause would require manufacturers "to supply small arms and light weapons only to governments, or to entities duly authorized by government." The clause would make it illegal, for example, to supply arms to the Kurds or religious minorities in Iran, in case Iranian persecution or genocide drove them to forcible resistance. The clause would have made it illegal for the U.S. to supply arms to the oppressed Kurds and Shia of Iraq before the Saddam Hussein regime was toppled.

Had the "non-state actors" provision been in effect in 1776, the transfer of firearms to the American patriots would have been prohibited. Had the clause been in effect during World War II, the transfer of Liberator pistols to the French Resistance, and to many other resistance groups, would have been illegal.

At the U.N. conference, the U.S. delegation stood firm against the "non-state actors" clause, rejecting compromise efforts to revise the language, or to insert it into the preamble of the Programme of Action. Although Canada pushed hard, the U.S. would not relent. U.S. Undersecretary of State John Bolton pointed out that the proposal "would preclude assistance to an oppressed non-state group defending itself from a genocidal government."

U.N. Deputy Secretary-General Louise Frechette (of Canada) explained that in some parts of the world, an AK-47 could be obtained for $15 or a bag of grain. Small-arms "proliferation erodes the authority of legitimate but weak governments," she complained.

U.S. delegate Faith Whittlesey replied that the U.N. "non-state actors" provision "freezes the last coup. It favors established governments, while taking away rights from individuals. It does not recognize any value higher than peace, such as liberty."[23]

According to the U.N., any government with a U.N. delegation is a "legitimate" government. This U.N. standard conflicts with the Declaration of Independence standard that the only legitimate governments are those "deriving their just powers from the consent of the governed."

A press release from Silent March complained that the U.S. had "rejected a call for states to stop arming guerrillas in other countries." The press release came after Undersecretary Bolton had explained that the U.S. objected to the provision because it "would preclude assistance to an oppressed non-state group defending itself from a genocidal government."[24]

Silent March promotes itself as a humanitarian group concerned about gun death, but this concern apparently vanishes when the victims are being murdered by governments. This is the moral upside-down world of the U.N. culture, in which victims who resist genocide, and governments that help the victims resist, are condemned as immoral.

Joining with Silent March and Iran to criticize the U.S. position was Gaspar Santos Rufino, vice-minister for defense of Angola:

> African leaders, in analyzing the causes of the proliferation and illicit trafficking of small arms, suggest that Member States and the suppliers should be more transparent in their conduct and go beyond national interests. This means, so far as possible, to impose limits on

the legal production of certain basic goods, to exercise rigorous control of their circulation, and even to destroy surplus production of goods.

It should be possible to do this with small arms and light weapons, as they are not basic goods and will not be missed by our people.[25]

Rufino, of course, is the defense minister of a communist dictatorship that was installed by the Cuban army's small arms and light weapons in 1975–76, and which has permitted exactly one election (criticized by some as fraudulent) in the last quarter-century.

Rufino complained: "In Angola, men with guns in their hands have opposed the legitimate Government for many years. It should be clear that it is imperative to destroy surplus arms, regulate their production in the legislation of manufacturing countries, and sell them to legally constituted and authorized entities."[26]

The "men with guns in their hands" are the men of UNITA, one of the groups that (along with Rufino's communist organization) fought against the Portuguese colonial regime until Portugal surrendered in 1975. Rufino's side would have lost the civil war that followed but for Fidel Castro's modern-day Hessians.

What makes Rufino's dictatorship—created by Cuban "men with guns in their hands"—legitimate? As Rufino shows, beneath the veneer of humanitarian rhetoric, the objective of small arms prohibition is to ensure that unpopular dictatorships enjoy a monopoly of force.

The push for banning gun ownership by "non-state actors" is based on the faulty premise that "the government" is equivalent to "the state." To the contrary, as the Declaration of Independence teaches, it is a self-evident truth that governments are created by the people of a state, in order to protect the human rights of the people.[27] As sovereigns, the people have the authority to change the government when they determine that the government is no longer fulfilling its function of protecting the people's rights. The people are the only true and legitimate rulers of a state, and the government is only their instrument and servant. To the extent that a government is not founded on the consent of the governed, it is illegitimate. As a U.S. federal district court put it, "the people, not the government, possess the sovereignty."[28]

The notion that gun possession by "non-state actors" is always illegitimate is directly contrary to the Second Amendment, which guarantees that the people retain the ultimate sovereignty. The conflict between the U.N.'s gun ban and the American Second Amendment reveals the essence of the modern U.N. vision: government is the master, and people are the servants.

Once we acknowledge that people may legitimately possess small arms in order to resist illegitimate governments, especially genocidal governments, then another favorite term of the prohibition lobby, "transparency," is easier to understand. Applied to individuals, transparency is a euphemism for the abolition of privacy. Applied to gun ownership, transparency means that governments keep track of everyone who owns a gun, and precisely what guns they own. In other words, transparency should be more properly defined as "government registration of private activities." No freedom-loving people would want to register the books they own or read, or their personal medical or health records. The same is true of firearms. Transparency has repeatedly been used by governments to facilitate confiscation of some or all guns—in democracies such as Bermuda, Canada, and England, and in dictatorships such as Nazi Germany, the Soviet Union, and the states conquered by them.

There is no legitimate reason for the government to monopolize firearms, newspapers, religious institutions, home ownership, or any other form of property that helps to preserve a free state. Government is responsible to the people, not to itself. Thomas Jefferson, James Madison, and their fellow patriots all understood this fundamental truth of political legitimacy and common heritage of all mankind. Indeed, America's Declaration of Independence and Bill of Rights are their legacy in enshrining our unique freedoms.

CHAPTER 4

Choking Off the Second Amendment in the United States

Did the work of the National Rifle Association members in the 2000 election matter? If Al Gore had won that election—and he would have won if the NRA had not put George W. Bush over the top in West Virginia, Missouri, Florida, Arkansas, and Tennessee—then the 2001 U.N. antigun conference would have had an entirely different result.

Rather than drawing a line in the sand against a binding international treaty, the U.S. delegation would have enthusiastically supported an extremely repressive treaty.

The Clinton-Gore administration was well aware—as a Kerry administration would also have been—of how effectively the U.N. can be used to impose extreme gun laws in the U.S. During the Clinton-Gore administration, when the draft protocol for the 2001 convention was being prepared in December 2000, it was the Colombian and Mexican delegations, not the American delegation, that offered optional language recognizing that some countries have legitimate traditions of sporting and other gun use.

Now you may wonder, what harm could signing a bad treaty do? After all, the U.S. Constitution requires that treaties be ratified by a two-thirds vote of the U.S. Senate.

There are many ways in which extreme U.N. gun laws could be enforced in the U.S., even without ratification of a repressive treaty by the U.S. Senate.

First of all, the president could call the document an "agreement" rather than a "treaty." Then, instead of needing two-thirds of the Senate, the document simply needs a majority in the U.S. House and Senate for approval. This tactic is precisely how President Bill Clinton convinced

Congress to ratify the North American Free Trade Agreement (NAFTA), which never could have won two-thirds' support in the Senate.

As a practical matter, if a president's party controls both houses of Congress, it is nearly impossible to stop him from building a majority for anything he wants—if the president is willing to commit every resource he has to getting the bill passed. That is how the Clinton gun ban was approved in 1994—by a Democrat president applying extreme pressure (both threats and promises) to normally pro-gun Democrat legislators.

Another back-door approach to extreme gun control would be an international treaty that, on its face, looks innocuous. The treaty might simply contain language about preventing arms transfers to criminals, and perhaps some requirements that countries enact strict controls on commercial firearms exports. (U.S. export controls are already the strictest in the world.) Then, a president might convince a majority of both houses—or two-thirds of the Senate—to make the document into law, since it appears to be harmless to U.S. rights.

The U.N. has a very long history of convincing nations to sign on to treaties with moderate, sensible language, and then—after ratification—twisting that language to impose extremist results.

Consider, for example, the U.N. Convention on the Elimination of All Forms of Discrimination Against Women (CEDAW). If you read the CEDAW, and you believe that a woman ought to be able to work in any job for which she is qualified, you would probably find little to criticize in the language. Not surprisingly, many nations ratified the CEDAW in the belief that they were simply affirming principles of nondiscrimination that they already believed in. The U.S., however, was more cautious, and did not ratify it.

As typical for U.N. conventions, CEDAW carried an attractive name, yet it has been perverted into a program for restricting freedom and eliminating choice for women and families. Patrick Fagan's excellent backgrounder for the Heritage Foundation details how U.N. bureaucrats in nations that have submitted to CEDAW are working to restrict religious freedom, eliminate parental choice about sex education classes, discourage the celebration of Mother's Day, deconstruct the two-parent family, and most of all make it legally, culturally, and economically burdensome for women to choose to stay home with their children.[1]

With truth-in-labeling, the CEDAW would be called "The Convention for the Gradual Replacement of Mothers by Government." The bureaucrats who implement it are profoundly antichoice on family issues, especially the choice of mothers to take care of their children personally.

The U.N. Convention on the Rights of the Child, for example, is being reinterpreted by U.N. bureaucrats in ways never agreed to by the governments that signed the convention. According to the U.N.'s Committee on the Rights of the Child, the convention means that all children, no matter how young, have—with no need for parental consent, or even in opposition to parental wishes—an unlimited right to reproductive and sexual services, and to freedom of association.

Obviously none of the 191 ratifying nations meant to accept such a radical destruction of parental rights. But, as one U.N. watchdog notes: "In light of such Committee actions, U.N. delegates fear it is impossible for countries to know what they are endorsing when they ratify international treaties. What is more, essential power may no longer rest with those who write treaties, but with those who get to interpret them."[2]

Thus, *any* U.N. firearms treaty that becomes law in the U.S. could become a platform for the imposition of extremist gun control, with U.N. bureaucrats, not U.S. voters, making the decisions.

Even worse, U.N. gun prohibition can be imposed in the U.S. without *any* form of approval from Congress. Let's suppose a gun-ban president, say Hillary Clinton, signs a U.N. antigun treaty, for ratification by Congress.

Now consider the Vienna Convention on Treaties, which has been ratified by the U.S. It provides the rules for how nations are supposed to abide by international treaties. One of the rules of the Vienna Convention is that once a nation has signed (not ratified, just signed) a treaty, the nation may not undermine the treaty.

So, relying on the signed but unratified treaty, President Hillary Clinton could start issuing executive orders to impose various gun laws because, she could claim, without executive orders the U.S. would be illegally undermining the treaty.

Would American courts enforce the Second Amendment to defend our rights against international gun control—either in the form of a treaty, or in the form of executive orders based on an unratified treaty?

Not necessarily. It's true that a treaty, even if ratified by the U.S. Senate, cannot directly repeal constitution rights.[3] Many judges, however, would interpret the Second Amendment so narrowly that the right to arms would always give way to the requirements of any "gun-control" treaty. Such judges believe in what they call a "living Constitution"—but what they really mean is a "dead Constitution." They reject a Constitution whose text and intent are the law of the land, favoring instead a Constitution that has no enduring meaning, but can be changed on the whim of a judge, based on the judge's determination of social policy.

Even worse, the very existence of international gun-control treaties, *even treaties that are never signed or ratified by the U.S.*, provides judges with a pretext for choking off Second Amendment rights.

The fact that many nations have nearly obliterated gun owners' rights and the right to self-defense is already an important reason, according to some judges, for interpreting the Second Amendment into protecting nothing at all. The existence of international gun control treaties reinforces their argument that the Second Amendment can be shriveled out of existence.

Supreme Court Justice Stephen Breyer told ABC's George Stephanopoulos that we must rise to "the challenge" of making sure the U.S. Constitution "fits into the governing documents of other nations."[4] In the case of *Knight v. Florida*, Justice Breyer wrote that it was "useful" to consider the death penalty jurisprudence in India, Jamaica, and Zimbabwe.[5] The notion that the U.S. Supreme Court should be guided by courts from the genocidal dictatorship of Robert Mugabe in Zimbabwe is outrageous. And while Jamaica and India have every right to enact their own laws for their own nations, so does the U.S. The American people will no longer be sovereign if courts start interpreting the U.S. Constitution based on the laws of other nations.

In *Grutter v. Bollinger*, in which the Supreme Court was asked to interpret the Fourteenth Amendment to the U.S. Constitution and the federal Civil Rights Act of 1964, Justices Ruth Bader Ginsburg, David Souter, and Breyer cited the Convention on the Elimination of All Forms of Discrimination Against Women.[6] And Justice Ginsburg, in a speech to the American Constitutional Society (a group of left-wing legal activists and academics), celebrated the Supreme Court abandoning the "Lone

Ranger mentality" and being "more open to comparative and international law perspectives."[7]

In the death penalty case *Atkins v. Virginia*, Justice John Paul Stevens wrote the opinion for the majority of the Court, and cited an amicus brief from the European Union. He quoted the E.U.'s statement that "within the world community, the imposition of the death penalty for crimes committed by mentally retarded offenders is overwhelmingly disapproved."

So according to Justice Stevens—and a majority of the Court—the European Union's disapproval is a good enough reason for the Supreme Court to change the meaning of our Constitution. The danger to the Second Amendment is quite obvious, since the E.U. also strongly disapproves of the American right to arms and the American right to self-defense.

Even more perilous, the international gun prohibition movement needs neither a treaty nor the cooperation of even one branch of our government in order to destroy the Second Amendment.

Formal legal documents—such as treaties, conventions, agreements, and declarations—are one source of international law. But international law is also based on "norms" or "customary law." In recent decades, activist lawyers have become extremely adept at fabricating norms and customary law out of thin air. Courts do not always go along with these nonsense-on-stilts arguments, but some could.

So even without a treaty, gun prohibitionists can argue in U.S. courts that international norms compel the court to interpret the Second Amendment, and the states' individual constitutional rights to arms, restrictively.

More ominously, a supposed international norm against civilian gun ownership—especially gun ownership for defense against criminals or a tyrannical government—could also be raised in a foreign court. In *The Second Amendment and Global Gun Control*, attorney Joseph Bruce Alonso describes how U.S. gun manufacturers could be sued in foreign courts.[8]

In a foreign court, the Second Amendment would provide no defense. Nor would any of the due process protections of the U.S. Constitution be applicable. American statutes such as the Protection of Lawful Commerce in Firearms Act would be irrelevant.

The prospect of destroying our Second Amendment through foreign lawsuits is already being developed. In the fall of 2005, the national government of Canada urged Canada's provincial governments to sue American gun companies in Canadian courts. (So far, none of the provinces have acted, but they could change their minds at any time, based on political calculation.)

Importantly, if one day U.S. gun controls are deemed a human rights violation, you can bet a wide variety of legal theories will spring up under which the American firearms industry could be sued in foreign or international courts.

University of Minnesota law professor Barbara Frye has been appointed the U.N. Special Rapporteur on the relationship between guns and human rights. In her role, she has served as an active ally of the gun prohibition movement. For example, in early 2005, she participated in a strategy session in Brazil in which various non-government organizations plotted how to pass a total gun prohibition referendum in that nation in October. The conference was sponsored by Brazil and Viva Rio, the group that pushed the handgun ban.

At the Brazil conference, Frye argued—and remember, she was speaking in her official capacity as the U.N.'s Special Rapporteur supplying an official report to the U.N. Human Rights Commission—that it is a human rights violation for a government not to impose some of the gun-control laws she favors. These controls include, but are not limited to, licensing for all gun owners, "safe storage" (that is, "lock-up-your-gun safety laws" preventing guns from being used in an emergency against an intruder), "and other appropriate measures to remove unwanted small arms from circulation."[9]

Frye, IANSA, and the rest of the U.N. gun-ban bureaucracy are also working on creating a claim that international law already forbids supplying arms to a serious abuser of human rights.[10] The theory could, perhaps, lead to the supplier being sued in a foreign court, or even criminally prosecuted in the International Criminal Court.[11]

Of course, it would be a good idea if the theory would be deployed against governments that actually are gross abusers of human rights—such as Sudan, Zimbabwe, or North Korea. But remember, according to the U.N., the worst human rights abuser in the world is Israel, and the fourth-worst is the U.S.[12]

Frye also says "there is a need to explore the boundaries of the right to self-defense as a general principle of criminal law and its specific application to small arms possession and use."[13] Since Frye is a member of IANSA—whose president, Rebecca Peters, denies that people have any right to self-defense, or to own firearms for self-defense—it is not hard to predict the result of the reexamination that Frye and the U.N. are conducting.

In the Orwellian world of the U.N., America's first freedom amounts to a human rights violation. The total gun prohibition that the U.N. has imposed on other nations, leaving them helpless against criminals, is precisely what the U.N. wants to impose on the U.S. After all, as Peters puts it, the United States has no right to be different from other countries.

The U.N. is the most lethal threat ever to our Second Amendment rights. Even if we avoid the worst possible results at the summer 2006 U.N. antigun conference in New York City, the U.N. and the international gun prohibition movement will continue their war against the Second Amendment. The danger to human rights in the U.S. and around the world grows more deadly every year. Already many thousands of people around the globe have been victims of genocide, because of the "success" of the U.N.'s war on gun ownership. To close our eyes and pretend "it can't happen here" would literally be a fatal error.

CHAPTER 5

Congress and the Second Amendment: Views of the Popular Branch

Highly contentious opinions handed down by the judicial branch cause some Americans to lose sight of the fact that the legislative branch interprets the United States Constitution when it legislates, rendering its own interpretations of what the Constitution permits or does not allow. Indeed, Congress enacts laws intended to protect constitutional rights and, in rare instances, declares the nature of those rights.

On four occasions in American history, Congress has enacted legislation that declared its unequivocal understanding of the meaning of the Second Amendment to the U.S. Constitution. The Second Amendment states: "A well regulated Militia, being necessary to the security of a free State, the right of the people to keep and bear Arms, shall not be infringed." The U.S. Congress adopted that wording and proposed it to the States in 1789 as part of the Bill of Rights, which the states ratified in 1791.

Until recent times, the Second Amendment was understood to mean what it said: it is the people who have the right to keep and bear arms and government may not infringe that right. The existence of this right would promote a well regulated militia composed of the armed populace, which is essential to the security of not just any state, but a *free* state.

That plain meaning of the Second Amendment is reflected in congressional action taken within vastly different historical contexts. Since it is elected (and hence held in check) by the people, Congress has never given any support for the newly minted argument that the Second Amendment fails to protect any right of the people, and instead ensures a nonsensical "collective right" of states to maintain militias. To the contrary, in the Constitution's vocabulary, states have powers, not rights, and federal–state powers regarding the militia are dealt with elsewhere in the Constitution.

On four occasions—in 1866, 1941, 1986, and 2005—Congress enacted statutes to reaffirm this guarantee of personal freedom and to adopt specific safeguards to enforce it.

These statutory declarations by Congress have been the subject of little or no comment by the judiciary or legal historians. The first two were enacted at times of great historical crisis. The 1866 declaration was enacted to protect the rights of freed slaves to keep and bear arms following a tumultuous civil war and at the outset of the subsequent, chaotic Reconstruction period. The 1941 enactment was intended to reassure Americans that preparations for war would not include repressive or tyrannical policies against firearms owners, and it was passed shortly before the Japanese sneak attack on Pearl Harbor, which forced the United States into World War II.

The two more recent enactments sought to reverse outrageous excesses involving America's legal system. In 1986, Congress reacted to overzealous enforcement policies under the federal firearms law by passing reform legislation. And in 2005, as a result of the misuse of the state and federal judicial systems aiming to destroy America's firearms industry, Congress stepped in to end this threat to the Second Amendment.

The hidden history of these four enactments of Congress makes absolutely clear that keeping and bearing arms is an individual right that may not be infringed by the government, whether federal or state.

THE FREEDMEN'S BUREAU ACT OF 1866: THE CONSTITUTIONAL RIGHT TO BEAR ARMS

Like the rest of the Bill of Rights, the Second Amendment was originally viewed by the Supreme Court as guaranteeing individual rights against action by the federal government, but not against the states. At the end of the War Between the States, slavery was abolished; however, Southern states continued to treat black freedmen as if they were still slaves, in part by prohibiting them from possessing firearms and sending militiamen to search freedmen cabins for arms.

In an effort to protect the Second Amendment rights of Southern blacks, Congress passed the Freedmen's Bureau Act in 1866, which declared protection for the "full and equal benefit of all laws and proceedings concerning personal liberty, personal security, and . . . estate . . . including the constitutional right to bear arms. . . ."[1] It also enacted the Civil Rights Act and proposed the Fourteenth Amendment to the states for ratification as an amendment to the Constitution.

The Fourteenth Amendment declares that all persons born or naturalized in the U.S. are citizens. It also prohibits the states from abridging "the privileges and immunities of citizens," and declares that no state shall "deprive any person of life, liberty or property without due process of law," or deny to any person "the equal protection of the laws."

The Freedmen's Bureau Act is key to understanding how Congress interpreted the Second Amendment some seventy-five years after it became part of the Constitution in 1791. It also demonstrates that the right to keep and bear arms was a fundamental right that the general clauses of the Fourteenth Amendment were intended to protect from violation by the states. Indeed, the same two-thirds of Congress that proposed the Fourteenth Amendment to the U.S. Constitution in 1866 also enacted the Freedmen's Bureau Act.[2]

This legislative history begins on January 5, 1866, when Senator Lyman Trumbull of Illinois introduced S. 60, the Freedmen's Bureau Bill, and S. 61, the Civil Rights Bill.[3] To exemplify the need for legislation, black citizens of South Carolina had assembled in a convention and adopted a petition to be submitted to Congress. It stated in part:

> We ask that, inasmuch as the Constitution of the United States explicitly declares that the right to keep and bear arms shall not be infringed—and the Constitution is the Supreme law of the land— that the late efforts of the Legislature of this State to pass an act to deprive us of arms be forbidden, as a plain violation of the Constitution. . . .[4]

The petition became the centerpiece of a speech on the Senate floor by Senator Charles Sumner of Massachusetts, urging protection of the freedmen, saying:

They also ask that government in that State shall be founded on the consent of the governed, and insist that can be done only where equal suffrage is allowed. . . . They ask also that they should have the constitutional protection in keeping arms, in holding public assemblies, and in complete liberty of speech and of the press.[5]

On January 30, Representative Thomas Eliot of Massachusetts, Chairman of the Select Committee on Freedmen, reported the Freedmen's Bureau Bill to the House of Representatives.[6] Eliot quoted from an ordinance of Opelousas, Louisiana, which contained the same deprivations of rights as under slavery, including the following:

No freedman who is not in the military service shall be allowed to carry firearms, or any kind of weapons, within the limits of the town of Opelousas without the special permission of his employer, in writing, and approved by the mayor or president of the board of police. Anyone thus offending shall forfeit his weapons, and shall be imprisoned and made to work five days on the public streets, or pay a fine of five dollars in lieu of said work.[7]

The bill was initially broadly worded, so to assure there would be no mistaking its intent, Rep. Nathaniel P. Banks of Massachusetts called for it to be amended explicitly to provide for everyone "the civil rights belonging to white persons, including the constitutional right to bear arms. . . ."[8]

Freedmen's Bureau Committee Chairman Eliot did just that on February 5 by offering a substitute for S. 60.[9] Among the clarifications was the following:

The next amendment is in the seventh section, in the eleventh line, after the word "estate," by inserting the words "including the constitutional right to bear arms," so that it will read, "to have full and equal benefit of all laws and proceedings for the security of person and estate, including the constitutional right to bear arms."[10]

In a speech urging adoption, Eliot quoted from a report to General O. O. Howard, Commissioner of the Freedmen's Bureau, which described the following conditions in Kentucky: "The civil law prohibits the colored man from bearing arms; returned soldiers are, by the civil officers, dispossessed of their arms and fined for violation of the law."[11] Commissioner Howard observed, "Thus, the right of the people to keep and bear arms as provided in the Constitution is *infringed*. . . ."[12]

The Freedmen's Bureau Bill, including the amendment characterizing "the constitutional right to bear arms" as a "civil right,"[13] passed the House by a landslide vote of 136 to 33.[14]

Senator Trumbull, as instructed by the Committee on the Judiciary, recommended that the Senate concur in the House amendments.[15] Trumbull explained,

> There is also a slight amendment in the seventh section, thirteenth line. That is the section which declares that negroes and mulattoes shall have the same civil rights as white persons, and have the same security of person and estate. The House have inserted these words, "including the constitutional right of bearing arms." I think that does not alter the meaning.[16]

Trumbull, the author of the Freedmen's Bureau and Civil Rights Bills, made it absolutely clear that general language about civil rights and personal security was intended to include the right to bear arms, regardless of whether that right was explicitly mentioned.

The Senate concurred in S. 60 as amended without a recorded vote.[17] The House then approved some unrelated Senate amendments.[18] With that, Congress had passed the Freedmen's Bureau Bill.

As passed, the Freedmen's Bureau Bill provided that, in areas where ordinary judicial proceedings were interrupted by the rebellion, the President should extend military protection to persons whose rights were violated. The text specified in part:

> Wherein, in consequence of any State or local law, ordinance, police or other regulation, custom, or prejudice, any of the civil rights or immunities belonging to white persons, including the right to make and enforce contracts, to sue, be parties, and give evidence, to inherit, purchase, lease, sell, hold and convey real and personal property, and

to have *full and equal benefit of all laws and proceedings for the security of person and estate, including the constitutional right of bearing arms,* are refused or denied to negroes, mulattoes, freedmen, refugees, or any other persons, on account of race, color, or any previous condition of slavery or involuntary servitude. . . .[19]

Meanwhile, discussion on the need to guarantee the right to keep and bear arms continued. Representative William Lawrence quoted General D. E. Sickles' General Order No. 1 for the Department of South Carolina as follows:

I. To the end that civil rights and immunities may be enjoyed . . . the following regulations are established for the government of all concerned in this department: . . .

XVI. The constitutional rights of all loyal and well disposed inhabitants to bear arms, will not be infringed. . . .

Those who had fought for the South in the Civil War were allowed the same right after taking the Amnesty oath or the Oath of Allegiance.[20]

This "most remarkable order," which was published in the headlines of the *Loyal Georgian*,[21] a prominent black newspaper, was thought to have been "issued with the knowledge and approbation of the President if not by his direction."[22] "A Colored Citizen" asked, "Have colored persons a right to own and carry fire arms?" The editor of the *Loyal Georgian* responded:

Almost every day we are asked questions similar to the above. We answer *certainly* you have the *same* right to own and carry arms that other citizens have. You are not only free but citizens of the United States and as such entitled to the same privileges granted to other citizens by the Constitution. . . .

The editor then quoted the following from a Freedmen's Bureau Circular:

Article II, of the amendments to the Constitution of the United States, gives the people the right to bear arms, and states that this right shall not be infringed. Any person, white or black, may be disarmed if convicted of making an improper or dangerous use of weapons, but no military or civil officer has the right or authority to disarm any class of people, thereby placing them at the mercy of others. All men, without distinction of color, have the right to keep and bear arms to defend their homes, families or themselves.[23]

President Andrew Johnson vetoed the Freedmen's Bureau Bill, although his objections had nothing to do with the reference to "the constitutional right to bear arms."[24] Lyman Trumbull criticized the veto, since the bill protected constitutional rights.[25] He quoted from a letter written by Colonel Thomas in Vicksburg, Mississippi, which stated that "nearly all the dissatisfaction that now exists among the freedmen is caused by the abusive conduct of this [State] militia," which typically would "hang some freedman or search negro houses for arms."[26]

The Senate attempted to override the veto, but mustered two votes less than the necessary two-thirds,[27] leaving no point in the House for conducting an override vote. This was the beginning of strained relations between Congress and the President, which would snowball into an unsuccessful attempt to impeach Johnson.

On March 7, Representative Eliot introduced a revised version of the Freedmen's Bureau Bill.[28] As before, it included "the constitutional right to bear arms" in the rights of personal security and personal liberty.[29]

Debate on the Civil Rights Bill was now in full swing. Representative John A. Bingham of Ohio quoted its provisions, including its guarantee of "full and equal benefit of all laws and proceedings for the security of person and property,"[30] and explained that "the seventh and eighth sections of the Freedmen's Bureau bill enumerate the same rights and all the rights and privileges that are enumerated in the first section of this [the Civil Rights] bill. . . ."[31] Bingham then quoted the seventh section of the first Freedmen's Bureau Bill, that provided that all persons shall "have full and equal benefit of all laws and proceedings for the security of person and estate, including the constitutional right of bearing arms. . . ."[32]

The Civil Rights Bill passed both the Senate and the House,[33] but on March 27 President Johnson vetoed it.[34] In the override debate in the Senate, Lyman Trumbull referred to the "inherent, fundamental rights which belong to free citizens or free men in all countries, such as the rights enumerated in this bill. . . ."[35] He quoted a prominent legal treatise as follows: "The absolute rights of individuals may be resolved into the right of personal security, the right of personal liberty, and the right to acquire and enjoy property."[36] The Civil Rights Bill was intended to protect these rights, which the Freedmen's Bureau Bill stated as including the right to bear arms.

The Senate successfully overrode the President's veto.[37] The *New York Evening Post* identified "the mischiefs for which the Civil Rights bill seeks to provide a remedy" as including "attempts to prevent their [blacks] holding public assemblies . . . keeping fire-arms. . . ."[38]

By April 9, the House had also overridden the President's veto, and the Civil Rights Act of 1866 became law.[39] As enacted, § 1 provided:

> [C]itizens, of every race and color, without regard to any previous condition of slavery or involuntary servitude . . . shall have the same right, in every State and Territory in the United States, to make and enforce contracts, to sue, be parties, and give evidence, to inherit, purchase, lease, sell, hold, and convey real and personal property, and to *full and equal benefit of all laws and proceedings for the security of person and property,* as is enjoyed by white citizens. . . .[40]

That remains the law today.[41]

Now that action on the Civil Rights Act was complete, Representative Eliot, on behalf of the Select Committee on Freedmen's Affairs, reported H.R. 613, the second Freedmen's Bureau Bill.[42] As before, the new bill recognized "the constitutional right to bear arms."[43]

Meanwhile, the proposed Fourteenth Amendment to the Constitution passed the House.[44] On May 23, Jacob Howard of Michigan introduced it in the Senate.[45] Senator Howard referred to "the personal rights guaranteed and secured by the first eight amendments of the Constitution; such as freedom of speech and of the press . . . the right to keep and bear arms. . . ."[46] Howard explained: "The great object of the first section of this amendment is, therefore, to restrain the power of the States and compel them at all times to respect these great fundamental guarantees."[47] No one in the Senate disputed that statement. What became the Fourteenth Amendment was clearly intended to protect the right to keep and bear arms from violation by the states.

The Freedmen's Bureau Bill was also debated in the House on May 23.[48] Representative Eliot observed that § 8, which explicitly recognized the right to bear arms, "simply embodies the provisions of the civil rights bill, and gives to the President authority, through the Secretary of War, to extend military protection to secure those rights until the civil courts are in operation."[49]

Eliot recited a Freedmen's Bureau report by General Clinton B. Fisk, who reported about black Union soldiers returning to their homes in Kentucky after the war ended:

> Their arms are taken from them by the civil authorities and confis-
> cated for the benefit of the Commonwealth. . . . Thus the right of the
> people to keep and bear arms as provided in the Constitution is
> infringed, and the Government for whose protection and preserva-
> tion these soldiers have fought is denounced as meddlesome and
> despotic when through its agents it undertakes to protect its citizens
> in a constitutional right.[50]

The freedmen, Fisk continued, "are defenseless, for the civil-law officers dis-arm the colored man and hand him over to armed marauders."[51] On May 29, the House passed H.R. 613, the Freedmen's Bureau Bill, by a vote of 96 to 32.[52] The House then took up the proposed Fourteenth Amendment.[53]

After further debate, the Fourteenth Amendment passed the Senate by a vote of 33 to 11,[54] a 75 percent margin, comfortably more than the required two-thirds to amend the Constitution. On June 13, the House passed the proposed Amendment by 120 to 32,[55] which was 79 percent of the votes, once more well beyond the necessary two-thirds.

A bill was also pending that mandated that the former Confederate states ratify the Fourteenth Amendment as a condition for reentry into the Union. As explained by Representative George W. Julian, the constitu-tional amendment was needed to prevent states from nullifying the Civil Rights Act:

> Although the civil rights bill is now the law . . . [it] is pronounced void
> by the jurists and courts of the South. Florida makes it a misdemeanor
> for colored men to carry weapons without a license to do so from a
> probate judge, and the punishment of the offense is whipping and the

pillory. South Carolina has the same enactments; and a black man convicted of an offense who fails immediately to pay his fine is whipped. . . . Cunning legislative devices are being invented in most of the States to restore slavery in fact.[56]

In other words, while the Civil Rights Act and the Freedmen's Bureau Bill were intended to guarantee the right to keep and bear arms and other rights, the Fourteenth Amendment was needed to leave no question as to the constitutionality of such enactments or proposed enactments.

On June 26, the Senate took up the Freedmen's Bureau Bill. Section 8, which included reference to "the constitutional right to bear arms," was renumbered as § 14.[57] The House rejected a motion by Senator Thomas Hendricks of Indiana to strike out the section on the basis that "the same matters are found in the civil rights bill substantially that are found in this section."[58]

The two bills protected the same rights, responded Senator Trumbull, but the Civil Rights Act applied in areas where the courts were operable, and the Freedmen's Bureau Bill would apply where the civil authority had not been restored.[59] The bill then passed without a roll-call vote.[60]

After being sent to a conference committee, the bill was reported, and the Senate concurred.[61] A motion in the House to table the bill lost by a vote of 25 to 102.[62] The report was then adopted without another roll call vote.

President Johnson then vetoed the second Freedmen's Bureau Bill,[63] but the House overrode the veto by 104 to 33, or 76 percent,[64] and the Senate did so by 33 to 12, or 73 percent.[65]

As finally passed into law on July 16, 1866, the Freedmen's Bureau Act extended the Bureau's existence for two more years.[66] The full text of § 14 of the Act declared:

> That in every State or district where the ordinary course of judicial proceedings has been interrupted by the rebellion, and until the same shall be fully restored, and in every State or district whose constitutional relations to the government have been practically discontinued by the rebellion, and until such State shall have been restored in such relations, and shall be duly represented in the Congress of

the United States, the right to make and enforce contracts, to sue, be parties, and give evidence, to inherit, purchase, lease, sell, hold, and convey real and personal property, and to have *full and equal benefit of all laws and proceedings concerning personal liberty, personal security,* and the acquisition, enjoyment, and disposition of estate, real and personal, *including the constitutional right to bear arms, shall be secured to and enjoyed by all the citizens* of such State or district without respect to race or color or previous condition of slavery. And whenever in either of said States or districts the ordinary course of judicial proceedings has been interrupted by the rebellion, and until the same shall be fully restored, and until such State shall have been restored in its constitutional relations to the government, and shall be duly represented in the Congress of the United States, the President shall, through the commissioner and the officers of the bureau, and under such rules and regulations as the President, through the Secretary of War, shall prescribe, extend military protection and have military jurisdiction over all cases and questions concerning *the free enjoyment of such immunities and rights,* and no penalty or punishment for any violation of law shall be imposed or permitted because of race or color, or previous condition of slavery, other or greater than the penalty or punishment to which white persons may be liable by law for the like offense. But the jurisdiction conferred by this section upon the officers of the bureau shall not exist in any State where the ordinary course of judicial proceedings has not been interrupted by the rebellion, and shall cease in every State when the courts of the State and the United States are not disturbed in the peaceable course of justice, and after such State shall be fully restored in its constitutional relations to the government, and shall be duly represented in the Congress of the United States.[67]

In short, the "full and equal benefit of all laws and proceedings concerning personal liberty, personal security, and . . . estate" included "the constitutional right to bear arms," and those rights "shall be secured to and enjoyed by all the citizens," who were entitled to "the free enjoyment of such immunities and rights." It is noteworthy that the same more than two-thirds of Congress that enacted this language of the Freedmen's

Bureau Act also enacted similar, albeit more general, language in the Civil Rights Act, which remains on the books today.

Even more significantly, more than two-thirds of Congress adopted the Fourteenth Amendment to the Constitution and submitted it to the states for ratification. If there was any Bill of Rights guarantee that the Fourteenth Amendment was intended to protect from state infringement, it would be first and foremost the Second Amendment right to keep and bear arms. Not even the First Amendment right to free speech was singled out for such special emphasis as was the Second Amendment.

Members of the Reconstruction Congress clearly read the Second Amendment to guarantee a fundamental right of "the people," i.e., individuals. It would be another century before the spread of the "collective right" view of the Second Amendment, under which the Amendment protects nothing more than some undefinable power of States to maintain militias or a nonsensical right to bear arms in a militia, which is inconsistent with any military force. Indeed, Congress in 1866 recognized "the constitutional right to bear arms" by all persons, even newly freed slaves, and further saw the need to protect this and other rights *from* the state militias.

This first Congressional action took place in a great historical epoch just after our bloody Civil War, yet at the beginning of a civil rights revolution. The next occasion in which Congress gave homage to the Second Amendment in a statutory declaration was in one of the darkest epochs in human history for civil rights abroad. It came just before America's entry into World War II.

THE PROPERTY REQUISITION ACT OF 1941: NO IMPAIRMENT OF THE RIGHT OF ANY INDIVIDUAL TO KEEP AND BEAR ARMS

Just shy of two months before Japan's infamous attack on Pearl Harbor, Congress enacted the Property Requisition Act of 1941. It authorized the president to requisition certain types of property seen as necessary for national defense in the event the United States was dragged into the war in Europe and Asia. The act declared that it must not be construed "to authorize the requisitioning or require the registration of any firearms possessed by any individual for his personal protection or sport," or "to impair or infringe in any manner the right of any individual to keep and bear arms. . . ."[68]

Before examining the deliberations in Congress that led to this enactment, some background as to why Second Amendment rights were a matter of concern is in order. This was the Age of Totalitarianism, featuring Nazi Germany, Fascist Italy, Imperial Japan, and Communist Russia. Mass murder and genocide characterized these regimes, under which depriving firearms from would-be victims was essential. The Nazi experience illustrates that point.

Americans reading the *New York Times* in November 1938 were horrified at the headlines reporting what became known as the Night of the Broken Glass: "Nazis Smash, Loot and Burn Jewish Shops and Temples Until Goebbels Calls Halt."[69] Homes were attacked and thousands of Jewish men arrested. Essential to the success of this pogrom was the prohibition on possessing arms:

> One of the first legal measures issued was an order by Heinrich Himmler, commander of all German police, forbidding Jews to possess any weapons whatever and imposing a penalty of 20 years confinement in a concentration camp upon every Jew found in possession of a weapon hereafter.[70]

The following year, after Hitler launched World War II by attacking Poland, Americans would read about a U.S. citizen originally from Poland being executed by the Nazis for "having concealed a considerable quantity of arms and ammunition in violation of German regulations."[71] And fast forwarding yet another year, with the collapse of France, the headlines read: "German Army Decrees Death for Those Retaining Arms and Radio Senders."[72] The *Times* observed:

> The best way to sum up the disciplinary laws imposed upon France by the German conqueror is to say that the Nazi decrees reduce the French people to as low a condition as that occupied by the German people. Military orders now forbid the French to do things which the German people have not been allowed to do since Hitler came to power. To own radio senders or to listen to foreign broadcasts, to

organize public meetings and distribute pamphlets, to disseminate anti-German news in any form, to retain possession of firearms—all these things are prohibited for the subjugated people of France, as they have been verboten these half dozen years to the people of Germany.[73]

Given these events, Americans were in no mood to accept inroads on their own Second Amendment rights. Domestic prohibitionists had turned from violent crime to subversion as the excuse for watering down the right to bear arms. Not unexpectedly, they found little support. The *Times* reported:

> In the face of pleas for compulsory registration of firearms as a defense measure against fifth columnists, the National Conference of Commissioners on Uniform State Laws voted today, by a large majority, to exclude from its proposed Uniform Pistol Act a clause compelling householders to register their weapons. . . . The suggested law retains the traditional right of the American citizen to keep arms as a matter of protection.[74]

Nonetheless, firearm registration was advocated by U.S. Attorney General Robert H. Jackson, who recommended to Congress laws making wiretapping easier, indeterminate criminal sentencing, and "a law for national registration of firearms now exempt from such listing."[75] That would have meant that ordinary rifles, pistols, and shotguns would have been required to be registered, as were machine guns under the National Firearms Act of 1934. That proposal, made in early 1941, set off alarm bells among firearm owners and their allies in Congress.

Indeed, Jackson had argued two years earlier in the U.S. Supreme Court that the Second Amendment right is "only one which exists where the arms are borne in the militia or some other military organization provided for by law and intended for the protection of the state."[76] In deciding *United States v. Miller* (1939), the Supreme Court disregarded that argument, ruling instead that the Second Amendment protects possession of a firearm that "is any part of the ordinary military equipment or that its use could contribute to the common defense."[77] *Miller* focused on the nature of the arm, not on whether the possessor was a militia member.

In mid-1941, citing intelligence from a "source close to one of the groups which has been agitating for registration of all firearms," C.B. Lister, secretary-treasurer of the National Rifle Association, warned Representative Edwin Arthur Hall of New York, that "an attempt might be made to incorporate such Federal registration of firearms in the pending tax bill."[78]

Soon after, in a hearing before the House Committee on Military Affairs, Representative Paul Kilday, a Democrat from Texas, attempted to ask questions of Undersecretary of War Robert P. Patterson, concerning a bill to allow the president to requisition property from civilians: "The reason I ask that is somebody made the boast they were going to get the other [firearms] legislation under this bill!" However, the committee then went into executive session, and the record does not reflect what happened next.[79]

As originally proposed in the Senate, the bill in question—S. 1579— gave the president wide powers to authorize the requisition of machinery and other property of value for the national defense on payment of just compensation. The House Committee on Military Affairs added the following qualifications to the bill:

> That nothing herein contained shall be construed to authorize the requisition or require the registration of any firearms possessed by any individual for his personal protection or sport (and the possession of which is not prohibited nor the registration thereof required); nor shall this Act in any manner impair or infringe the right of any individual to keep and bear arms.[80]

The Committee Report included this explanation about the reason for adding the above provision:

> It is not contemplated or even inferred that the President, or any executive board, agency, or officer, would trespass upon the right of the people in this respect. There appears to be no occasion for the requisition of firearms owned and maintained by the people for sport and recreation, nor is there any desire or intention on the part of the Congress or the President to impair or infringe the right of the

people under section 2 [*sic*] of the Constitution of the United States, which reads, in part as follows: 'the right of the people to keep and bear arms shall not be infringed.' However, in view of the fact that certain totalitarian and dictatorial nations are now engaged in the willful and wholesale destruction of personal rights and liberties, our committee deem it appropriate for the Congress to expressly state that the proposed legislation shall not be construed to impair or infringe the constitutional right of the people to bear arms. In so doing, it will be manifest that, although the Congress deems it expedient to grant certain extraordinary powers to the Executive in furtherance of the common defense during critical times, there is no disposition on the part of this Government to depart from the concepts and principles of personal rights and liberties expressed in our Constitution.[81]

While the declaration about the right to keep and bear arms was welcome, supporters of the Second Amendment were not so sure that no one contemplated future infringements. When the bill hit the House floor on August 5, Congressman Hall described what was happening abroad and anticipated violations here as follows:

Before the advent of Hitler or Stalin, who took power from the German and Russian people, measures were thrust upon the free legislatures of those countries to deprive the people of the possession and use of firearms, so that they could not resist the encroachments of such diabolical and vitriolic state police organizations as the Gestapo, the Ogpu, and the Cheka. Just as sure as I am standing here today, you are going to see this measure followed by legislation, sponsored by the proponents of such encroachment upon the rights of the people, which will eventually deprive the people of their constitutional liberty which provides for the possession of firearms for the protection of their homes.

I submit to you that it is a serious departure from constitutional government when we consider legislation of this type. I predict that within 6 months of this time there will be presented to this House a measure which will go a long way toward taking away forever the individual rights and liberties of citizens of this Nation by depriving the individual of the private ownership of firearms and the right to use weapons in the protection of his home, and thereby his country.[82]

Representative Walter G. Andrews of New York responded that the bill was strongly advocated by Undersecretary of War Patterson.[83]

The Senate then considered the House amendment. Senator Tom Connally of Texas described it as "safeguarding the right of individuals to possess arms."[84] Senator Albert B. Chandler of Kentucky argued that "we have no reason to take the personal property of individuals which is kept solely for protection of their homes."[85] Delegates to a conference committee were appointed.[86]

The conference committee deleted the ban on registration, but kept the declaration against infringing the right to bear arms.[87] In support of that version, Representative A.J. May, a Kentucky Democrat and conference manager, recalled the remarks in executive session of the Undersecretary of War in the Military Affairs Committee:

> Judge Patterson before the committee stated in answer to a question that the War Department had been considering regulations with respect to the requisitioning of personal property, that it had not yet occurred to them . . . that they might be called upon to register arms. If they were called upon to register arms, I do not think they would go out and say to every farmer in this country, to every workingman in this country, to every citizen, businessman, or whatever profession or calling he may have, that he must register the weapons he might have in his home, but to guard against that we undertook to give these brethren here concerned about their guns the proper kind of protection, and we did it in the language of the Constitution, or as nearly as we could, and I quote from the report: "Nothing contained in this act shall be construed to impair or infringe in any manner the right of any individual to keep and bear arms."[88]

Congressman May added his understanding of the Second Amendment as follows: "the right to keep means that a man can keep a gun in his house and can carry it with him if he wants to; he can take it where he wants to . . . and the right to bear arms means that he can go hunting . . . and that nobody has any right, so long as he bears the arms openly and unconcealed, to interfere with him."[89]

Commenting on registration, Representative Dewey Short of Missouri explained, "The method employed by the Communists in every country that has been overthrown has been to disarm the populace, take away their firearms with which to defend themselves, in order to overthrow the Government."[90] Representative Paul Kilday of Texas put it in historical perspective:

> For a period of perhaps 15 years there has been an element in this country seeking to require the registration of all firearms. That bill has been offered in almost every Congress during that period of time. It has never been reported out of the Committee on the Judiciary, and we now have another one of those subterfuges of getting under the name of national defense something that they have not been able to get over a period of years.
>
> I call attention to section 4 of this act, which provides that the President shall have the power to administer the provisions of the act, through any officer or agency that he may determine and to require such information as he may deem necessary in carrying out the provisions of the act. That gives the power to require the registration of every firearm in the United States because knowledge of the location and the owner would be the first information necessary for requisition.[91]

Merely enacting the words of the Second Amendment in the bill, Kilday noted, would provide no real protection:

> We are in the ridiculous position of being asked to vote for an amendment which copies the language of the Constitution into an act of Congress. . . . At the proper time I propose to offer a motion to recommit the conference report to the conference committee, to the end that they may pass on this and incorporate my amendment which provided that the bill shall not be construed to give the Government the power to requisition a firearm possessed by an individual, nor to

require the registration of it. That must be put in here in order to make the bill constitutional. Judge Patterson testified. His one example was that they might need shotguns, and he felt that if they need shotguns they should have the right to take them from anybody.[92]

Kilday was referring to the remarks in executive session by Undersecretary of War Patterson in the Military Affairs Committee. Kilday further recalled, "Judge Patterson said they had already made their plans to require registration.... Remember that registration of firearms is only the first step. It will be followed by other infringements of the right to keep and bear arms until finally the right is gone."[93]

Noting that the Russian Communist experience taught the wisdom of Second Amendment protection for "our right to bear arms as private citizens," Representative Lyle H. Boren, an Oklahoma Democrat, averred that "the gun I own in my home is essential to maintaining the defense of my home against the aggression of lawlessness."[94] He added about the American way of life:

> I propose to defend it against the soldiers of a Hitler and against a government bureaucrat. All the invasions threatened against American democracy are not from without. I feel that the defense of democracy is on my doorstep and your doorstep as well as on the world's battlefields.... I rebel against the destruction of freedom in America under the guise of emergency.[95]

Representative John W. Patman, a Texas Democrat, noted the constitutional safeguard provided by the framers against abuse of power by the president, who controlled both the army and the state militias when federalized:

> The answer was, "The people have a right to bear arms. The people have a right to keep arms; therefore, if we should have some Executive who attempted to set himself up as dictator or king, the people can organize themselves together and, with the arms and ammunition they have, they can properly protect themselves....
> If we permit the people here in Washington to compel the people

all over the Nation to turn in their arms, their ammunition, then the Chief Executive, whoever he is, gets control of the Army and the militia, how will the people be able to protect themselves?[96]

Patman characterized the bill's language as "meaningless," repeating the Second Amendment guarantee. "The Constitution guarantees to the people those rights which they have asserted in this bill."[97]

"The Constitution guarantees to every citizen the right to keep and bears arms," asserted Representative John J. Sparkman, an Alabama Democrat. But he conceded that Undersecretary Patterson had stated that, if "it is necessary to take our shotguns, we ought to have the power to do it." Indeed, Sparkman even said that "if in order to defend this country it is necessary to come into my home and take my shotgun, my pistol, my rifle, or anything else I have . . . I say you are welcome to do it."[98] What distinguished this from totalitarianism was left unclear.

That argument fell on deaf ears, and the motion to recommit the bill to committee then passed by 154 to 24.[99] The resulting new conference report restored the ban on firearm registration.[100]

As passed and signed by President Franklin Roosevelt, the Property Requisition Act authorized the president to requisition broad categories of property with military uses from the private sector on payment of fair compensation, subject to the following:

Nothing contained in this Act shall be construed

(1) to authorize the requisitioning or require the registration of any firearms possessed by any individual for his personal protection or sport (and the possession of which is not prohibited or the registration of which is not required by existing law), [or]

(2) to impair or infringe in any manner the right of any individual to keep and bear arms. . . .[101]

This law bore witness to the value that any war would be fought to preserve the Bill of Rights and other liberties, not to destroy them. And it was fitting that the Second Amendment would be declared to be of special importance as war clouds loomed, for Americans who were accustomed to keeping and bearing arms would make superior riflemen. In fact, the National Rifle Association played an instrumental role in training civilians in marksmanship throughout the war.

In less than two months after passage of the Act, the Japanese attack on Pearl Harbor would drag the United States into World War II. It was then a fight to the death to preserve freedom, and it would be victorious.

THE FIREARMS OWNERS' PROTECTION ACT OF 1986: THE RIGHTS OF CITIZENS TO KEEP AND BEAR ARMS

The world had changed considerably by the time Congress enacted the Gun Control Act of 1968. A new generation of zealots pushed the envelope against constitutional rights in favor of unprecedented powers being grabbed by the federal government. The Gun Control Act intruded into traditional areas of state regulation and created numerous victimless crimes, such as making it a felony to transfer a firearm to a person in another state, to sell an unspecified number of guns without a license, or to do other harmless acts without any intent to violate the law.

By this time, prohibitionists denied that the Second Amendment protected any individual right whatsoever. U.S. Attorney General Ramsey Clark led the charge for a bill that required the registration of all firearms and to imprison those who failed to comply.[102] After Michigan Congressman John Dingell, a Democrat, recalled how the Nazis used registration records to confiscate firearms, the Johnson administration produced a report reaching the preposterous conclusion that "there is no significant relationship between gun laws and the rise of dictators."[103] NRA officials testifying before the committee recalled the language of the Property Requisition Act, but the prohibitionists were in denial.

The prohibitionists' registration bill was defeated. Moreover, as passed, the Gun Control Act included a preamble that eschewed any intent to burden law-abiding citizens, although it included no explicit reference to the Second Amendment. In the ensuing years, however, experience substantiated the predictions of the act's opponents that the law would be used to ensnare innocent citizens. The enforcement policies of the Bureau of Alcohol, Tobacco, and Firearms (BATF) led to numerous abuses that would be well documented in Congressional hearings beginning in the late 1970s.

Increasing awareness in Congress of the need for reform led to the enactment of the Firearms Owners' Protection Act of 1986 (FOPA). FOPA represents the third time Congress made clear by statute that the Second Amendment enshrines an individual right. Actually, FOPA declared that the existing Gun Control Act and its enforcement by BATF needed correction in light of several constitutional rights as follows:

> The Congress finds that
>
> (1) the rights of citizens
> - (A) to keep and bear arms under the second amendment to the United States Constitution;
> - (B) to security against illegal and unreasonable searches and seizures under the fourth amendment;
> - (C) against uncompensated taking of property, double jeopardy, and assurance of due process of law under the fifth amendment; and
> - (D) against unconstitutional exercise of authority under the ninth and tenth amendments; require additional legislation to correct existing firearms statutes and enforcement policies; and
>
> (2) additional legislation is required to reaffirm the intent of the Congress, as expressed in section 101 of the Gun Control Act of 1968, that "it is not the purpose of this title to place any undue or unnecessary Federal restrictions or burdens on law-abiding citizens with respect to the acquisition, possession, or use of firearms appropriate to the purpose of hunting, trap shooting, target shooting, personal protection, or any other lawful activity, and that this title is not intended to discourage or eliminate the private ownership or use of firearms by law-abiding citizens for lawful purposes.[104]

The finding in FOPA that the Second Amendment guarantees the rights of citizens to keep and bear arms was supported by a comprehensive report by the Senate's Subcommittee on the Constitution, which stated:

> The conclusion is thus inescapable that the history, concept, and wording of the second amendment to the Constitution of the United

States, as well as its interpretation by every major commentator and court in the first half-century after its ratification, indicates that what is protected is an individual right of a private citizen to own and carry firearms in a peaceful manner.[105]

In FOPA's substantive reforms, Congress implemented its recognition that the Second Amendment guarantees individual rights by deregulating substantially the purchase, sale, and possession of firearms, and by requiring proof of a "willful" or "knowing" violation for conviction under the law.

FOPA further enforced Second Amendment rights and reflected Congress's traditional rejection of registration in the following provision:

> No such rule or regulation prescribed after the date of the enactment of the Firearms Owners' Protection Act may require that records required to be maintained under this chapter or any portion of the contents of such records, be recorded at or transferred to a facility owned, managed, or controlled by the United States or any State or any political subdivision thereof, nor that any system of registration of firearms, firearms owners, or firearms transactions or dispositions be established.[106]

Another important FOPA reform was the provision preempting state laws that prohibit travelers from transporting firearms throughout the United States.[107] This reflected Congress's recognition that the Second Amendment protects the individual right to keep and bear arms, which was made applicable to the states through the Fourteenth Amendment. Idaho Senator Steve Symms introduced this provision with the explanation, "The intent of this amendment . . . is to protect the Second Amendment rights of law-abiding citizens wishing to transport firearms through States which otherwise prohibit the possession of such weapons."[108] In the House, Rep. Tommy Robinson of Arkansas stated that "our citizens have a constitutional right to bear arms . . . and to travel interstate with those weapons."[109]

FOPA, which was signed into law by President Ronald Reagan, represents a high water mark for protection of Second Amendment rights by the U.S. Congress. When the Clinton administration pursued anti-Second Amendment policies, the American electorate cleaned house beginning in 1994, making further passage of prohibitionist legislation in Congress difficult. At the state level, the passage of "Right-to-Carry" laws ushered in further defeats for the prohibitionists, who then turned to the courts. They launched frivolous lawsuits against the firearms industry, hoping to bankrupt it and destroy the Second Amendment through judicial fiat.

THE PROTECTION OF LAWFUL COMMERCE IN ARMS ACT OF 2005: TO PRESERVE A CITIZEN'S ACCESS TO FIREARMS

The prohibitionist attempt to bypass the legislative process and ban guns through litigation led Congress to enact the Protection of Lawful Commerce in Arms Act ("PLCAA") in 2005.[110] This Act represents the fourth occasion in the history of the U.S. Congress in which that body interpreted the Second Amendment to protect individual rights.

PLCAA is self-described as: "An Act to prohibit civil liability actions from being brought or continued against manufacturers, distributors, dealers, or importers of firearms or ammunition for damages, injunctive or other relief resulting from the misuse of their products by others." The bill was in response to more than thirty lawsuits brought by municipalities against the firearms industry aimed at ruining the industry and shutting down firearms commerce. The legislation was supported by the National Rifle Association, the Department of Defense, the National Association of Manufacturers, the U.S. Chamber of Commerce, United Mine Workers of America, and other business and union organizations.

PLCAA begins with findings that go directly the heart of the matter:

Congress finds the following:

(1) The Second Amendment to the United States Constitution provides that the right of the people to keep and bear arms shall not be infringed.

(2) The Second Amendment to the United States Constitution protects the rights of individuals, including those who are not members of a militia or engaged in military service or training, to keep and bear arms.[111]

The Act recognizes that having arms is a constitutional right, and thus it makes no sense to sanction lawsuits against federally licensed manufacturers merely for making this constitutionally-protected product. Moreover, Congress asserted its constitutional power to protect Second Amendment rights.

Lawsuits were filed against the firearms industry for damages and other relief for the harm caused by criminals and other third parties who misuse firearms.[112] However, the manufacture, importation, possession, sale, and use of firearms and ammunition are heavily regulated by federal, state, and local laws.[113]

The Supreme Court of Illinois recognized this plain fact in 2004, ruling in *Chicago v. Beretta* (2004):

> It seems that plaintiffs seek injunctive relief from this court because relief has not been forthcoming from the General Assembly. We are reluctant to interfere in the lawmaking process in the manner suggested by plaintiffs, especially when the product at issue is already so heavily regulated by both the state and federal governments. We, therefore, conclude that there are strong public policy reasons to defer to the legislature in the matter of regulating the manufacture, distribution, and sale of firearms.

Indeed, the federal Gun Control Act was originally passed under the Commerce Clause, adding further justification for this act. As the findings stated, businesses "are engaged in interstate and foreign commerce through the lawful design, manufacture, marketing, distribution, importation, or sale to the public of firearms or ammunition that has been shipped or transported in interstate or foreign commerce," and they should not be liable for the harm caused by unlawful misuse of firearms that function as designed and intended.[114]

Such imposition of liability on an industry abuses the legal system, erodes public confidence in the law, "threatens the diminution of a basic constitutional right and civil liberty," destabilizes other industries in the free enterprise system of the United States, and "constitutes an unreasonable burden on interstate and foreign commerce of the United States."[115]

Such liability actions, commenced by the federal government, various state politicians, urban officials, and gun-ban groups, were unprecedented and not a bona fide expansion of the common law. The sustaining of these actions by a "maverick" judge or jury would expand liability in a manner never contemplated by the Constitution's framers or by the federal or state legislatures. Congress's enforcement power under the Fourteenth Amendment was made clear in the further finding: "Such an expansion of liability would constitute a deprivation of the rights, privileges, and immunities guaranteed to a citizen of the United States under the Fourteenth Amendment to the United States Constitution."[116] Those rights include the right to keep and bear arms and the right to due process of law.

The liability actions at issue "attempt to use the judicial branch to circumvent the legislative branch of government to regulate interstate and foreign commerce through judgments and judicial decrees," undermining the separation of powers, federalism, state sovereignty, and comity between the sister states.[117]

PLCAA also included purposes clauses that further defined its constitutional bases. The immediate purpose was to prohibit causes of action against the firearms industry for harm caused by criminals and others who unlawfully misuse firearms.[118]

The values of the Second Amendment were reflected in the goal "to preserve a citizen's access to a supply of firearms and ammunition for all lawful purposes, including hunting, self-defense, collecting, and competitive or recreational shooting," and "to guarantee a citizen's rights, privileges, and immunities, as applied to the States, under the Fourteenth Amendment to the United States Constitution, pursuant to section 5 of that Amendment."[119] Section 5 is the Enforcement Clause, which allows Congress to enforce rights against state violation.

Besides preventing such lawsuits from imposing "unreasonable burdens on interstate and foreign commerce,"[120] the law also protects the First Amendment rights of members of the firearms industry, including their trade associations, "to speak freely, to assemble peaceably, and to petition the Government for a redress of their grievances."[121]

PLCAA's substantive provision stated: "A qualified civil liability action may not be brought in any Federal or State court." Any such pending action "shall be dismissed immediately."[122] The rest of the law defined the nature of the prohibited civil action in contrast with the types of traditional actions, which would remain unaffected.

Debate on the bill focused on the substantive liability issues and proposed amendments. The propositions contained in the findings and purposes that the Second and Fourteenth Amendments guarantee an individual right to keep and bear arms went virtually uncontested.

Senator John Thune of South Dakota set the tone when he averred, "This bill is about law abiding gun owners, it is about law abiding gun dealers, it is about law abiding gun manufacturers who are having that Second Amendment right infringed upon by those who are trying to destroy an industry. . . ."[123] And Senator Larry Craig of Idaho—the bill's chief sponsor—maintained, "The Constitution also, I believe, imposes upon Congress the duty to protect the liberties enshrined in the Bill of Rights which includes the Second Amendment. If the firearms manufacturers are driven out of business, that Second Amendment will be nothing more than an illusion."[124]

Opponents of firearm ownership previously denied that the Second Amendment protected any individual rights, but in this debate hypocritically attempted to wrap themselves in the Amendment. New York Senator Chuck Schumer, a consistent firearm prohibitionist, uttered these words: "The right to guns is a good thing. I support the Second Amendment." He then contradicted those words by vehemently urging defeat of the bill.[125]

The bill would pass the Senate with sixty-five yeas and thirty-one nays, a very comfortable margin.[126] This victory never would have been achieved without Majority Leader Bill Frist of Tennessee and his tireless efforts to ensure that the bill received a fair hearing and that it was not "poisoned" with antigun amendments. Sen. Max Baucus of Montana helped Senator Craig marshal this reform effort through the Senate, aided by strong support from Senate Majority Whip Mitch McConnell of Kentucky and Senate Republican Conference Chairman Rick Santorum of Pennsylvania. A filibuster-proof sixty votes were needed to ensure PLCAA's passage; of course, this would have been impossible without support from senators from both parties and that certainly included Minority Leader Harry Reid of Nevada.

In House debate, Representative Lamar Smith of Texas averred that "to allow frivolous lawsuits to constrain the right of Americans to lawfully use guns is both irresponsible and unconstitutional."[127] Noting the need to stop "this abuse of the legal process," Representative Sam Graves of Missouri explained: "This bill will protect the firearms industry from lawsuits based on the criminal or unlawful third party misuse of their products. This law is necessary to prevent a few state courts from undermining our Second Amendment rights guaranteed by the Constitution."[128]

Representative Joe Schwarz of Michigan said it in a nutshell when he explained, "The Second Amendment was not written as a mere exercise in constitutional thought. It had a practical purpose: first, to ensure that citizens would have the tools to protect their families and their homes and, second, to ensure that an armed militia could be called up to defend the country in emergencies."[129]

The PLCAA—with Cliff Stearns of Florida and Rick Boucher of Virginia its chief sponsors—passed the House overwhelmingly with 283 yeas and 144 nays[130] and was promptly signed into law by President George W. Bush. The anti-Second Amendment litigators who earlier filed the frivolous lawsuits the act was designed to eliminate, filed motions claiming that the PLCAA was unconstitutional.

Future history will determine if Congress will deem it necessary once again to protect the Second Amendment rights of American citizens. When Congress construes a Bill of Rights guarantee broadly, it reflects the interests of the people at large, who influence Congress through the rights of petition and suffrage.

Congress has reaffirmed and embellished the Second Amendment on four occasions. In the Freedmen's Bureau Act of 1866, Congress guaranteed to the freed slaves "full and equal benefit of all laws and proceedings concerning personal liberty, personal security, and . . . estate, . . . including the constitutional right to bear arms." Again, in the war-time Property Requisition Act of 1941, Congress prohibited any construction that would "require the registration of any firearm possessed by any individual for his personal protection or sport" or would "infringe in any manner the right of any individual to keep and bear arms."

In the Firearms Owners' Protection Act of 1986, Congress found that "the rights of citizens . . . to keep and bear arms under the Second

Amendment to the United States Constitution" required legislation to correct the Gun Control Act and BATF enforcement policies, and enforced this with a prohibition on the registration of firearms owners. And finally, in the Protection of Lawful Commerce in Arms Act of 2005, Congress sought to protect the supply of firearms, declaring that the Second Amendment "protects the rights of individuals, including those who are not members of a militia or engaged in military service or training, to keep and bear arms."

As the branch elected by the people, the U.S. Congress fulfills its proper function when it declares and protects the constitutional rights of the people. This role is essential to the checks and balances necessary to prevent power from being concentrated in one branch of government. Great weight should be accorded to the repeated determinations by Congress, over a long historical period and in vastly different historical circumstances, that the right to keep and bear arms is a fundamental, individual right that the government may not infringe.

CHAPTER 6

U.N. Gun Prohibition: One Country at a Time

The United Nations has not yet succeeded in imposing worldwide gun prohibition, but several countries provide a preview for what the U.N. wants. In these countries, the U.N. has imposed total gun prohibition, enforced with severe penalties and house-to-house military searches, notwithstanding plain evidence that such a policy leaves innocent families defenseless against violent criminals. These violent criminals often work together with corrupt governments that refuse to protect the innocent. The U.N.'s imposition of gun prohibition, and its cooperation with international human trafficking, violates several human rights Declarations and Treaties created by the U.N. itself.

CAMBODIA

When Cambodia was a French colony, from 1863 to 1953, the French rulers passed many laws to prevent the Cambodian peasants from arming.[1] On April 17, 1975, a revolutionary war brought the Cambodian communist party to power, and the state of Democratic Kampuchea came into existence. The new government of Pol Pot and his Khmer Rouge perpetrated a reign of terror against unarmed civilians, resulting in the deaths of more than two million people.[2]

On December 25, 1978, an invasion by Vietnam ended Pol Pot's regime, but continued genocide at a slower pace, killing approximately a quarter million people.[3] A period of internecine factional fighting ended on October 23, 1991, when the four warring factions[4] signed the Paris Peace Agreements[5] and invited the U.N. to help restore peace and supervise free elections in the country. The Paris Agreements gave the U.N. a broad mandate to disarm and demilitarize the warring factions, and to improve human rights. UNTAC, the U.N. Transitional Authority in Cambodia, was created.[6]

The terms of the Paris Agreements stipulated that troops from all four factions would be disarmed and demobilized by the U.N., which meant collecting more than 300,000 conventional arms from an estimated 425,000 combatants (203,300 regular army and 220,290 militia).[7] In theory, when that goal was reached, there would be a "neutral security environment as a prelude to activities aimed at creating a neutral political environment,"[8] thereby enabling Cambodians to vote in national elections without coercion. This would represent a major step toward democratization and a humanitarian climate.

The Khmer Rouge ("PDK"), however, refused to disarm, and the remaining factions grew reluctant to proceed with their own disarmament. The phenomenon of "decaying consent" has occurred before in disarmament programs.[9] Leaders of warring factions may sign an agreement, but ground forces refuse to adhere to those agreements when doing so threatens their survival.

The UNTAC program is the *only known instance in which there was an attempt to record empirical data using weapon injuries as an outcome measure after microdisarmament.* David Meddings and Stephanie O'Connor compared the incidence of weapon injuries before and after the UNTAC disarmament.[10] They estimated that "around 25–50 percent" of Cambodia's combatants were "believed to have been disarmed" during the peacekeeping operation. Although a stable government was left in place at the time of departure of the U.N., "the annual incidence of weapon injuries was higher than the rate observed before the peacekeeping operation."[11]

Because of continued violence, the U.N. issued another disarmament imperative just prior to the 1993 election. Yasushi Akashi, the Secretary-General's Special Representative to Cambodia, issued a directive that rendered unlicensed civilian firearm possession illegal, as of March 18, 1993, although the Paris Agreements had given UNTAC no legal authority to issue such a decree. Penalties for violation of the U.N. directive included confiscation of arms and imprisonment for a period of six months to three years.[12]

Five years after the U.N.-imposed gun-licensing law, violent crime was still rising in Cambodia.[13] Gun-rights advocates rightly argue that gun-licensing or registration laws can set the stage for gun confiscation, since the government will know where to find all legally owned guns. In Cambodia, gun confiscation followed the U.N.'s gun-licensing fiat. In 1999, the Cambodian government, with U.N. support, banned all firearms, blaming the nation's crime problem on "the large number of guns in circulation, thought to be about half a million...."[14] Eventually, the *BBC News* reported, there would be house-to-house searches and a ban on all arms, including firearms previously registered and even arms carried by off-duty police and soldiers. [15]

At the 2001 U.N. Conference on the Illegal Trade in Small Arms and Light Weapons in All its Aspects, Sar Kheng, Cambodian Minister of the Interior, said that "illegally held arms" (i.e., all non-government arms) were "major obstacles to efforts to reconstruct and rehabilitate the country and to the building of democracy and respect for human rights."[16] He explained:

> The Government of Cambodia has designated management of all arms and explosives as its major task, and has instituted several measures, such as collecting and confiscating all arms, explosives and ammunition left by the war; instituting practical measures to reduce the reckless use of arms; and strengthening the management of weapons registration. Those who possessed weapons during the civil war wish to continue possessing them for self-protection. On the other hand, criminals have no intention of giving up their weapons, because they need them to carry out their criminal offences. However, with assistance from the European Union and from non-governmental organizations (NGOs), there has been some success in raising the awareness of the problem among a majority of Cambodians.[17]

As of February 2002, reportedly 112,562 of Cambodia's "small arms" had been confiscated.[18]

Although the current Cambodian government is not engaged in genocide, it nevertheless has a poor human rights record and is attempting to eliminate the political opposition with threats of violence. And, as the U.N. admitted in its International Drug Control Programme report, Cambodia has become a center for "illicit drug production and trafficking, smuggling and exploitation of human beings, kidnappings, prostitution, illegal gambling, arms trafficking and extortion," and much of this criminal behavior is "protected by Cambodian officials."[19] The government's involvement in the international crime of the trafficking of women for sexual exploitation is an extreme violation of human rights.[20]

The Cambodian people have suffered decades of political and criminal violence. Many Cambodians have personally learned how to use arms for protection against criminals, so it seems doubtful that disarmament plans, even those enforced by government coercion, will persuade the populace to surrender all their arms. As the Working Group for Weapons Reduction in Cambodia (WGWR) survey noted, "it is increasingly common in Cambodian society for people to believe that weapons are needed to protect businesses and homes."[21]

The authors of *Small Arms Survey 2002* admitted, "Most people, while broadly supportive of the weapons collection process, remain reluctant to participate in it themselves so long as the rule of law is not fully established in the country and there is a lack of public trust in the security forces."[22]

As the great British philosopher John Locke once explained, the foundation of the people's political sovereignty is their God-given property right to their own bodies.[23] Accordingly, when Cambodians choose to retain their arms so that they may defend themselves and their families against programs of rape and other government-sanctioned violent crimes, they are, in effect, choosing to retain their sovereignty.

The root of the crime problem in Cambodia is the tyrannical government that steals land from peasants, cooperates with organized crime, and enriches itself by participating in the sex-trade enslavement of women and children. It is entirely reasonable for the Cambodian people to want firearms to protect their families and to guard against the recurrence of a genocide like the one that took place the last time they were disarmed.[24]

Sadly, yet another disarmament program is being instituted in Cambodia. On Jan. 13, 2003, the Japanese government announced it would provide up to $3.6 million to implement the euphemistically-named "Peace Building and Comprehensive Small Arms Management

Program in Cambodia."[25] The new disarmament program, in the Bakan district, pays for public works construction of medical clinics, schools, roads, or bridges, if the locals surrender a sufficient number of firearms.[26] In other words, if a community does not surrender its only practical means of protecting itself from genocide, common criminals, and government-sponsored criminals, the government will not build any schools, clinics, roads, or bridges.

The rationale for the latest disarmament program is that "small arms have been sometimes used for criminal objectives, which severely harm the security and social stability of Cambodia, and thus the reduction of arms has been considered as one of the first prioritized social actions toward sustainable peace in Cambodia."[27]

To the contrary, the reduction of civilian arms in Cambodia was the *sine qua non* for the Khmer Rouge genocide, and continuing efforts to disarm Cambodia's citizens have contributed to the continuing criminal victimization of the Cambodian people by their government.

Less coercive programs, such as community-arms surrenders, are also contrary to the Universal Declaration of Human Rights. A corrupt government that profits from the kidnapping of teenage girls for slavery in the sex trade is grotesquely violating the Universal Declaration, including Article 4 ("No one shall be held in slavery or servitude; slavery and the slave trade shall be prohibited in all their forms."); Article 9 ("No one shall be subjected to arbitrary arrest, detention or exile.); Article 13 ("Everyone has the right to freedom of movement and residence within the borders of each state."); Article 16 ("The family is the natural and fundamental group unit of society and is entitled to protection by society and the State."); and Article 23 ("Everyone has the right . . . to free choice of employment . . . Everyone who works has the right to just and favourable remuneration ensuring for himself and his family an existence worthy of human dignity").

In community gun-surrender programs, wealthy foreign organizations tell people, in effect, "We will build you a bridge—if you give up your ability to protect your daughters from sex-trade kidnappers," or "if you give up your ability to protect your families against the genocide and tyranny that occurred here not too long ago." Offering such choices is completely inconsistent with respect for human rights.

ALBANIA: HOUSE-TO-HOUSE GUN CONFISCATION

The collapse of several elaborate pyramid schemes in November and December 1996, which impoverished the Albanian people, many of whom lost their entire life savings,[28] led to widespread anarchy and the toppling of the Sali Berisha administration. During the anarchy, "virtually all inmates escaped from the Albanian prisons."[29] The combination of a sudden upsurge in violence and well-placed mistrust of the corrupt Albanian government caused civilians to loot 1,300 armories, removing approximately 550,000 to 1,500,000 arms, plus millions of rounds of ammunition, as well as explosives. [30]

In February 1998, the Albanian government requested aid from the U.N. to retrieve the balance of the missing arms. Jayantha Dhanapala, Undersecretary-General for Disarmament Affairs, led a fact-finding mission in Albania in mid-June 1998. The two initial proposals were: (1) the creation of a paramilitary force that would carry out house-to-house searches and confiscation, or (2) a compensated gun surrender program, which the U.N. expected would create an increase in black market gun trafficking into the region.[31]

At first, the U.N. tried a different approach: a voluntary arms collection program that would be linked to building community development projects such as roads, schools, and communications systems, and strengthening the capabilities of local police in order to improve security. There was also an intense public information and education campaign, including TV and radio spots, posters, T-shirts, and musical concerts.[32]

In 2000, the voluntary program in Gramsch was escalated into a national house-to-house gun confiscation program. In conjunction with the U.N.'s Weapons in Exchange for Development (WED) program, the Albanian government created a task force of 250 police, to visit every household in the country and demand the surrender of arms.[33] During the visit, the head of the family would be expected to hand them over and would sign a document stating that his home was gun-free. If he were later found to possess arms or ammunition, he would be subject to arrest, prosecution, and incarceration for up to seven years.[34]

The WED program expired in July 2002, as did the amnesty period for voluntary surrender of firearms, yet an estimated 200,000 arms were still unaccounted-for among the civilian population.[35] So a few months before WED was set to expire, the Albanian government enthusiastically embraced another collection program aided by the U.N. On March 12, 2002, the U.N. Development Programme (UNDP) approved the new Small Arms and Light Weapons Control (SALWC) program. Targeting 18 districts, or about half the country, the program aimed for "the surrender and collection of the greatest number of weapons."[36] Due to a shortage of funding, the SALWC project tried to foster competition in arms surrenders; only the locales most successful in collecting arms would earn public works projects. A new feature of SALWC was "development and establishment of a pilot database project as the basis for a centralized, government-operated weapons control system."[37]

Johan Buwalda, program manager for UNDP's WED program, commented, "It is not only weapons collection. It is also weapons control. So we will assist the police in setting up a database, storing these data, managing the data. . . ."[38] In other words, the U.N. was building experience in creating a registry of law-abiding gun owners.

Alfred Moisiu, President of Albania, observed that many Albanians were reluctant to disarm: "Most people are not agreeing to hand over the arms, the weapons, because the situation is still not secure here in our country." Moisiu acknowledged that his countrymen believed that unilateral disarmament endangered law-abiding citizens who surrendered their arms, because criminals will always be able to acquire weapons.[39]

It is reasonable for Albanians to be skeptical about trusting the government. As Human Rights Watch reported, in Albania, there is "impunity for police abuse, failures of various government branches to uphold the rule of law, trafficking in human beings, and widespread violations of children's rights. . . ."[40]

Organized crime syndicates have trafficked more than 20,000 Albanian women to Greece for sexual exploitation. Albanian children are also trafficked for what amounts to *de facto* slavery for the crime syndicates, "to be used in labour, to beg in public places or clean car windows at traffic lights. In other cases, Albanian criminal networks have trafficked babies, which according to the police authorities are sold for US $200."[41]

Rather than persisting in a futile attempt to disarm the public, it would be more effective for government to control police abuses, to pay better attention to fundamental human rights, to spend its resources on required infrastructure, and to reduce the civilian need for arms by protecting the people against slave traffickers.

The coercive disarmament programs, such as military-style house-to-house search-and-seizure, are an assault on human rights. They are characteristic of a police state and have sometimes been precursors of genocide.[42] U.N.-sponsored house-to-house military invasions for gun confiscation violate Article 12 of the Universal Declaration of Human Rights, which states, "No one shall be subjected to arbitrary interference with his privacy, family, [or] home. . . . Everyone has the right to the protection of the law against such interference or attacks."

BOUGAINVILLE

Bougainville is an island near Papua New Guinea (PNG), with a population of approximately 200,000. Named for French sailor Captain Louis de Bougainville who, in 1768, established trade with the islanders, it is the largest island in the Solomon chain.

For years, Bougainville was controlled by various colonial powers. During World War II, of course, it saw extremely fierce combat, as the last Japanese stronghold in the Solomons. After the war, Bougainville was placed under Australian control as a U.N. Trust territory. Against the wishes of its people, Bougainville found itself ruled by Papua New Guinea when PNG gained independence from Australia in 1975, despite the fact that the Bougainvilleans are more closely related to the Solomon Islanders culturally, ethnically, and geographically. PNG lies more than 900 kilometers away. [43] In defiance, Bougainville declared itself the independent Republic of the North Solomons 15 days before PNG gained independence.[44]

In 1960, copper was discovered on Bougainville, and in 1963, the company that eventually evolved into what today is known as Rio Tinto (a leading international mining conglomerate, based in London and Australia) commenced operations.

Land is of utmost importance to the people of Bougainville. Inheritance is maintained through the matrilineal clan system, passing from mother, who is both titleholder and custodian of the tribal land, to eldest daughter.[45]

When, in January 1965, it became apparent that a large open-pit copper mine was to be established, local villagers protested. A hearing was held in the Warden's Court in the town of Kieta,[46] and the court awarded a mining license to Conzinc Riotinto of Australia (a subsidiary of the mining company now called Rio Tinto). Under the court's interpretation of Australian law, what is "on top of the land" belonged to the villagers, but what was underneath—the copper deposits—belonged to the government, and not to the titleholders of the land.

That ruling ran contrary to traditional Bougainvillean ownership. It was also contrary to traditional Anglo-American common law, by which subsurface and mineral rights belong to the owner of the surface land. To the villagers, it was incomprehensible how, after countless generations, the land was no longer theirs.

When the bulldozers came, Bougainvillean landowning women resisted, and lay down with their babies in front of the machines.[47] While Americans sympathized with the brave, unarmed Chinese student who stood in front of a tank in Tiananmen Square, there were no journalists to document similarly brave acts in Bougainville.

Construction of the mine proceeded, accompanied by chemical defoliation of an entire mountainside of pristine rain forest (i.e., the "top of the land" which belonged to the villagers), and huge amounts of toxic mine waste were dumped onto the land and into major rivers. According to a lawsuit filed in November 2000 in the U.S. District Court for the Northern District of California, by 1988,

> the mine . . . dug a crater six kilometers long, four kilometers wide and a half a kilometer deep. . . . [It] produced over one billion tons of waste . . . . [V]ast tracts . . . are still barren and devoid of vegetation many years after closure of the mine. . . . Thirty kilometers of the river valley system was converted into moonscape. . . . What the people of Bougainville see is one of the worst human-made environmental catastrophes of modern times. But the mine turned out to be an enormous source of income for PNG. Rio Tinto gave the PNG government 19 percent of the mine's profits, which at the time, amounted to one-third of the government's income—ample incentive for PNG to overlook environmental damage.[48]

In response, Francis Ona, the son of a dispossessed village chief, formed the Panguna Landowners Association (soon to be known as the Bougainville Revolutionary Army). Ona and his followers shut down the mine on December 1, 1988, using explosives stolen from the mining company to destroy a transmission tower that supplied power to the mine.

In April 1990, the PNG government, with the assistance of the Australian government, imposed a total blockade of the island in an attempt to reopen the mine, and to prevent Ona and the BRA from acquiring arms.[49] Women and children were most affected by the blockade: pregnant women died in childbirth, and young children died from easily preventable diseases. According to the Red Cross, the blockade resulted in the deaths of more than 2,000 children in just the first two years of operation.

The blockade of Bougainville—which supposedly ended during a 1994 ceasefire, but which nevertheless continued informally until 1997— was directly responsible for the deaths of an estimated 15,000 to 20,000 people. PNG thus ranks among the more successful mass-murderers of the twentieth century, having wiped out 10 percent of the Bougainville population.

Instead of forcing the populace into submission, the blockade had just the opposite effect. In May 1990, Ona declared the independence of the Republic of Meekamui ("The Sacred Island").[50]

Meanwhile, control of Bougainville became even more important economically; an aerial survey in the late 1980s had discovered rich deposits of other minerals, including gold and even offshore oil.

The U.N. was apprised of events taking place in Bougainville at least as early as 1991. That summer, a BRA delegation to the U.N. Committee hearing in Geneva on the Rights of Minorities and Indigenous Peoples accused the PNG government of numerous atrocities committed against the islanders.[51] Some of these—extrajudicial executions, "disappearances," ill-treatment, and arbitrary arrests and detentions, including women and children—were detailed by Amnesty International.[52]

In his address to the parliament of Rwanda on May 7, 1998, Kofi Annan offered an apology: "All of us who cared about Rwanda . . . fervently wish that we could have prevented the genocide. . . . In their greatest hour of need, the world failed the people of Rwanda."[53] There was no apology forthcoming for Bougainville, however—just silence, and the determination to disarm the surviving islanders.

To help neutralize the BRA, Papua New Guinea created, funded, and armed the Bougainville Resistance Force (BRF), ensuring its loyalty to the central government, and placed a bounty on Ona's head.

The BRA proved more than a match, however, as they were not only expert guerrilla fighters, but expert in psychological warfare. According to PNG officer Yauka Aluambo Liria, who documented the early years of the Bougainville campaign, it was not long into the fighting that rumors began to spread among the PNG troops about the magical "puri puri" powers possessed by the BRA members from the inner jungles, which enabled them to change into dogs and scout PNG positions, steal weapons, and even kidnap PNG soldiers.[54]

The Bougainville Revolutionary Army even learned how to produce indigenous copies of the M-16 rifle. Completely cut off from imports by the lack of funds and by the blockade, the BRA used material and equipment salvaged from mining operations, and materials left on the island after World War II (including thousands of tons of ammunition and machine-gun parts salvaged from wrecks). Initially, the BRA manufactured crude single-shot firearms, but they soon learned to build more sophisticated guns.[55]

Despite being isolated from the rest of the world, and lacking friends, funds, and sophisticated armament factories, the BRA prevailed. They outmaneuvered trained, well-armed soldiers wielding M79 grenade launchers and mortars, who were backed up by Australian-supplied Iroquois helicopters outfitted with automatic weapons.[56]

Having failed in the military arena, PNG switched tactics. On August 30, 2001, an unrealistic Bougainville Peace Agreement was signed by Bougainvilleans who had strong political ties to PNG.[57] Bougainvilleans loyal to revolutionary leader Francis Ona did not sign. The agreement put a formal end to hostilities, provided for the establishment of an autonomous Bougainville government, and a referendum on full independence from PNG that was to be held within ten to fifteen years.

The most important part of the Peace Agreement (at least to PNG, Australia, and the U.N.)—and what the independence was utterly contingent upon—was the Rotakas Record of May 3, 2001, an agreement that laid out a "phased weapons disposal plan," and which, upon implementation, would result in complete disarmament of the BRA.[58] Some of its details were reported by Papua New Guinea's *Post-Courier*:

> The weapons disposal plan includes . . . collecting all weapons from ex-combatants and locking them in the containers with robust but simple padlocks. The unit commanders will retain the keys and trunks but allow UN officials to verify the exercise. During the second stage, the weapons would be double-locked in larger containers with one key held by the local commander and one by the UN. . . . After the PNG Security Forces withdraw from each command area, the Company Commanders shall deliver arms held by them to one central collection point in each command area. . . . The decision on how these weapons should be finally dealt with will be made within one month of the constitutional amendments coming into effect.[59]

In short, this meant that BRA company commanders were no longer in control of their arms. There was also the implied threat is that if their arms were not forthcoming, neither would be the independence referendum.

What is the purpose of disarming a people who are headed toward greater autonomy and freedom? Upon independence, disarmament would be a moot point because Bougainville would then be self-governed, and the Bougainvilleans would be free to do whatever they liked, including retaining their arms.

One of the witnesses to the signing of the Bougainville Peace Agreement was New Zealand Foreign Minister Phil Goff, whose country agreed to provide 200 containers (basically, large trunks) for the storage of arms to be handed in by Bougainvillean ex-combatants. As the first batch of fifteen gun lockers were flown in on November 20, 2001, Goff declared: "The challenge now lies with the Bougainvilleans, particularly ex-combatants, to show their commitment to the Weapons Disposal Plan as expressed in the Bougainville Peace Agreement."[60]

The real challenge, however, was to convince Bougainvilleans who used those arms to halt the plunder of their land to unilaterally disarm. Francis Ona, whose independence movement controlled up to 20 percent of Bougainville, refused to participate in the peace process. The June 11, 1999,

Sydney Morning Herald quoted a defiant Ona as stating, "There are thousands of homemade weapons hidden in the villages and they will never be handed back until Bougainville becomes independent."[61]

The process of independence moved another step forward on January 23, 2002, when the PNG parliament unanimously voted in favor of constitutional amendments relating to Bougainville. One of these amendments would permit Bougainville to become autonomous under PNG, and the other would permit Bougainville to hold its referendum for independence in ten to fifteen years. Bougainville would be given control of its own foreign affairs, banking system, aviation, and shipping rights. Also, the "legislation allows Bougainville to have its own disciplined forces. . . ."[62]

That begs the question: if Bougainville is to have its own "disciplined forces," why should citizens be forced to reacquire firearms, after the second reading in parliament turns the amendments into law?

If peace was the real objective, why not disarm all combatants? Why not disarm, especially, the aggressors—the governments of Papua New Guinea and Australia—instead of only the victims who fought back? Why insist on disarmament first and postpone a referendum on independence for ten or more years, when independence was clearly the key to a lasting peace? Why should the people of Bougainville believe that once they were disarmed and helpless, the government of PNG would honor its promise ten or fifteen years in the future?

After the signing of the peace agreement, a total of 1,639 guns were registered and placed into locked containers. When it became obvious that the PNG government would not obey the peace agreement, at least two break-ins occurred where the sequestered arms were stored.[63] The first time, 110 weapons were removed. After the second break-in, an additional 360 were discovered missing. As Philip Alpers and Conor Twyford pointed out, "With so much energy being directed at weapons disposal, potential existed for community-wide resentment to develop as other needs were not met, or were met more slowly than expected."[64] That is exactly what came to pass.[65]

It has become clear that both the Australian and the PNG governments are loathe to hold the promised referendum on the future of the islanders. This is a violation of the Universal Declaration of Human Rights, which requires that "the will of the people shall be the basis of the authority of government; this will shall be expressed in periodic and genuine elections which shall be by universal and equal suffrage and shall be held by secret vote or by equivalent free voting procedures."[66] The kleptocracy's theft of the resources of the Bougainvilleans, and consequent impoverishment of the people, are inconsistent with the International Covenant on Economic, Social, and Cultural Rights, which recognizes "the inherent right of all peoples to enjoy and utilize fully and freely their natural wealth and resources."[67]

Unfortunately, the collection of firearms—rather than the restoration of human rights, or attention to basic human needs—is the first priority of the U.N. mission on Bougainville. As actually administered, the current "peace" program in Bougainville, like its predecessors, is relentlessly focused on removing arms from civilians and is indifferent to improving the lives of the population, including women and children.

CHAPTER 7

United Nations Corruption

T he United States pays a whopping 22 percent of the annual budget of the U.N., including payments to U.N. peacekeeping operations and to U.N. agencies and organizations. American taxpayers spent 1.6 billion dollars on the U.N. in 2004[1] in what amounts to an extremely poor use of our resources. As a deeply corrupt organization, the U.N. spends money (that is, U.S. taxpayer money) on waste, fraud, and abuse—as is common in large, corrupt bureaucracies.

Yet the massive waste, fraud, and abuse at the U.N. pales in comparison to other forms of corruption. The Oil-for-Food program was supposed to aid the poor people of Iraq; instead, it was used to help Saddam Hussein oppress and murder the Iraqis, protect himself by bribing foreign governments, and finance terrorism against Americans.

Even worse than the Oil-for-Food program is the most corrupt U.N. program of all—its so-called peacekeeping mission. U.N. peacekeepers often sexually abuse women and children, while the U.N.'s bureaucracy turns a blind eye. Yet American taxpayers pay for 27 percent of the U.N.'s "peacekeeping" budget.

The culture of rape among the U.N. peacekeepers has been significantly abetted by Kofi Annan, first in his role as director of U.N. peacekeeping operations from 1993 to 1996, and then in his role as U.N. secretary-general from 1997 to the present.[2]

The *Christian Science Monitor* has written that "wherever the U.N. has planted its flag in recent years, violations of women seem to follow."[3] The *Christian Science Monitor* summarized some of the abuses by the U.N.:

- A prostitution ring in Bosnia involved peacekeepers, while Canadian troops there were accused of beatings, rape, and sexually abusing a handicapped girl.

- Local U.N. staff in West Africa reportedly withheld aid, such as bags of flour, from refugees in exchange for sexual favors.

- Jordanian peacekeepers in East Timor were accused of rape.

- Italian troops in Somalia and Bulgarian troops in Cambodia were accused of sexual abuses.[4]

According to Sarah Martin, of the group Refugees International, "This is a problem in every mission around the world."[5] According to the *Washington Post*, "Pamela Shifman, a UNICEF expert on sexual exploitation of children, said abuses are pervasive among U.N. peacekeepers deployed in countries that have been afflicted by grinding poverty and years of conflict."[6]

Credible allegation of sex abuse by U.N. peacekeepers have been made regarding Cambodia, Mozambique, Somalia, Bosnia, Sierra Leone, East Timor, and Kosovo. These allegations "include sex-trafficking, prostitution rings, rapes, pedophilia, even abandoning 'peacekeeper babies.'"[7]

The pattern of sex abuse by peacekeepers finally garnered headlines in the summer of 2004, when investigative journalists uncovered the abuses taking place in the Democratic Republic of the Congo.[8] But the pattern of abuse was far older, dating back, at the least, to the first year that Kofi Annan took over as head of U.N. peacekeeping.

CAMBODIA

In the book *Emergency Sex and Other Desperate Matters*, three United Nations employees describe what "peacekeeping" really meant when U.N. peacekeepers showed up in Cambodia in 1993.

When a nation supplies peacekeepers to the United Nations, the U.N. pays a $1,028 monthly per-soldier fee to the nation's government, in effect buying mercenaries from those various governments.

According to the book, the first set of peacekeepers sent to Cambodia by the Bulgarian government were not soldiers but were prison and psychiatric ward inmates who were promised freedom in exchange for serving six months as U.N. peacekeepers. The Bulgarian government no longer had to pay to confine these criminals and lunatics. Instead, it made a profit by receiving U.N. money for their services in Cambodia. Then, according to the authors, "A battalion of criminal lunatics arrives in a lawless land. They get drunk as sailors, rape vulnerable Cambodian women. . . ."[9]

Similar abuses were documented in a 1993 report by Human Rights Watch.[10]

When whistleblowers came forward to protest the sex abuse by U.N. troops, Yasushi Akashi, the head U.N. official in Cambodia, brushed them off, claiming, "Boys will be boys."[11] That response might be adequate to thirteen-year-old boys skipping school to play football. It is not an acceptable response to thirty-year-old men raping thirteen-year-old girls.

BOSNIA

Kathryn Bolkovac is a mother of three, and a former American police-woman from Nebraska. She is also the human rights activist who exposed U.N. complicity in forced prostitution of fifteen-year-old girls in Bosnia. U.N. forces had been sent to Bosnia in part to protect women from human trafficking. In October 2000, Mrs. Bolkovac wrote an e-mail to the head of the U.N. mission in Bosnia-Hercegovina, Jacques Paul Klein, blowing the whistle on U.N. participation in the very abuses it was supposed to be fighting.

According to Mrs. Bolkovac, U.N. employees were frequent customers at brothels and strip clubs whose "employees" were foreign women who were, in essence, held prisoner and beaten and raped if they did not prostitute themselves, or if they attempted to escape.

Bolkovac kept up her pressure for an investigation. In 2002, she told the U.N. that there were females who were willing to testify about their abuse by U.N. forces. She urged the U.N. to conduct an internal investigation. Instead, she was told that she herself was a victim of "psychological burnout."[12] She was fired by the private contractor that hired her to provide services to the U.N. The contractor claimed she falsified her time sheets, a charge she successfully refuted in a lawsuit.[13]

Not only were the U.N.'s international staff patronizing brothels of captive children, some of the staff were working with corrupt local police as active participants in human trafficking. Yet according to the U.S. House International Relations Committee, the "U.N. quashed an investigation into involvement of U.N. police in the enslavement of Eastern European women in Bosnian brothels."[14]

Reporter Kate Holt of the British newspaper *The Independent* has investigated U.N. peacekeeper abuse all over the world.[15] Holt recalls a March 1998 conversation with U.N. staff in Sarajevo. One of the staffers mentioned that in "the infamous Arizona Market, near Brcko in northeastern Bosnia, young girls [from Romania, Moldova, and other Eastern European countries] were paraded weekly for sale and purchased by bar owners who put them to work as sex slaves."

In 1999, Holt found that some U.N. "employees were heavily involved in providing a market for this [sex slave] trade. Every young girl I spoke to in these bars told me that, of the six to eight men they were forced to sleep with each night, the majority were U.N. employees."

Holt met with Kathy Bolkovac, who "was willing to reveal that very senior levels of the U.N. mission were involved in this sickening trade."

Holt also met with a Bosnian photographer who said he had been beaten up and his camera was stolen after he photographed "a very senior member of the U.N. one night in a bar with a very young Romanian girl." The same night that Holt met with the photographer, she "received an anonymous phone call saying 'don't continue with your investigations or you will find yourself in trouble.'"

Bosnia was not the only place where U.N. peacekeepers ran a child prostitution ring. They did the same on the Eritrea/Ethiopia border, and in Mozambique.[16]

KOSOVO

In 2001, independent human rights investigators proved the extensive U.N. involvement in running houses of prostitution with victims of human trafficking not only in Bosnia, but also in Kosovo.[17]

U.N. participation in human trafficking in Kosovo was to have ended by reforms enacted after the first round of exposure by the whistleblowers. But as a May 2004 report by Amnesty International detailed, the women and child prostitutes "are threatened, beaten, raped, and effectively impris-oned by their owners." Further, "With clients including international police and troops, the girls and women are often too afraid to escape, and the authorities are failing to help them. It is outrageous that the very same people who are there to protect these women and girls are using their posi-tion and exploiting them instead—and they are getting away with it."[18]

In November 2004, the *Christian Science Monitor* reported on contin-uing U.N. involvement in sex trafficking in Kosovo.[19] Kosovo follows the typical pattern of human trafficking. Foreign women—including girls as young as fourteen—are lured from their homelands with promises of jobs. Instead, they are sold like slaves, usually to work in the sex industry. They are not allowed to leave, and are beaten up if they try to escape. They are also told that if they escape, their family back home will be attacked or killed.[20]

In August 2005, three Pakistani U.N. police officers in Kosovo were arrested for human trafficking. Avni Arifi, a senior adviser to Kosovo's prime minister, said the three were "not isolated cases." Kosovo's prime minister, Bajram Kosumi, stated, "Unfortunately we do not have exact data about human trafficking here. But I can say that the citizens of Kosovo do not trust UNMIK's (U.N. Mission in Kosovo) structures in some fields."[21]

WEST AFRICA

U.N. peacekeepers arrived in Liberia in 1996. Most were from Nigeria, and they reportedly encouraged nine- or ten-year-old girls from a nearby refugee camp to have sex with them, in exchange for rice or a bit of cash. Ghanian peacekeepers did the same, except they would give the little girls an entire can of rice, rather than just a handful. As a result, the girls started coming to the Ghanian camp instead of the Nigerian one.

"One day dead little girls started appearing on the path from the dis-placed persons camp to the Ghanian camp. . . . The girls had been decapi-tated and their heads inserted inside their nine-year-old genitals." A U.N. investigator concluded that the Nigerians were warning the girls not to go the Ghanian camp for the extra food.

"And these are the peacekeepers," the authors of *Emergency Sex and Other Desperate Matters* note.[22] The book recounts an incident in which

Liberian refugees were fleeing from a rebel army until U.N. peacekeepers intercepted them and told them to stay put in a village. Then the peacekeepers withdrew, leaving the refugees behind to be soon slaughtered by the rebels. Further south, the peacekeepers refused to allow any refugees to flee through U.N. defensive lines, thereby leaving the refugees nowhere to escape the rebels.[23]

The sexual abuse in Liberia was hardly untypical. A 2002 report by Save the Children detailed how staff from more than forty international "aid" agencies—including the United Nations High Commissioner for Refugees (UNHCR)—raped and sexually abused refugees in Liberia, Sierra Leone, and Guinea. The report also accused the U.N. of trying to cover up the problem.[24]

In 2001, the United Nations High Commissioner for Refugees and Save the Children conducted a joint investigation of the abuses. They found widespread problems, including "humanitarian" workers who refused to give out food or supplies unless the refugees submitted to sex. The report, a draft of which was released in February 2002, contained extensive recommendations. [25]By October 2002, the High Commissioner for Refugees could point to an extensive list of reforms that had been implemented.[26]

But in March 2005, the *Washington Post* reported on a February 8, 2005, internal U.N. letter, which stated that in Gbarnga, Liberia, "girls as young as 12 years of age are engaged in prostitution, forced into sex acts and sometimes photographed by U.N. peacekeepers in exchange for $10 or food or other commodities." Further, the letter reported that in Robertsport, Liberia, community leaders said that U.N. peacekeepers were "using administrative building premises and the surrounding bush to undertake sex acts with girls between the age of 12–17."[27]

DEMOCRATIC REPUBLIC OF THE CONGO

Although solid reports of widespread sexual abuse by U.N. employees and peacekeepers dated back at least to 1993, it was not until 2004 that significant media attention was finally focused, as a result of the massive sexual abuses perpetrated in the Democratic Republic of the Congo (DRC).

Sadly, many of the crimes perpetrated by the U.N. in the Congo have been made possible with American taxpayer dollars. Through 2005, the

U.S. had spent $759 million on Congo peacekeeping, and plans to spend an additional $207 million in 2006.[28]

The head of U.N. operations in the Congo, incidentally, is William Lacy Swing, who had previously been appointed by President Clinton to serve as U.S. Ambassador to the Congo, and before that, as U.S. Ambassador to Haiti.

Journalist Kate Holt, who had first investigated the U.N.'s culture of rape in Bosnia in 1998, arrived at a U.N. refugee camp in Bunia, Congo, in February 2004. She almost immediately found that women and girls in the camp were sneaking out nightly to have sex with U.N. personnel, in exchange for a bag of peanuts or a couple of eggs.

"When it became evident the U.N. was reluctant to act on the information I had given it, I decided I had no choice but to publish," Holt reports. "Only then did the U.N. say it was going to start a full investigation."[29]

Holt, by the way, was not the only person whose warnings were ignored by the U.N. "A local children's rights organization said it investigated allegations of rape purportedly by U.N. peacekeepers and turned the findings over to the U.N.," she says. "But the organization said so far, it has seen no results."[30]

Returning to the Congo in July, she "became aware that the problem was not just there [Bunia] but was endemic to every town where the U.N. was based in the DRC—and that the U.N. had first received reports of abuse as far back as 2002. These reports, filed to Kinshasa, had been buried, and no action had been taken."[31] Holt says she received two threatening phone calls, and a note warning, "If you continue your investigations against the U.N., there will be trouble for you."[32]

Holt wrote that she "was also approached by several people in the U.N. who were increasingly horrified as to how widespread the problem was and how so much of the information was apparently being covered up. With long U.N. careers behind them, they were risking their jobs to give me information, but felt that the levels of abuse and corruption had to be exposed if the U.N. was to continue to function with any degree of integrity."[33]

Other journalists have also found that children engaging in "voluntary" sex with U.N. troops in exchange for a bit of food, or a dollar, was common.[34] Some of the girls engaged in what is called "survival sex" were as young as eleven. [35]

The U.N. employees who exposed the truth should be commended for serving the original, noble purposes for which the U.N. was created. The U.N. has many good employees, however, the bad ones are allowed to run rampant by a system of corruption that reaches all the way to the office of the secretary-general. Many of the good employees were subjected to death threats for providing information to U.N. investigators.[36]

In July 2004, a draft internal U.N. report of worldwide peacekeeping concluded, "Sexual exploitation and abuse, particularly prostitution of minors, is widespread and long-standing. . . . Moreover, all of the major contingents appear to be implicated."[37] The U.N. had announced a series of steps to halt the abuses, including tough language about "zero tolerance" for sex abuse, but these "had largely faded away" by October 24, when a U.N. special commission headed by Jordan's Prince Zeid al-Hussein showed up to investigate.[38]

A November 8, 2004, draft of the prince's report (which was leaked to the press) concluded that sexual abuse "appears to be significant, wide-spread and ongoing."[39] According to the report, "In some cases, U.N. officials allegedly raped women and girls and then offered them food or money to make it look as if they had engaged in prostitution."[40] In other words, "The situation appears to be one of 'zero-compliance with zero-tolerance' throughout the mission."[41]

ABANDONING BABIES

All the rape and prostitution result in many native women bearing "peace-keeper babies"—notwithstanding the U.N. practice of distributing one condom per day to each peacekeeper.

On the U.N. Web site, you can read all sorts of documents with soaring rhetoric about the inviolable rights of women, but in practice, the U.N. does not seem to believe that women who are impregnated by U.N. rapists have any rights.

Brian Ross, the ABC News reporter for a *20/20* investigation of sex abuse in the Congo, explains, "There is no evidence that we could find that anyone in the U.N. is making a serious or systematic effort to identify the fathers or to hold them accountable. In fact, the head of the U.N. Congo mission admits they have no effective paternity policy."[42]

Ross continues:

The babies themselves are seriously at risk. Keep in mind that their mothers are among the poorest people in the world, quite literally. And they are living in a war zone, which is the reason for the U.N. intervention. In this context, the babies abandoned by peacekeepers will suffer deeply entrenched poverty in the care of their struggling mothers. There is no institutional support system for them provided by the U.N. or any of its affiliated groups. [43]

In February 2005, Ross's *20/20* broadcast brought the story of the U.N. sex abuse in the Congo to a wide American audience. ABC interviewed William Lacy Swing, the appointee from the Clinton State Department who was now running the U.N. mission in the Congo. According to ABC, "Swing said the problem was just recently brought to his attention, and that only a small percentage of the 11,000 U.N. personnel in Congo were involved."[44]

Swing's statement appears incorrect on both counts. The problem was, in fact, brought to his attention at least as early as 2002, by a report sent to U.N. headquarters in Kinshasa (Congo's capital), which reported on sexual abuses in the town of Goma, perpetrated by Moroccan peacekeepers. Swing and MONUC (the Mission of the U.N. in the Democratic Republic of the Congo) did nothing in response to the report.[45]

Because of MONUC's continuing failure to act, *The Independent* conducted its own investigation in early 2004 and published the results. The attendant publicity finally led the U.N. to begin an investigation.[46] Around June 8, 2004, Swing cabled U.N. headquarters with information about fifty allegations of abuse, of which 80 percent were against children. Among the allegations was a "prostitution network of minors at MONUC airport, reportedly operated by various MONUC contingents and personnel."[47] In other words, the U.N.'s own airport in the Congo was the base for a U.N.-run child prostitution network.

The U.N.'s Offices of Oversight Services (OSIS) was ordered to conduct an investigation. But as reported in the *New York Sun*, "this investigation was fatally flawed. No witness protection was offered to girls coming forward and according to a confidential U.N. report leaked in July, witnesses had been bribed to change their testimony and threatened with retaliatory attacks should they continue to pursue their claims." Although there were allegations of sex abuse by the U.N. all over the Congo, the OSIS was ordered to investigate only the claims from the Bunia region.[48] The OSIS report was kept secret until early 2005, although it was completed much earlier.[49]

A Canadian critic noted that the report claimed that the U.N. had taken "appropriate action" in response to the abuses, but Kofi Annan's office was unable to describe what any of those actions were.[50]

Swing's claim about "a small percentage" of U.N. personnel rings true only to the extent that the U.N. has succeeded in hiding data from the public. In an online exchange with viewers, ABC reporter Brian Ross explained: "We are not in a good position to quantify a percentage of implicated peacekeeping troops. Clearly, there are hundreds of allegations which may imply a large number of U.N. personnel involved in misconduct. *Without a greater degree of transparency on the part of the U.N., it is not possible to* quantify the number implicated in the hundreds of allegations."[51]

In other words, the organization that is so determined to create transparency (that is, universal gun registration, as a prelude to a worldwide gun registry) for ordinary citizens can't stand the idea of transparency for itself—especially for public investigation of violent sex crimes against children perpetrated by its employees.

Like Kofi Annan, William Swing was a master about making promises to help victims of the U.N., and then doing nothing. ABC reports:

> Swing promised that the United Nations would make an effort to find the young women Bourguet photographed and include them in the U.N. victim support program. No such actions have yet been taken. In fact, none of the victims interviewed for this story had received any help, of any kind, psychological or financial, from the United Nations.[52]

Continuing media exposure of U.N. sex assaults in the Congo and elsewhere resulted in stern denunciations from U.N. bureaucrats. "I am afraid there is clear evidence that acts of gross misconduct have taken place," fulminated Kofi Annan. "This is a shameful thing for the United Nations to have to say, and I am absolutely outraged by it."[53]

The tough language was reminiscent of Captain Renault's claim in *Casablanca* that he was "shocked" to find out that gambling was taking place in Rick's nightclub—as a croupier handed him his winnings. Annan, remember, had been head of U.N. peacekeeping in 1993, when reports of U.N. peacekeepers raping children in Cambodia were brushed off as "boys will be boys."

Throughout late 2004 and the first part of 2005, the U.N. bureaucracy issued numerous promises of reform, for "zero tolerance" for sex abuse, and so on, [54] but after leading his own investigation, Jordan's Prince Zeid al-Hussein told the media in 2005 that the U.N. member states were uninterested in real reform. "The entire responsibility for this mess is with the member states." His calls for reform were met with what he called "utter silence." He scheduled meetings to discuss reform, and no one would attend.[55] Prince Zeid explained to the Security Council that the U.N. had been covering up abuses by peacekeepers ever since its inception sixty years ago.[56]

Today, as before, the worst thing that is likely to happen to a U.N. peacekeeper who sexually abuses someone is that he will be sent home. As before, hardly any of the few peacekeepers who are sent home are punished, or even charged.[57] The main countries that supply peacekeepers are Pakistan, Morocco, and Bangladesh—none of which treat women decently in their own countries.

Although it was expected that Kofi Annan would fire William Lacy Swing, the head of the U.N. mission in the Congo, Swing kept his job. But the U.N. did dismiss one "troublemaker" in the summer of 2005.

One of the coauthors of *Emergency Sex and Other Desperate Measures: A True Story from Hell on Earth*, which detailed the incompetence and abuses of U.N. peacekeepers, was New Zealand doctor Andrew Thomson. Although he had worked for the U.N. for twelve years and his contract had been renewed annually, he was terminated without explanation.[58]

Another coauthor, Kenneth Cain, left the U.N. in 1996. Cain explains that most U.N. employees come from a corrupt national elite that can get away with anything, as long as they do not offend someone more powerful. At the U.N., they have created a similar culture. "They are perfectly happy to release documents that promise or imply efforts to reform—and time after time it dies before the ink is dry. . . . The United Nations promulgates human-rights standards to the whole world. But when you try to hold them to the very same standards, it's impossible."[59]

Rape, kidnapping, human trafficking, and pederasty committed by peacekeepers are violations of human rights standards created by the U.N., including the Convention on the Rights of the Child, Convention on the Elimination of All Forms of Discrimination Against Women, and the Universal Declaration of Human Rights.

OIL-FOR-FOOD

The U.N. peacekeepers' sexual abuse of destitute women and children is sometimes called the "sex-for-food" scandal. The term is a variant of a more widely known U.N. scandal, the Oil-for-Food program.

After the 1991 Gulf War, Iraqi dictator Saddam Hussein agreed to a ceasefire on the part of coalition forces—which could have easily deposed his criminal regime—in exchange for complete dismantlement of his weapons of mass destruction (WMD) program. The burden was explicitly on Saddam to prove that he had disarmed. He was given a fifteen-day deadline to declare all of his WMD facilities and weapons, and required to "unconditionally accept" total destruction of his WMDs.[60]

Saddam thumbed his nose at one U.N. resolution after another, and never complied with the U.N.'s repeated disarmament demands. The economic sanctions imposed as a result of his invasion of Kuwait had little impact on Saddam personally. As head of what was in effect an organized criminal gang that looted Iraq, he always made sure there was enough money to pay for his palaces and luxuries. The sanctions did, however, put a crimp in his WMD plans, and in his efforts to rebuild the Iraqi military. The sanctions also had a significant impact on the ordinary people of Iraq.

The United States supported a U.N. proposal for a strict policy to allow some oil sales by Iraq, with the revenue being carefully monitored to assure that it was spent for the benefit of the Iraqi people, and not for Saddam. He rejected the proposal out of hand.

In 1996, the U.N. caved in, and created the Oil-for-Food program (OFFP). Although ostensibly meant to help the Iraqi people, it was almost instantly taken over by Saddam, and used to finance his dictatorship and for the extensive bribery of foreign governments, and of the U.N.[61]

The bank chosen to administer the program was a Parisian institution that was already a major holder of Saddam's government accounts.[62] Saddam was allowed to be the exclusive decision maker on who would get oil contracts and contracts to supply goods to Iraq. Within the U.N., it was "assumed from the beginning that Iraq would corrupt it [OFFP] from the start."[63] A U.S. House International Relations subcommittee concluded:

> Once firmly ensconced as gatekeeper of contracts, Saddam Hussein's strategy of corrupting the program was relatively simple and was achieved by a number of means: fraudulent orders for humanitarian goods paid for, but never delivered; a partial delivery of humanitarian goods with proceeds shared among regime elements; goods shipments with obscure descriptions to hinder timely inspections; overpricing of humanitarian goods designed to hide kickbacks; after sale service fees of as much as 30%, a portion of which was paid as a kickback; overcharging for shipping costs and outright theft of goods destined for the Iraqi people.[64]

The U.N. staff in Baghdad knowingly allowed itself to be infiltrated by Saddam's intelligence service, and allowed their communications with the outside world to be monitored by Iraqi intelligence. Rather than working to force Iraq to comply with U.N. resolutions, the U.N. Baghdad staff acted as a public relations arm for the dictator—demanding that sanctions be lifted even though Saddam was still in violation of every U.N. resolution. The few conscientious U.N. employees who did speak up were quashed by the management, and told that they were spies.[65]

Benon V. Sevan was appointed by Annan in October 1997 as executive director of the Iraqi OFFP. Sevan actively obstructed all inquires into corruption.[66] It later turned out that Sevan was being bribed by Saddam, from whom he received special oil allocations for 13 million barrels.[67]

When the United States and Britain slowed down U.N. processing of OFFP contracts, so they could be examined more carefully, Annan objected.[68]

According to the U.S. General Accounting Office, Saddam reaped 10.1 billion dollars from OFFP,[69] and used OFFP to acquire materials that were ostensibly for civilian use, but were in fact used to build up his WMD programs.[70]

Among the uses to which Saddam put the OFFP revenues were $25,000 rewards to the families of Palestinian terrorist bombers.[71] He was very public about his reward payments to the terrorists, yet his funding of terrorism never received the slightest condemnation from the U.N.

Other revenues from OFFP corruption appear to have funded the terrorist insurgents currently fighting against the elected Iraqi government and its coalition allies.[72] Stated another way, the U.N. facilitated Saddam's acquisition of the enormous funds that are still paying for the killers of U.S. troops.

By early 1998, Iraq had stepped up its defiance of U.N. weapons inspectors. Kofi Annan's response was to speak before the Security Council on February 1, 1998, and ask that OFFP be doubled.[73] After praising Saddam as "A man I can do business with," [74] Annan resolved the inspections crisis by making a deal with Saddam that U.N. inspectors would be accompanied by diplomats, including some friendly to the dictator. These diplomats gave the Iraqis advance warning of inspections, so that suspicious WMD facilities could be cleared before the inspectors arrived. Annan's staff condemned the U.N. inspectors as "cowboys" who had been insufficiently deferential to the Saddam government's feelings.[75]

By 2000, the corruption in OFFP had grown to an enormous size. At the same time, Annan bragged to the Security Council that he had reformed OFFP to make it transparent. [76]Yet, when records of the Saddam government were pored over by investigators, it was discovered that Saddam had given Benon Sevan vouchers for millions of barrels of oil.[77] It was also discovered that kickbacks had been paid to more than 2,000 companies, with companies from France, Russia, and China receiving preferential treatment.[78]

Also receiving Iraqi OFFP bribes were Vladimir Zhirinovsky (deputy chair of Russia's parliament, the Duma), France's former U.N. ambassador Jean-Bernard Merimee, and George Galloway (a pro-terrorist, viciously anti-American member of the British Parliament).[79]

Annan at first resisted making any U.N. documents available to outside investigators. Under enormous pressure from Congress, Annan ultimately allowed outside access to the documents. But first, Annan's chief of staff, S. Iqbal Riza, directed the shredding of thousands of papers related to OFFP.[80]

THE COTECNA CONNECTION

Cotecna is a Swiss company that was interested in acquiring a U.N. contract to monitor the OFFP spending. Kofi Annan had friends at Cotecna, and he asked them to help find work for his son, Kojo.[81]

Kojo Annan was paid $400,000 by Cotecna. He had been hired to help them obtain a multi-million dollar contract, which he did, and yet he was kept on the payroll even after the contract had been awarded.[82] Kofi Annan later claimed that he had no idea that Kojo had gotten a job with Cotecna.[83] He also claimed that he thought his son's involvement in Cotecna had ended in 1999, even though Kojo was still on the payroll in 2004. When the scandal broke, Benon Sevan (understandably) ordered Cotecna not to cooperate with investigators.

Annan has claimed that he received an "exoneration" by the Independent Inquiry Committee (IIC) headed by Paul Volcker.[84] In fact, Robert Parton, a former FBI agent who was the senior investigator of Kofi Annan's participation in the OFFP had stated that Annan lied. [85]According to a U.S. House of Representatives International Relations subcommittee, Parton stated that Volcker and the other senior members were "unwilling to reach any conclusion that would result in significant adverse consequences for the secretary-general." [86]

The International Relations subcommittee concluded that the problems of OFFP are not aberrational, but are endemic and the inevitable result of the U.N.'s structure:

> The U.N.'s capacity to punish wrongdoing within its ranks also suffers from a lack of a functioning independent administrative justice system, allowing crimes or malfeasance to go unpunished, and when cases are brought up, they frequently are riddled with procedural errors such that many are overturned on appeal by the United Nations' own supreme tribunal. Each of the deficiencies detailed in this report has individually and collectively contributed to the culture of impropriety and the lack of accountability that undergirded the oil-for-food era. The very fact that the IIC had to be created is a sign of the U.N.'s inability to investigate and expose its own wrongdoing.

Problems associated with the OFFP are not isolated or unique to that particular U.N.-administered program. The OFFP, and the myriad of problems associated with it, are symptomatic of a pervasive mismanagement and failure of leadership at the U.N.

Among the management and organizational weaknesses are a lack of appropriate and effective internal or external independent oversight (including both audit and investigations); the near absence of adequate internal controls within the Secretariat; and a lack of appropriate and modern accountability mechanisms, including a functioning whistleblower protection policy; a code of ethics; an ethics training and certification regime; a financial disclosure process and policy; and a freedom of information policy.

In addition to being decades behind other public institutions in its business processes, internal controls, and accountability mechanisms, the U.N. suffers from a lack of proper leadership and commitment to excellence by the organization's senior most leadership.[87]

When Iraqi and U.S. forces drove out terrorists from their stronghold in Fallujah in late 2004, Secretary-General Annan objected to the operation. Today, he continues to undermine Iraqi freedom at every turn.

SCANDAL AFTER SCANDAL

The Congo rape scandal and the Oil-for-Food scandal have become well known to the American public; however the U.N. is such a factory of corruption and malfeasance that it appears to be producing scandals so fast it is hard to keep up.

One of the newest financial scandals involves the United Nations Procurement Division, which spends most of the U.N.'s money, and whose responsibilities include spending over $1.3 billion annually in supplies for peacekeepers. So far, eight officials of the Procurement Division have been suspended. One of them, Alexander Yakovlev, has pled guilty in Federal District Court to bribing contractors.[88] Problematic contracts issued by the procurement division may amount to several hundred million dollars. An outside report from Deloitte Consulting said that the Procurement Division is incompetent, and is easy pickings for corruption.[89]

Claudia Rossett is an investigative reporter who has been examining the U.N. for the *Wall Street Journal*, *New York Sun*, and *Fox News*. She writes that the procurement scandal "suggests that the U.N.'s failures of governance are not confined to such special projects as the Oil for Food program. If anything, Oil for Food looks more and more like a large outcropping of U.N. business as usual."

She points out that one of the companies at the center of the procurement scandal was IHC Services—which turns out to exist only as some kind of front for other interests. She concluded, "it appears the U.N. has been serving as a bazaar in which corruption, conflicts of interests and shadowy financial networks have found ways to set up shop. Behind the maze, who was the real owner of IHC during its nine years of doing big business with the U.N.? The U.N. won't say, and quite possibly does not even know. Its policy, in fact, was not even to ask."[90]

A special U.N. commission also has been investigating the assassination of political leaders in Lebanon, including former Prime Minister Rafik Hariri. The head of the investigation is German prosecutor Detlev Mehlis. The trail of evidence uncovered by the Mehlis investigation leads straight to Syria's dictatorship, which ruled Lebanon as a colony for decades until being forced out in early 2005.

When the Mehlis commission was created, Kofi Annan promised that he would not alter a single word in the Mehlis report. But when Mehlis produced its draft report, Annan ordered it to be censored, to remove text implicating the brother of Syrian dictator Bashar Assad, as well as other top officials in the Assad tyranny.[91]

CONCLUSION: PREYING ON THE WEAK

There is currently lots of talk about reforming the U.N., but the body has been "reformed" many times. The U.N. goes through the motions of faux reform approximately once every eight years. Back in 1998, when Annan was busy crushing another effort at reform, he complained, "I think we should be allowed to focus on our work and not face constant harassment of reform, reform, reform."[92]

In the long run, the U.N. only gets worse and worse. None of the reforms address the fundamental problem: the majority of U.N. member states are dictatorships with a strong interest in ensuring that the U.N. bureaucracy complies with their wishes.

The Deloitte Consulting study concluded that "staff members feel unprotected when reporting violations of codes of conduct." Rather, they are inhibited from reporting wrongdoing by "fear of retaliation."[93]

Peter Dennis, a law student at NYU Law School, worked at refugee camps in Sierra Leone in 2003 on behalf of the Foundation for International Dignity. In a *Washington Post* op-ed titled "The U.N., Preying on the Weak," he summarized the fundamental problems at the U.N.[94]

> Anyone who was shocked by the most recent revelations of sexual misconduct by United Nations staff has never set foot in a U.N.-sponsored refugee camp. Sex crimes are only one especially disturbing symptom of a culture of abuse that exists in the United Nations precisely because the United Nations and its staff lack accountability. . . .
>
> [T]he recent stonewalling over a series of scandals from the United Nations—from oil-for-food to a sexual harassment imbroglio involving a high U.N. official—are typical of a bureaucracy dedicated to self-preservation. This code of behavior travels rapidly down the organizational chart. The message is: cover your tracks and the United Nations will obstruct your prosecution.

Unlike Bill Clinton, I do not think that "Kofi Annan's a good guy who deserved the Nobel Peace Prize."[95] Yet while the problems at the U.N. in the last decade often involve Kofi Annan, it would be a mistake to conclude that the problems revolve around him alone. The gun-banning, genocide-abetting Annan did not rise to his position by force or trickery. He was put there because the U.N. system—that is, the U.N. bureaucracy and the U.N. member states—wanted him. Annan never had a significant career as a diplomat, or any other real-world role. Since 1962, he worked within the U.N. bureaucracy, learning the skills of flattery, evasion, doublespeak, and deception necessary to rise to the top. He is the epitome of the modern U.N.

His record as head of peacekeeping operations in 1993–96 was perfectly plain: genocide in Rwanda and Bosnia, as disarmed victims relied on phony promises of U.N. protection, and obstruction of any effort to call attention to the problem. Rape, slavery, and kidnapping by the peacekeepers under Annan's supervision in Cambodia continued unabated, with their violent crimes dismissed by one of Annan's underlings as "boys will be boys."

Sweden's former deputy Per Ahlmark explains:

That is the culture of the U.N.: believe the best of the barbarians, do nothing to provoke controversy among superiors, and let others be the butt of criticism afterwards. Even subsequent revelations about Annan's responsibility for the disasters in Rwanda and Bosnia did not affect his standing. On the contrary, he was unanimously reelected [as Secretary-General in 2000] and awarded the Nobel Peace Prize.[96]

The record of 1993 to 1996 was clear, and Annan was rewarded in 1996 with selection as Secretary-General. When such a man rises to the top, the system that elevated him must bear the primary blame.

The U.N. aid worker, New Zealand doctor and whistleblower Andrew Thomson tells the same story, from the perspective of an idealistic U.N. staffer dismayed by the reality of the U.N.:

"On the one hand you can be in charge of the peacekeepers, as he was in the 90s when these catastrophes happened, and get promoted to the top job in the organization. . . .

"But if, like myself, you work in those mass graves with the result of those catastrophes, and then write about it, with the stories of all the victims and survivors I worked with, you get fired. If that's the message they're sending then I have more concerns for the United Nations than I have for myself." Thomson said the decision not to renew his contract was a "classic case of trying to shoot the messenger." He said he was accused of being disloyal to the U.N. by "the very people responsible for allowing the worst abuses to take place."[97]

The pervasive corruption of the U.N.—of which Kofi Annan is more a symptom than a cause—is ultimately the result of a huge institution that has no meaningful system of accountability. At the U.N., there are no checks and balances that apply to democratic nations and institutions.

It should not be surprising then, that the U.N. has declared global war on gun ownership, because gun ownership is the ultimate protection against tyranny.

CHAPTER 8

United Nations and Genocide: A Historical Perspective

The United Nations was founded to prevent the recurrence of global disasters such as World War II and, in particular, to prevent future tyrants from emulating the genocides perpetrated by Adolf Hitler and Hideki Tojo.

In 1948, the United Nations General Assembly adopted the Convention on the Prevention and Punishment of the Crime of Genocide, which was ratified by enough states in 1951 that it became binding international law.[1] The Convention not only outlaws genocide, it also forbids any government from assisting a genocide in any way. Further, the Genocide Convention requires signatory states to act to stop genocides in progress.

Yet despite the promising start, the U.N. has proved almost entirely useless in preventing crimes against humanity. Indeed, it has barely ever tried, and its agenda to ensure that victims are disarmed and defenseless can only lead to future genocides.

University of Hawaii political science professor R.J. Rummel, the world's leading statistical scholar of mass murders by governments, estimates that during the twentieth century, governments murdered approximately 169,198,000 victims. That figure does not include people killed by warfare; if you add war deaths, the death by government total rises by 33 million more. Indeed, dictatorships are the major cause of violent death in the world, far exceeding all other causes.

Professor Rummel's book, *Statistics of Democide: Estimates, Sources, and Calculations on 20th Century Genocide and Mass Murder*, includes data on mass murders throughout the twentieth century. These are *some* of the genocides that took place between 1946-1987, after the creation of the U.N.:

In Asia[2]

- Vietnam (1,678,000)

- North Korea (over 2 million)

- Pakistan (1,503,000, mainly from West Pakistan's 1971 mass murder of over a million Bengalis and Hindus in East Pakistan, which is now the independent nation of Bangladesh)

- Iraq (the 1966–88 murder of over 100,000 Kurds and southern Shiites)

- Communist China (73 million)

- Cambodia (by the Khmer Rouge from 1975–79: 2,035,000; by the Vietnamese-allied military government that took power afterwards: 230,000)

- Afghanistan (by Communist government which took power in 1978 coup: 237,000)

- Soviet Union (22.485 million; as with other countries on this list, the figure is only for murders from 1946 onward, after the U.N. had been created)

- Indonesia (1965: 509,000 communists and ethnic Chinese)

- East Timor (1975–98: 150,000 killed by the Indonesian government)

In Europe[3]

- Poland (885,000 from 1945 to 1948)

- Czechoslovakia (185,000)

- Romania (435,000)

- Bulgaria (185,000)

- Yugoslavia (1,072,000 from 1944 to 1987, under the Tito dictatorship; in the 1990s, about 25,000–100,000 murdered in Bosnia-Herzegovina)

In Africa[4]

- Ethiopia (725,000, by communist dictatorship that took power in 1974)

- Rwanda (600,000 to 1,000,000 Tutsi and moderate Hutus killed in 1994)

- Uganda (301,000 by Idi Amin; 262,000 after Amin)

- Burundi (1967-87 murders of Hutus: 150,000)

- Sudan (starting in 1955 and continuing to the present: murders of non-Arab Africans, Christians, and animists, over one million deaths)

Professor Rummel summarizes the statistics: from 1945 through 1987, there were about 114 million people who were murdered by governments. Of those 114 million, about 104 million were killed by Communism, a political system that imposed repressive gun laws wherever it obtained power. Rummel estimates that since 1987, between three million and six million more people have been mass-murdered by governments.[5]

To read the list of genocides above is to read a list of U.N. failures. Never, anywhere in the world, in the U.N.'s six decades of existence, has it acted to stop a genocide in progress. To make matters worse, the U.N. has become, in practice, a genocide enabler. Formerly, tyrants preparing for genocide carried out civilian disarmament themselves. Now, genocide perpetrators have U.N. assistance in disarming their victims.

RWANDA

Not too long ago the U.N. facilitated the genocide against the disarmed people of Rwanda,[6] a nation which had been ruled since 1973 by the dictator Juvénal Habyarimana, a member of the majority Hutu tribe. The Tutsi minority comprised about 10 to 15 percent of the population.

Rwanda had an ideal gun control system by U.N. standards: a 1979 law nearly completely outlawed civilian gun possession. Of course, the government still had guns, and every family had a machete—an essential daily tool for the small farming villages where almost all Rwandans lived.

Years of oppression drove the many Tutsi and moderate Hutus to join the Rwandan Patriotic Front (RPF), a group of rebel militias that operated out of nations bordering Rwanda.

The Rwandan government had long been calling for killing the Tutsis, and, ever since achieving independence from Belgium in 1959, had carried out many mass murders of Tutsis, as well as many other forms of ethnic persecution. In 1992, President Habyarimana escalated the rhetoric even further, with insistent calls for Tutsi extermination. His propaganda was reinforced by two major radio stations; Radio Rwanda and Radio Milles Collines constantly called the Tutsis "cockroaches" and called for their extermination in songs and comedy routines.

All of the several Hutu political parties had one thing in common: their platforms demanded the killing of Tutsis, in meticulous and explicit detail.[7] At political rallies and meetings, Hutus were told to stop being friends with Tutsis, or sharing farm work with them, because one day the Hutus would have to kill the Tutsis.[8]

In 1990, the Habyarimana clan had formed a group of organized violent gangs called the *interahamwe*, founded on the principle of hatred of Tutsis and obedience to the Habyarimana dictatorship. (Foreign observers refer to these gangs as "militias," but they obviously had nothing in common with legitimate militias, created for community self-defense.)

After an April 1993 visit to Rwanda, the U.N.'s Special Rapporteur of the Commission on Human Rights documented the extensive massacres and other killings of Tutsis that were taking place. He did not conclude that the massacres constituted genocide, but did raise the possibility. His report was "largely ignored" by the United Nations.[9]

U.N. peacekeepers were sent to Rwanda late that year. On January 11, 1994, the head of the U.N. mission in Rwanda, Canadian General Roméo Dallaire, send an urgent message to the U.N. headquarters in New York. The message was directed to the Department of Peacekeeping Operations, which was headed by Kofi Annan.

Dallaire reported what he had learned from an informant, who had been put in touch with Dallaire by a "very, very important government politician." A large organized gang called the Hutu Interhamwe was receiving training in Rwandan government army camps. The Interhamwe were being prepared to register all Tutsi in the region of Kigali, the capital city.

The informant suspected that the purpose of registering Tutsis was "for their extermination." He also knew where the Interhamwe had huge caches of arms, and he offered to tell the U.N., so that the peacekeepers could seize them. Dallaire informed Annan's office that he intended to seize the caches that were about to be used for genocide.

Annan's office had every reason to believe Dallaire. The personal representative of the U.N. secretary-general had cabled Annan's office to say that he had met with the prime minister designate of Rwanda, who had "total, repeat total confidence in the veracity" of the informant. The previous year, the U.N. had received reports of 2,000 Tutsis being murdered. The United Nations Human Rights Commission, in a 1993 investigation of Rwanda, had warned that the nation was at risk of genocide. Senior Rwandan military officers had written to General Dallaire in December 1993 to tell him about a plan to mass murder Tutsis. And a Hutu radio station was broadcasting intense hate propaganda, inciting the Hutus against the Tutsis.

Despite all the evidence, Annan's assistant in New York, Iqbal Riza, ordered General Dallaire to leave the arms alone, and chastised him for even thinking of seizing them. Instead, he was ordered to pass along his information only to the U.S., French, and Belgian embassies, and to the president of Rwanda.

In February, Dallaire's office cabled New York again, warning of "catastrophic consequences" if the peacekeepers stood idle. Again, Annan's office ordered Dallaire to stand down.

The genocide began on April 6, 1994, perpetrated by the *interahamwe* and the Rwandan army. Almost all the killers used machetes, although a few used spears, clubs, or bows. The Rwandan army and the *interahamwe* used firearms, including machine guns, for crowd control, but hardly ever for actual killing. Sometimes educated people who had been especially vociferous in agitating for genocide would be given a gun by the government, so they could kill without getting blood on their clothes. As the genocide spread nationwide, it was carried out by entire Hutu villages, which would assemble every morning and spend the day murdering and looting. Sometimes they were led by the army or the *interahamwe*, but more often they were on their own.[10]

On April 7, the killers struck the Rwandan prime minister, her five children, and the ten Belgian soldiers who were guarding her. After the Belgians surrendered, the entire contingent was murdered.

In the first few days, tens of thousands of Tutsis and moderate Hutus were slaughtered. General Dallaire cabled the U.N. to ask for reinforcements and the authority to take forceful action against the genocide. Annan's department replied that Dallaire should do nothing that would "compromise your impartiality." As Dallaire later explained, if the U.N. peacekeepers in Rwanda had been joined by 300 U.S. Marines in neighboring Rwanda, and by 900 French soldiers (a force which the French eventually sent in June), the genocide could have been stopped.

The U.N. ordered Dallaire to focus solely on evacuating foreigners, with the explicit instruction "no locals." Annan and his staff did not want to compromise their neutrality by helping the genocide victims.

In response to the U.N. evacuation of foreigners only, the radio stations told the Hutu mobs, "The foreigners are departing. They had material proof of what we are going to do, and they are leaving Kigali. This time around they are showing no interest in the fate of the Tutsis." The U.N. evacuation further emboldened the killers.[11]

Early on in the genocide, thousands of Rwandan civilians had gathered in areas where U.N. troops had been stationed, thinking they would be protected. They were not. When the U.N. forces departed, Hutu mobs moved in to slaughter all the Tutsis left behind.

If the Rwandans had known that the U.N. troops would withdraw, they would have fled, and some might have survived. "The manner in which troops left, including attempts to pretend to the refugees that they were not in fact leaving, was disgraceful," an independent report later concluded.[12]

By the end of April, 100,000 Rwandans had been murdered. But at the Security Council in New York, the Clinton administration joined other nations in refusing to use the word *genocide*, because admission that genocide was taking place would create a legal obligation on the U.N., the United States, and other nations to try to prevent it.

Eventually, the U.N. authorized the dispatch of 900 French soldiers, who in late June occupied a quarter of the country, and began running the country in collaboration with the Rwandan Hutu government that had perpetrated the genocide.

The genocide ended on July 4, 1994, when the Hutu government was ousted by the RFP militias of Tutsis and moderate Hutus. There were 800,000 Rwandans, mostly Tutsi, dead. The 103 days of murder were the fastest genocide in world history.

The main impact of the French who had been dispatched by the U.N. was to cover the retreat of the murderous Hutus into the Congo.[13] The disarmed civilian population had been left by the U.N. to die; the mass murders ended because the genocidal regime was overthrown by forces of arms—by what the U.N. condemns as "illegitimate" arms because they are possessed by "non-state actors."

Kofi Annan repeatedly interfered with and obstructed investigations about the handling of the Dallaire cable. When a Belgian commission began investigating the Rwanda genocide, Annan forbade Dallaire to testify, because the testimony was not "in the interest of the organization."[14]

THE SREBRENICA GENOCIDE

"The spread of illicit arms and light weapons is a global threat to human security and human rights," insists Annan.[15] It would be far more accurate to say, "The U.N.'s disarmament policy is a global threat to human security and human rights." It was the U.N.'s lethal policy that was directly responsible for the deaths of thousands of innocents in Srebrenica, Bosnia in 1995. A future of U.N. gun control is a future filled with thousands more Srebrenicas.

Srebrenica was the best-known atrocity in a genocide campaign run by Yugoslav president Slobodan Milosevic and facilitated by the U.N. Located near the eastern border of Bosnia-Herzegovina, the silver-mining town of Srebrenica was once part of the Republic of Yugoslavia. Yugoslavia had been created by the Treaty of Versailles in 1919, and until the country broke up in 1991, it was the largest nation on the Balkan peninsula, composed of six republics: Serbia, Croatia, Bosnia-Herzegovina, Macedonia, Slovenia, and Montenegro, as well as two provinces, Kosovo and Vojvodina.

Yugoslavia was turned into a Communist dictatorship in 1945 by Marshal Tito, whose iron hand kept ethnic tensions in check until his death in 1980. His successors feared civil war, so a system was instituted according to which the collective leadership of government and party offices would be rotated annually. But the new government floundered, and in

1989, Serbian president Milosevic began reimposing Serb and Communist hegemony. Slovenia and Croatia declared independence in June 1991.

Slovenia repelled the Yugoslav army in ten days, but fighting in Croatia continued until December, with the Yugoslav government retaining control of about a third of Croatia. Halfway through the Croat-Yugoslav war, the U.N. Security Council adopted Resolution 713, calling for "a general and complete embargo on all deliveries of weapons and military equipment to Yugoslavia" (meaning rump Yugoslavia, plus Croatia and Slovenia).[16] Although sovereign nations are normally expected to acquire and own arms, Resolution 713 redefined such weapons as "illicit" in the eyes of the U.N.

It was universally understood that the Serbs were in control of most of the Yugoslavian army's weaponry, and that the embargo therefore left them with military superiority. Conversely, even though the embargo was regularly breached, it left non-Serbs vulnerable. The U.N. had, in effect, deprived the incipient countries of the right to self-defense—even though every nation is guaranteed a right to self-defense by Article 51 of the U.N. Charter.[17]

Macedonia seceded peacefully from Yugoslavia in early 1992, but Bosnia-Herzegovina's secession quickly led to a three-way civil war between Bosnian Muslims ("Bosniacs"), Serbs (who are Orthodox), and Croats (who are Roman Catholic). The Bosnian Serbs received substantial military support from what remained of old Yugoslavia (consisting of Serbia and Montenegro, and under the control of Slobodan Milosevic).

Security Council Resolution 713 now operated to make it illegal for the new Bosnian government to acquire arms to defend itself from Yugoslav aggression. This was rather ironic, since Bosnia did not even exist as an independent nation when Security Council Resolution 713 was passed in 1991. But since Bosnia had declared independence from Yugoslavia, and Yugoslavia's murderous government was subject to the U.N. arms embargo, the U.N. insisted that the embargo also applied to Bosnia.

The Bosnian Muslims were told that they did not need arms of their own; instead, they would be protected by U.N. and NATO peacekeeping forces.[18] Bosnia-Herzegovina president Izetbegovic "was in favour of the UNPROFOR [United Nations Protection Force] proposal, which, as he understood it, meant that the Bosniacs would hand their arms over to UNPROFOR in return for UNPROFOR protection."[19]

Creation of "safe areas" pursuant to Resolution 819, which was adopted by the Security Council in April 1993, also proved disastrous. Safe areas were "regions, which should preferably be substantially free of conflict beforehand, where refugees could be offered a 'reasonable degree of security' by a brigade of peacekeeping troops."[20]

The concept of a safe area, however, was a pacifist fantasy, with little resemblance to the reality on the ground. Even the U.N. forces were not safe; they could not protect themselves, let alone anyone else. In fact, the U.N.'s so-called peacekeepers were so inept and passive that the Bosnian Serbs often took them hostage, sometimes by the hundreds, in a single operation.[21] The U.N. hostages would then be used by the Bosnian Serbs to deter the U.N. and NATO from taking more aggressive action.

The first, and so far only, contested case involving the scope of the duty to prevent genocide was *Bosnia v. Yugoslavia*, in which Bosnia sued Yugoslavia in the United Nations' International Court of Justice.[22] In April 1993, the International Court of Justice (I.C.J.) ruled, with only one dissenter, that Yugoslavia was perpetrating genocide, and ordered it to stop.[23] Of course Yugoslavia ignored the court order.

A few months later, Bosnia brought forward additional legal claims, including a request to have the U.N. embargo declared illegal, as a violation of the Genocide Convention. The majority of the I.C.J. dodged the question, stating that it had no jurisdiction over the Security Council's embargo.

Judge Elihu Lauterpacht wrote a separate opinion, which was the first international court opinion ever to address the legal scope of the Genocide Convention's affirmative duty "to prevent" genocide. Judge Lauterpacht cited the findings of a special rapporteur about the effect of the arms embargo, and pointed to the "direct link . . . between the continuation of the arms embargo and the exposure of the Muslim population of Bosnia to genocidal activity at the hands of the Serbs."[24]

Normally, Security Council resolutions are unreviewable by the I.C.J.; however, Judge Lauterpacht ruled that the prevention of genocide is *jus cogens*, or "just law."[25] He concluded that the Security Council arms embargo became void once it made U.N. member-states "accessories to genocide."[26]

Formal repeal of the Security Council embargo was impossible, because Russia threatened to veto any action harmful to its client-state Serbia. However, Judge Lauterpacht's opinion stated that the U.N. embargo was already void, as a matter of law, the moment it came into conflict with the Genocide Convention.

By the summer of 1995, the population of Srebrenica, a designated safe area, had swelled with refugees. By the time of the massacre, it was an island of Bosniacs in Bosnian Serb territory, an island the U.N. had sworn to protect.

But the U.N. would not honor its pledge. As the BBC later reported, "A former U.N. commander in Bosnia has told a Dutch parliamentary inquiry into the Srebrenica massacre that it was clear to him that Dutch authorities would not sacrifice its soldiers for the enclave."[27]

And, indeed, on July 11, 1995, Bosnian Serb forces entered Srebrenica without resistance from Bosniac or U.N. forces; not a shot was fired. (The Bosniac general in Srebrenica had recently been recalled by his government, leaving the Bosniac forces leaderless.) The peacekeepers ignored the pleas of the Muslims in the camp not to abandon them.[28]

Ethnic cleansing and genocide followed. The men and boys were separated from the women, then taken away and shot.

Knowing that remaining in the U.N. safe area would mean certain death, some 10,000 to 15,000 Bosniac males fled into the surrounding forests, escaping to the Bosniac-held town of Tuzla. Only about 3,000 to 4,000 were armed, mostly with hunting rifles. These were the men who survived what has since become known as the six-day "Marathon of Death." [29]

And the rest? Laura Silber and Allan Little, in their book *Yugoslavia: Death of a Nation*, describe the slaughter in the forest: "Some were killed after having surrendered, believing the U.N. would protect them. . . . Serb soldiers, some even dressed as U.N. peace-keepers driving stolen white U.N. vehicles, would guarantee the Muslims' safety. Then they would shoot."[30] In this way, over 7,500 men and boys were killed.

The Srebrenica massacre was Europe's worst atrocity since World War II, but it was only one small part of the genocide and ethnic cleansing of Bosnia. Approximately 200,000 people were killed; another million became refugees.[31]

Three months after the massacre at Srebrenica—lightning speed for the U.N.—a unanimous Security Council rescinded its arms embargo against the nations of the former Yugoslavia.[32]

Who was responsible for the Srebrenica genocide and the rest of the genocide in Bosnia? Primarily, of course, the Yugoslav government and its Bosnian Serb allies. Many of the perpetrators are being prosecuted before the International Criminal Tribunal for the Former Yugoslavia (ICTY) at the Hague.[33] Bosnian Serb general Radislav Krstic, the senior commander of the Srebrenica genocide, was found guilty by the ICTY on August 2, 2001, and sentenced to a forty-six-year prison term.[34] (The ICTY has no death penalty.)

Ex-Yugoslav president Slobodan Milosevic is among the former leaders currently being prosecuted for genocide and for crimes against humanity.

A large share of the blame for Srebrenica was placed on the Dutch government and ill-prepared Dutch peacekeepers, as detailed in an April 2002 report by the Netherlands Institute for War Documentation.[35] Dutch prime minister Wim Kok and his entire cabinet resigned in shame a week later.

The Convention on Genocide makes "complicity in genocide" a punishable act.[36] The U.N.'s reflexive attempt at disarmament prior to the massacre at Srebrenica might be said to fulfill the definition of complicity: "a state of being an accomplice; partnership in wrongdoing."[37] Even if not legally complicit, the U.N. undeniably functioned as a facilitator of genocide.

The U.N. was hardly ignorant of the murderous Serb intent. Prior to Srebrenica, the U.N. knew about other mass killings committed by the Serbs against the Bosniacs between 1991 and 1994. One of the largest took place in April 1992 in the town of Bratunac, just outside Srebrenica; approximately 350 Bosnian Muslims were tortured and killed by Serb paramilitaries and special police.[38]

The U.N. was fully aware of Milosevic's designs for a "Greater Serbia" (incorporating portions of Bosnia), and was also fully aware of the disparity in military capabilities between Milosevic and his intended victims.

In short, the U.N. was aware of Milosevic's propensity for ethnic cleansing, and had ample reason to know that its actions would create a situation ripe for genocide. The atrocities at Srebrenica could not have been perpetrated by the Serbs on such a grand scale had not the U.N. and its policies first prepared an enclave of victims, most of them disarmed.

If the U.N. were genuinely interested in protecting people from geno-cide, then the person who supervised the incompetent, genocide-facilitating actions of the organizaton's so-called peacekeepers would be fired. During the Srebrenica genocide, the U.N. Undersecretary-General for Peacekeeping Operations was Kofi Annan.

The only consequence he suffered for his deadly incompetence was being promoted to Secretary-General, and then being awarded the Nobel Peace prize on December 10, 2001.

In 1998, three years after the Srebrenica massacre, he did offer an apology:

> The United Nations . . . failed to do our part to help save the people of Srebrenica from the Serb campaign of mass murder. . . . In the end, the only meaningful and lasting amends we can make to the citizens of Bosnia and Herzegovina who put their faith in the international com-munity is to do our utmost not to allow such horrors to recur. When the international community makes a solemn promise to safeguard and protect innocent civilians from massacre, then it must be willing to back its promise with the necessary means. Otherwise, it is surely better not to raise hopes and expectations in the first place, and not to impede whatever capability they may be able to muster in their own defense.[39]

The apology would have been meaningful if Annan changed the policies of the U.N., rather than continuing to impose those morally bankrupt ones that led to genocide in Bosnia. In fact, just months after the show of contrition, Kofi Annan and the U.N. were back at work preventing prospective genocide victims from defending themselves, this time in East Timor.

EAST TIMOR

Slightly larger than the state of Maryland, the island of Timor lies in Southeast Asia, 400 miles northwest of Australia. The Portuguese first visi-ted the island in the early 1500s. Beginning in the eighteenth century, the Dutch competed with the Portuguese for control of Timor. In the middle of the nineteenth century, they divided the island between them. When the Dutch East Indies gained independence in 1949 as the nation of Indonesia, West Timor was absorbed into Indonesia, and Portugal retained the eastern part of the island as its colony.

Portuguese occupation of Timor was characterized by the exploitation of its people through oppressive taxation, forced labor, and other human-rights abuses. Portugal's harsh treatment of the Timorese led to widespread resentment, and, eventually, violent rebellion. Although Portugal was able to suppress the rebellions, resistance continued.

Portugal's fascist government was toppled on April 25, 1974, by the Carnation Revolution, a relatively nonviolent military coup. The new government in Lisbon was dedicated to democracy and to the decolonization of Portugal's overseas territories.

Thirsting for freedom, the Timorese leadership began preparing for liberation. Kay Rala Xanana Gusmao (now the president of Timor) recalled, "our only ideology was *ukun rasik an*, self-determination." He believed the only choice the Timorese had was between freedom and "total extermination." It was only by defying a United Nations gun-control campaign that the Timorese won their freedom, and avoided total extermination.

When Portugal officially abandoned its colonies in 1975, East Timor declared independence. But a few days later, on December 7, Indonesia invaded. Within six months, there were 35,000 Indonesian troops in East Timor, and 10,000 more were standing by in West Timor.

The armed occupation lasted twenty-four years. In an attempt to bring East Timor to its knees, Indonesia resorted to forced sterilization (paid by for the World Bank), mass starvation, rape, murder, torture, and conventional and napalm bombing directed at isolated villages, most of which were leveled to the ground.[40]

Between 1975 and mid-1999, more than 200,000 East Timorese—a third of its preinvasion population of 700,000—had been killed. The overwhelming majority of casualties were civilians. It is estimated that 100,000 East Timorese were killed by Indonesian troops just in the first year of the invasion. That, combined with the twin policies of forced sterilization and the migration of Indonesians into East Timor, led observers to the conclusion that Indonesia intended ethnic cleansing for the Maubere people.[41]

What did the U.N. do? In effect, nothing. Toothless resolutions decreed that Indonesia should withdraw from East Timor. There were no sanctions. The U.N. refused to use the word *genocide* to describe the rampant murder that was being perpetrated in East Timor.

In effect, the U.N. response to Indonesia's genocide in East Timor was to pass a sternly worded resolution warning that if Indonesia did not stop, it would pass another sternly worded resolution—all of which was consistently ignored by Indonesia.

Even so, Timorese resistance stiffened. What the East Timorese people needed were loaded firearms, not empty words from the U.N. In spite of the resources expended by Indonesia to prosecute the war—a cost of up to $1 million (U.S.) per day—the Armed Forces for the National Liberation of East Timor (*Falintil*) waged a successful guerrilla campaign, using arms left over from the days of Portuguese rule, or stolen from Indonesian troops.

In the eyes of the U.N., once those arms fell into the hands of *Falintil*, they crossed the line from what the U.N. defines as "licit" guns, into "illicit" guns.

It is here that the hypocrisy and inconsistency of U.N. policy becomes apparent. The U.N. equates "licit gun" with "government gun," and "illicit gun" with "antigovernment gun." As Charles Scheiner, national coordinator for the East Timor Action Network (ETAN), correctly pointed out, however, "The guns used by the Indonesian military to kill 200,000 East Timorese civilians were almost all 'legal' . . . [but] the line between legality and illegality is irrelevant to the victims. . . ."[42]

That line in the sand—distinguishing licit from illicit—legitimizes possession of firearms owned by governments and people approved by those governments, rendering firearm possession by all others illegitimate. Yet it was illegitimate transfers that armed *Falintil*. Measured against U.N. standards, the *Falintil* guerrillas—as "non-state actors"—were in unlawful possession of the firearms they used to defend their country and their people when there was no one else to do so. Similarly illegitimate by that same U.N. standard was the French Underground that resisted the Nazis, almost every anticolonial movement in the world, and the American Revolution.

According to the U.N. Institute for Disarmament Research, "the ready availability of weapons makes it far too easy for substate groups to seek remedy for grievances through the application of violence."[43]

In other words, the U.N. lamented that it was "far too easy" for *Falintil* to resist Indonesia's genocide. Although the U.N. did offer resolutions telling Indonesia to get out of East Timor, those words were meaningless without the force supplied by *Falintil*'s illicit arms.

James F. Dunnigan, the military historian and editor of StrategyPage.com, pointed out why *Falintil*—a guerrilla army comprised of both men and women, equipped with only small arms and support from the civilian populace—prevailed against the might of Indonesia: "The basic idea behind guerilla war is to keep your force intact, not to fight the enemy. Guerillas who keep those priorities straight are successful. The East Timor separatists used a sound strategy, and eventually, the situation became intolerable for the occupying power. . . . That was how the American Revolution was fought. Washington didn't have to win, or even fight, battles, he just had to keep the Continental army intact until the British parliament got tired of paying for the North American war."[44]

In 1999, the Indonesian government, headed by B. J. Habibie, finally agreed to an East Timorese vote on self-determination: autonomy under Indonesian rule, or complete independence.

Indonesia, though, had merely changed tactics. The *Sydney Herald* (April 29, 1999) detailed Indonesia's "three-pronged attempt" to sabotage the referendum process: "to first destabilize the situation in East Timor sufficiently to prevent a referendum; second, to terrorise the population sufficiently to ensure a pro-integration outcome in case a referendum takes place; and third, to 'Timorise' the conflict by presenting to the world a picture of 'warring Timorese factions.'"[45]

So the Indonesian military set about training militias in East Timor.[46] These bore no resemblance to the American model our Founding Fathers had in mind, our well-armed citizenry that provides homeland security. Indonesia's militias consisted of armed gangs of thugs, perpetrating mayhem and rape, and intimidating anyone believed to be in support of independence. While Jakarta tried to cast *Falintil* as the cause of continued violence in East Timor, it was evident that the violence was orchestrated by the Indonesian army and its militia thugs.[47]

In April 1999, Indonesian Foreign Minister Ali Alatas demanded that the East Timorese give up their arms as a precondition for peace.[48] East Timor resistance leader Xanana Gusmao refused. He reiterated that *Falintil* guerrillas were never involved in acts of terrorism but had always acted in self-defense. They should therefore be treated as "an army of liberation and not as a band of bandits." He did, however, agree to a U.N.-brokered compromise between East Timor and Jakarta: *Falintil* and the Indonesian militias were to refrain from carrying arms except in designated areas called "cantonments."[49]

While *Falintil* remained passive in accordance with the truce, the Indonesian military continued to encourage militia misbehavior, leaving the undefended East Timorese populace easy prey.[50] Because independence depended on the referendum, which in turn depended on the cantonment of *Falintil*, East Timorese leaders had no choice.

On May 5, 1999, agreements were signed allowing the referendum to go forward, and on June 11, U.N. Resolution 1246 formally established the U.N. Mission in East Timor (UNAMET) for the purpose of organizing and supervising the referendum process.[51] The "responsibility . . . to maintain peace and security in East Timor . . . in order to ensure that the popular consultation [the vote] is carried out in a fair and peaceful way and in an atmosphere free of intimidation" was placed on the Indonesian government.[52]

Remember, all this was taking place just a few months after Kofi Annan had apologized for the U.N.'s failure to protect the disarmed genocide victims in Bosnia.

Now, after decades of genocide perpetrated by Indonesia against the Timorese, the ever-helpful U.N. insisted that the vast majority of the Timorese people be deprived of armed protection. They were supposed to rely on the Indonesian government to protect them.

The Indonesian army and its militias, with a long record of broken promises of nonaggression, now had a monopoly of power in East Timor, and their terror campaign persisted. One knowledgeable Western security expert predicted, "If independence wins, these autonomy guys will go berserk."[53]

On August 30, 1999, the referendum was held. The turnout was huge, and the vote was 78.5 percent for independence.[54] *Falintil* remained in cantonment, muzzled.

Until the eve of the referendum, the Indonesian military and police continued to promise to curb the violence and to honor a free vote. And as predicted, once East Timor voted to cut its ties with Indonesia, the

Indonesian military set loose their vengeful militias on a defenseless populace. They hunted down independence supporters and their families, and torched villages.

According to the *New York Times*, one militiaman said that his orders were "to kill anyone on the street who stood for independence." And, he added, "if they could not hold onto East Timor, they would leave behind a wasteland devoid of schools, society, structure or a population." [55]

Falintil remained passive, in compliance with U.N. orders.[56]

The extraordinary restraint exhibited by *Falintil* during the ensuing chaos earned high praise from U.N. officials: "Throughout all this emergency they have not moved. The Indonesians want them to come out and attack so they can blame the chaos on *Falintil*."

As the world took notice, international pressure was finally brought to bear on Jakarta. Three weeks after the referendum, the first wave of Australian, New Zealand, and British troops—the core of the U.N. peacekeeping force—arrived in Dili, the capitol of East Timor. Within a week, 3,000 troops had arrived, with a final target of 8,000.[57]

It was good these Australian, New Zealand, and British troops finally arrived to stop the Indonesian depredations. But it is difficult to think of any good reason why the people of East Timor should have been forced to meekly submit to three weeks of mass murder, rape, and pillage while people in other countries pondered what to do. It was the U.N.'s obsession with disarmament that allowed the murder, rape, and pillage.

University of Minnesota law professor Barbara Frye, the U.N. Special Rapporteur on how small arms are used in human rights violations, and a member of the international gun prohibition lobby IANSA,[58] writes, "While male-dominated society often justify small arms possession through the alleged need to protect vulnerable women, women actually face greater danger when their families and communities are armed."[59]

To see how catastrophically and callously wrong Frye is, one need only consider the examples detailed in this book: the woman and girls raped, kidnapped, and murdered in East Timor, in Rwanda, in Bosnia, in Kosovo, in Albania, in Liberia, in Sierra Leone, in the Congo—because neither they nor anyone else in their family had a firearm to protect them. Because they were disarmed at the behest of the U.N. And quite often, the criminal perpetrators were U.N. staff and peacekeepers.

After the Commonwealth troops arrived, the U.N. again ordered *Falintil* to disarm completely. Again, they refused. Recognizing the high cost of confiscating *Falintil's* arms, U.N. peacekeepers backed off. On October 5, 1999, Australian Army Col. Mark Kelly, spokesman for the international peacekeeping force Interfet, made a face-saving statement: "The ongoing discussions we will have with the *Falintil* leadership will look towards the eventual disarming. We have got a requirement to disarm those people under our [U.N.] mandate."[60]

By December, it was decided that *Falintil* would be transformed into East Timor's "legally constituted police force."[61] If the U.N. could not disarm *Falintil*, then the group could be legitimized in U.N. eyes by morphing it into the East Timor Defence Force.

On February 1, 2001, the *Falintil* guerrilla force became the world's newest internationally recognized army. Its mission was declared by its new commander, Brigadier-General Taur Matan Ruak: "to guarantee the defence of our homeland, of the new sovereign state of Timor, fully respecting the new democratic institutions and the political representatives democratically elected by our people."[62]

Meanwhile, the U.N. continued to work toward its goal of total gun prohibition for civilians. As a price of independence, the Timorese were forced to accept Regulation Number 2001/5, On Firearms, Ammunition Explosives and Other Offensive Weapons in East Timor, enacted into law on April 23, 2001, by the U.N. Transitional Administration in East Timor.[63] In May 2002, East Timor (now Timor-Leste) became the world's newest nation.

SUDAN

In September 2004, the United States government explicitly invoked the Genocide Convention to call upon the U.N. to stop the genocide in Sudan. The call by the U.S. was the *only* time any party to the Genocide Convention has ever invoked the Genocide Convention to call upon the U.N. Security Council to take action against a genocide.

Did the U.N. then stop the genocide in the Sudan? Of course not. Did the organization even use the word *genocide* to describe the genocide in the Sudan? Of course not. Did the U.N. respond to the mass murder of unarmed civilians by pushing for more gun control? Of course.

In 1989, Sudan's elected government was overthrown in a military coup by the National Islamic Front, which created a racist, Islamist tyranny in Khartoum. The Institute for the Study of Genocide reports that, "Animated by a radical Islamism and a sense of Arab racial superiority, the movement engaged in genocide almost from the time it seized power."[64] Now, genocide in Sudan continues "by force of habit."[65]

The first genocide was perpetrated against the people of the Nuba Mountains, in central Sudan. Afterwards, the Arab Sudanese dictatorship carried out genocide against the Christian and animist black Africans who live in southern Sudan, killing about 2.2. million, and driving 4.5 million from their homes.[66] Victims who were not killed were often sold into slavery. Rape was used extensively as an instrument of state terror.

Fortunately, rebel groups among the south Sudanese had arms. Although there were not enough arms for the innocent civilians to protect themselves, the southern rebel groups were able to keep up an armed resistance. Under intense pressure from President George W. Bush, the Khartoum government finally accepted a cease-fire in late 2004. The government has promised that in 2010, the south Sudanese will be able to vote on a referendum for independence. But never have the Khartoum dictatorship's promises been of any value.

Today, it is not clear whether the peace agreement will hold; the leader of the southern rebels, who was supposed to become vice president of Sudan, died in a suspicious helicopter accident in the summer of 2005.

While armed rebels have, at least temporarily, stopped the genocide in South Sudan, the situation is even worse in the western Sudan. The three states of western Sudan are collectively known as "Darfur." As in the south, much of the population is black African. Unlike in the south, the black Africans of Darfur are Muslims.

Also inhabiting Darfur are Arab nomads, who have a long-standing conflict with black African pastoralists there. The Arabs consider the blacks to be racially inferior, and fit only for slavery. "Beginning in the mid-1980s, successive governments in Khartoum inflamed matters by supporting and arming the Arab tribes, in part to prevent the southern rebels from gaining a foothold in the region. . . . Arabs formed militias, burned African villages, and killed thousands. Africans in turn formed self-defense groups, members of which eventually became the first Darfur insurgents to appear in 2003."[67]

These so-called Janjaweed militias are like the terrorist gangs created by the Indonesian government—little different from state terror organizations such as Hitler's SS or Stalin's NKVD.

Because of the abuses of the tyrannical Islamist government in Khartoum, two movements seeking independence for Darfur were created in February 2003: the Sudan Liberation Army (SLA), and the Justice and Equality Movement (JEM). In April 2003, the rebels successfully attacked a government airfield, provoking massive retaliation by the Khartoum government.[68]

On the ground, the main force of the government's attack on the black Africans of Darfur is Arab militia known as the Janjaweed (literally, "evil men on horseback" or "devil on a horse").

The Janjaweed have caused the deaths of up to 400,000 black Sudanese, have raped many thousands, and have forced two million black Sudanese into refugee camps.[69] "When the Janjaweed attack, they do unmistakably hurl racial abuse at their victims, alleging in particular that Africans are born to be slaves: 'Slaves, run! Leave the country. You don't belong; why are you not leaving this area for Arab cattle to graze?'"[70]

The Janjaweed attacks on villages were supported with aerial bombing by the Sudan Air Force.[71] There were no reports of response to these attacks from villagers or from the JEM or SLA. The rebel groups did not appear to have antiaircraft weapons, such as surface-to-air missiles. The rebels did, however, possess small arms and light weapons, including firearms.[72]

Salah Gosh, head of Sudan's national security, admitted that the government, indeed, bombed the villages, noting: "The [rebel] militia are attacking the government from the villages. What is the government going to do? It will bomb those villages."[73] Notably, the majority of villages bombed were villages where there were no armed rebels.[74] Thus, the destruction of the villages should be seen not as an overzealous form of counterinsurgency warfare, but rather as a deliberate attempt to destroy an entire society. The ethnic cleansing of Darfur had been so thorough that, literally, there were no villages left to burn.[75]

Although ethnic cleansing is not uncommon where the population supports an antigovernment insurgency, it can also lead to deaths of innocent civilians on a large scale. Intentionally targeting civilians has long been recognized as a violation of the laws of warfare. An Amnesty International report noted "international law also makes it clear that use of such tactics does not provide the other side with a license to kill civilians."[76]

The Sudanese government tells the international community that the central government is not responsible for the Arab versus African violence in Darfur. However, Human Rights Watch observed that "Government forces not only participated and supported militia attacks on civilians, they also actively refused to provide security to civilians seeking protection from these militia attacks."[77]

Despite promises from the Sudanese government, the attacks on Darfur grew even worse in early 2005. The U.S. Department of State reported that brutal attacks were still occurring, and that "attacks on civilians, rape, kidnapping and banditry actually increased in April."[78] According to the *Sudan Tribune*, "Attention to Darfur's staggering death toll—which has grown to approximately 400,000 over the course of more than two years of genocidal conflict—has increased in the past several months."[79] U.N. Undersecretary for Humanitarian Affairs Jan Egeland warns that the death rate might increase to 100,000 per month if the humanitarian relief collapses.[80]

Egeland notes, "The only thing in abundance in Darfur is weapons."[81] However, these arms are distributed unevenly among Darfur's population. Despite the U.N. arms embargo,[82] Sudan has been funding its arms buildup using income from its oil sector to supply the Arab militia friendly to Khartoum.[83] According to Amnesty International, the Janjaweed are so well supplied that the majority of them have five or six guns per person.[84]

But in Sudan, it is virtually impossible for an average citizen to lawfully acquire and possess the means for self-defense. According to the national gun-control statutes,[85] a gun licensee must be over thirty years of age, must have a specified social and economic status, and must be examined physically by a doctor. Females have even more difficulty meeting these requirements because of social and occupational limitations.

When these restrictions are finally overcome, there are additional restrictions on the amount of ammunition one may possess, making it nearly impossible for a law-abiding gun owner to achieve proficiency with firearms. A handgun owner, for example, can only purchase fifteen rounds of ammunition a year. The penalties for violation of Sudan's firearms laws are severe and can include capital punishment.

The U.N. and the international gun-prohibition groups complain that Sudan's gun laws are not strict enough—but the real problem with the laws is that they have been—and are—enforced arbitrarily. A U.S. Department of State document stated: "After President Bashir seized power in 1989, the new government disarmed non-Arab ethnic groups but allowed politically loyal Arab allies to keep their weapons."[86] Meanwhile, there are many reports that the Arab militia have been armed and supplied by the government in Khartoum.[87]

After a village had been softened up by government air bombardment, the Janjaweed enter and pillage, killing and raping in order to displace the population and steal the land.[88] The villagers were generally unarmed.[89]

Amnesty International reported the testimony of a villager who complained, "none of us had arms and we were not able to resist the attack."[90] One underarmed villager lamented, "I tried to take my spear to protect my family, but they threatened me with a gun, so I stopped. The six Arabs then raped my daughter in front of me, my wife and my other children."[91]

In cases when the villagers were able to resist, the cost to the marauders rose: Human Rights Watch reported that "some of Kudun's residents mobilized to protect themselves, and 15 of the attackers were reportedly killed."[92]

The Pittsburgh *Tribune-Review* asked a U.S. State Department official why there were no reports of the Darfur victims fighting back. "Some do defend themselves," he explained. But he added that the perpetrators have helicopters and automatic rifles, whereas the victims have only machetes.[93]

A teenage girl with a gun might not be the ideal soldier. But she is certainly not the ideal rape victim. It is not particularly difficult to learn how to use a firearm to shoot a would-be rapist from a distance of fifteen or twenty-five feet away. With an AK-47 type rifle, which is plentiful in some areas of the Third World, self-defense would be quite easy. Would every one of the Janjaweed Arab bullies who enjoy raping African girls be brave enough to dare trying to rape a girl who was carrying a rifle or a handgun?

The *Tribune-Review* asked an Amnesty International representative, Trish Katyoka, whether the Darfur victims should be armed.[94] Her response is worth analyzing sentence by sentence.

She began: "We at Amnesty International are not going to condone escalation of the flow of arms to the region." The answer is not surprising. In the last decade, Amnesty International has become a leading worldwide advocate for total gun prohibition—a stance contrary to its declared policy of opposing government abuses of human rights.

Amnesty International is a member of Rebecca Peters' gun prohibition group IANSA (International Action Network on Small Arms). Amnesty International also has its own special Web site dedicated to arms prohibition, (http://www.controlarms.org).

"You are empowering (the victims) to create an element of retaliation," the AI representative insisted. Her answer shows a serious confusion about self-defense. "Retaliation" is taking revenge for a misdeed after the fact. Self-defense is prevention of an imminent, unlawful, violent attack. Protecting a girl from an imminent gang rape has nothing to do with retaliation.

"Whenever you create a sword-fight by letting the poor people fight back and give them arms, it creates an added element of complexity. You do not know what the results will be." Ms. Katyoka summarized: "Fighting fire with fire is not the solution to genocide. It is a dangerous proposition to arm the minorities to fight back."

According to the Institute for the Study of Genocide, there is no reason to believe that the Darfur genocide will ever stop; the U.N. sent several thousand African Union troops to protect the international aid workers (but *not* to protect the Darfuris) and the AU force has proven incapable of even protecting the aid workers. Many Darfuris are now starving to death and dying of epidemics in remote refugee camps that the Sudanese dictatorship has cut off from all outside supply.[95] The IGS argues for NATO intervention, which appears to have no likelihood of ever taking place— and is especially unlikely in light of the French government's current, lucrative commercial arrangements for oil extraction in Sudan.

The U.N.'s actions are patently ineffectual. The Security Council "demanded" that the Khartoum tyranny disarm the Janjaweed, and the Khartoum dictators replied that they would not.

In March 2004, the U.N. Humanitarian Coordinator for Sudan, Mukesh Kapila, spoke the truth by stating, "The only difference between Rwanda and Darfur is the numbers involved." Rejecting Sudanese government claims that Darfur is simply in a state of civil war, with some civilians being accidentally injured therein, Kapila stated that Darfur "is more than just a conflict, it is an organized attempt to do away with a group of people." In response, the Sudanese government demanded that the U.N. get rid of Kapila, and the U.N. acceded, forcing him to resign.[96]

The Security Council's toothless demand, its referral to the International Criminal Court, and its authorization of the pathetic African Union force to protect only foreigners in Darfur might be regarded as feeble—but at least well-intentioned—efforts to try to take small steps against the genocide.

But the actions of the secretary-general appear to be of a different character altogether. Some of the Darfur refugees are currently being held in what the Institute for the Study of Genocide calls "concentration camps run by Janjaweed and Sudanese army guards, where murder and rape are standing orders." [97]

With the Sudan dictatorship already killing people in concentration camps, the secretary-general's solution is . . . more concentration camps! In 2004, the special representative of the secretary-general signed a Sudanese government plan for the creation of safe areas where the Darfuris would be "guarded" by the Sudanese army—the same Sudanese army that has been carrying out genocide against these same Darfuris, who are now refugees only because the Sudanese army abetted the Janjaweed in burning down all the Darfuri villages.

The special representative of the secretary-general who signed the safe areas plan was Jon Pronk, who in 1995 was the Dutch Development Cooperation Minister, with authority over the safe areas scheme in Bosnia that led to 8,000 Bosnians being murdered by the Serbs while the Dutch peacekeepers stood idle.[98]

Eric Reeves, a scholar with the Institute for the Study of Genocide, predicts that not only will the Darfur genocide continue, but that a new genocide will begin soon against the people of oil-rich eastern Sudan.[99]

If the Darfuris in the refugee camps possessed firearms, the refugees would hardly be able to march on Khartoum and overthrow the government, but they would be able to drive off the Janjaweed who come to a camp for plunder, murder, and rape.

Interestingly, the U.N. has, on at least one occasion, admitted that some communities in the world have survived only because they were armed. However, the U.N. views this as a problem to be solved, not something to be celebrated. A 2002 U.N. book setting out future global gun control plans explained the need for "long-term strategies to reverse the culture of violence and gun dependency through strategic education and socio-economic development projects in communities that are dependent on arms traffic *or that survive due to their access to and/or use of small arms.*"[100]

Considering how many million people did not survive the genocides of the last sixty years while the U.N. did nothing effective to save those disarmed victims, the U.N. should focus on protecting disarmed victims, rather than on disarming the communities that found a way to "survive due to their access and/or use of small arms."

Abandoned by the world, the people of Sudan have every moral right, every right under natural law, and every right under the Universal Declaration of Human Rights and other international human rights instruments to use firearms to save their lives. That the international gun prohibition movement would deny the right to possess defensive arms even by the victims of genocide, and even when the rest of the world has forsaken those victims, seems to me clear evidence that the international gun prohibition is neither "pro-life" nor "pro-choice," but is instead morally blinded by its obsessive hatred of guns and gun owners. The U.N. is complicit in genocide, and the international gun haters are complicit in evil.

CHAPTER 9

More Gun Control for Genocide Victims

While unwilling to say the word *genocide* about Sudan, the United Nations is very vocal about gun control in places like Sudan, saying we need a lot more of it. The U.N. has been promoting regional gun prohibition plans around the world.

In the Great Lakes and Horn of Africa regions, the prohibition plan is "The Nairobi Protocol for the Prevention, Control and Reduction of Small Arms and Light Weapons in the Great Lakes Region and the Horn of Africa."[1] The protocol was signed on April 21, 2004, by representatives of eleven nations: Burundi, Democratic Republic of the Congo, Djibouti, Eritrea, Ethiopia, Kenya, Rwanda, Seychelles, Sudan, Uganda, and Tanzania. The Nairobi Protocol will become legally binding when it is ratified by two-thirds of the signatories.[2]

Of the signatories, only Eritrea (which won independence in 1991 in a revolutionary war against Ethiopia) has been democratic for at least half its existence as an independent nation. The majority of signatories of the Nairobi Protocol have witnessed genocide in their nations within the last several decades, including the current genocides being perpetrated in the Democratic Republic of the Congo, Ethiopia, and Sudan.

To prevent genocide, the U.N. should encourage the dictatorships of east Africa to respect the human rights, but instead it pushes for more stringent gun controls on the people of Rwanda, and on people in other nations targeted for genocide.

In the U.N.-sponsored Nairobi Protocol, the genocidal and dictatorial governments of east Africa, together with a few nominally or actually democratic governments, promised to incorporate in their national laws the prohibition of civilian possession of small arms. Terms included:

- the total prohibition of civilian possession of semiautomatic rifles;

- centralized registration of all civilian-owned small arms;

- competency testing of prospective small arms owners;

- restrictions on owners' rights to relinquish control, use, and possession of small arms; and

- restriction on the number of small arms that may be owned.[3]

The protocol also requires "heavy minimum sentences for . . . the carrying of unlicensed small arms," as well as programs to encourage citizens to surrender their guns, widespread searches for firearms, and educational programs to discourage gun ownership.[4]

In other words, the U.N. is successfully pushing for gun control in four east African nations with *current, ongoing* genocides, and in several others with recent histories of mass murder. Quite plainly, the U.N. believes that resisting an actual genocide in progress is not a sufficient reason for someone to want to own a gun.

A set of mandatory antigun laws—mostly similar to east Africa's Nairobi Protocol—is also being pushed in southern Africa, for the nations in the Southern African Development Community (SADC).[5] The large majority of the fourteen governments that have signed the U.N. antigun protocol are notoriously corrupt.[6] Few of them are democratic. Two of them—Zimbabwe and Congo—are the sites of genocides currently taking place. The U.N. has not stopped the genocides—but it has worked to make sure that the victims are defenseless.

ECOWAS

Over in West Africa, the U.N. is promoting an even more extremist antigun agenda among the Economic Community of West African States (ECOWAS). The ECOWAS antigun protocol calls for the *total prohibition* of firearms imports, except for firearms that governments buy for their own use.

Sixteen nations make up ECOWAS. In two of them—Mali and Niger—

the Tuareg tribesmen of the desert north successfully took up arms to defend themselves against the depredations of the kleptocracy based in the capital city. Because the Tuareg were able to defend their rights with arms, they were able to force governments in the southern capital to stop stealing foreign food aid, which was supposed to be sent to starving people in the north.[7] The ECOWAS Protocol, if successful, will ensure that starving people in West Africa will never again be able to take up arms against such corrupt governments.

The human rights organization Genocide Watch has created a model of the eight stages of genocide: classification, symbolization, dehumanization, organization, polarization, preparation, extermination, and denial.[8]

According to Genocide Watch, Ivory Coast (Côte d'Ivoire) has entered the critical stage: preparation.[9] No wonder the Ivory Coast was in such a hurry to make sure that no guns were supplied to citizens anywhere in West Africa, lest some of those guns be sold or donated to the victims of the Ivory Coast government's persecutions.

In Guinea, the National Alliance for Democracy and Development warns:

> There is a looming Rwanda-type genocide if nothing is done to prevent ethnic conflict in Guinea. The small elite of the minority Soussou that controls the country will not hesitate to use genocide to keep power in Guinea. General Lansana Conte is ready to use state resources and authority to incite and force his minority over-armed Soussou ethnic group to kill other Guineans to preserve the power.[10]

With genocide "looming," the U.N. has nonetheless worked to ensure that Guinea's victims will be unable to resist.

In Liberia in the 1990s, two sides of the army fought a civil war, and perpetrated what was called "attempted genocide" against civilians in tribes that supported the other faction.[11] U.N. peacekeepers prevented innocent civilians from fleeing, and then abandoned them so that they were mass murdered.

In Nigeria, the nation's Christians and animists are under constant attack by violent Islamist extremists funded by pro-terrorist Arab groups. For example, in November 2002, Muslim rioters killed more than 200

Christians, in anger over an article in a Lagos newspaper that said that Mohammad would have wanted to marry a Miss World contestant. When the Nigerian government refused to protect the Christians, Nigerian Archbishop Most Rev. John Olorenfemi Onaiyekan told Nigerian Christians: "It is a Christian duty to protect yourselves."[12]

But the good people of Nigeria will be unable to protect themselves, as the ECOWAS Protocol will ensure that law-abiding citizens cannot obtain arms for self-defense.

Under the Utopian vision of the U.N. and gun prohibition groups like IANSA, citizens need not protect themselves, because the government will. But in Nigeria, the government refuses to protect people—and in many other countries of Africa, it is the genocidal government *from* which people need protection.

As for relying on the U.N. for protection, the situation hasn't improved since 1994, when the U.N. forces fled in Rwanda, or 1995, when the U.N. forces fled in Bosnia. In both countries, the U.N. lured unarmed victims to "safe" areas, then abandoned them, turning them into easy prey for genocide.

Let's look at what happened in Sierra Leone—another ECOWAS country where the U.N. intends to disarm every innocent civilian.

In May 2000, Sierra Leone "nearly became the U.N.'s biggest peace-keeping debacle" as Dennis Jett explains in his book, *Why Peacekeeping Fails.* Five hundred U.N. "peacekeepers" were taken hostage by rebels of the Revolutionary United Front (RUF).[13] The RUF has been described by Human Rights Watch as a "barbarous group of thugs," who "lived off the country's rich diamond fields and terrorized the population with its signature atrocity of chopping off arms and hands of men, women, and often children."[14]

Jett continues: "The RUF troops are unspeakably brutal to civilians, but will not stand up to any determined military force. Yet the U.N. peacekeepers, with few exceptions, handed over their weapons including armored personnel carriers and meekly became prisoners." It was only the deployment of Britain's troops to the former colony that saved civilian lives and averted a "complete U.N. defeat."

As the U.N. aims to disarm the citizens of sub-Saharan African, it is targeting the victims of some of the world's worst tyrannies and dictatorships. Of the sub-Saharan countries, only ten are rated as "free" by the Freedom House annual report, *Freedom in the World 2005*. Another eighteen are "partly free"—mostly dictatorships in which government abuse is significant but not always pervasive. And nineteen are rated "not free."[15]

The Universal Declaration of Human Rights recognizes the fundamental right of people victimized by those nineteen tyrannies to revolt against the government that is destroying their inalienable human rights. Instead, the U.N. would disarm the victims of government abuse, leaving them defenseless against governments that pose a significant danger of genocide.

THE HUMAN RIGHTS ALTERNATIVE TO GENOCIDE

In an excellent article in the *Notre Dame Law Review*, David Kopel, Paul Gallant, and Joanne Eisen argue that genocide victims have a fundamental human right to possess arms, under international law. They point out that nearly every nation in the world has signed the Convention on the Prevention and Punishment of the Crime of Genocide.[16]

The Convention states: "The Contracting Parties confirm that genocide, whether committed in time of peace or in time of war, is a crime under international law *which they undertake to prevent* and punish."[17] International law is clear that the duty to prevent is real, and is entirely distinct from the duty to punish.[18]

The Genocide Convention prohibits more than the direct killing of humans. Other actions—if undertaken with genocidal intent—can constitute genocide. For example, rape would not normally be genocide, but if a political or military commander promoted the widespread rape of a civilian population—with the intent of preventing normal reproduction by that population—then the pattern of rape could constitute genocide.[19]

Similarly, though many governments do not provide their citizens with minimal food rations or medical care, such omissions are not genocide. On the other hand, if a government eliminated food rations to a particular group but not to other groups, and the change in rations policy was undertaken with the intent of exterminating that group by starvation, then the government's termination of food aid could constitute genocide.[20]

Thus, if a government enacted or applied arms control laws for the purpose of facilitating genocide, then the government's actions would constitute genocide.[21] The Universal Declaration of Human Rights, which was adopted by the U.N. in 1948, never explicitly mentions "genocide," but a right to resist genocide is an inescapable implication of the rights which the Declaration does affirm.

First, the Declaration affirms the right to life.[22] Of course, the right to life is recognized not just by the Universal Declaration, but also by several other international human rights instruments.[23]

Second, the Declaration affirms the right to personal security.[24] The right of self-defense is implicit in the right of personal security, and is explicitly recognized by, *inter alia*, the European Convention on Human Rights[25] and by the International Criminal Court.[26]

The Preamble of the Universal Declaration of Human Rights recognizes a right of rebellion as a last resort: "Whereas it is essential, if man is not to be compelled to have recourse, as a last resort, to rebellion against tyranny and oppression, that human rights should be protected by the rule of law...."[27] The drafting history of the Universal Declaration clearly shows that the Preamble was explicitly intended to recognize a preexisting human right to revolution against tyranny.[28]

Finally, Article 8 of the Universal Declaration states: "Everyone has the right to an effective remedy."[29] The Universal Declaration therefore comports with the long-established common-law rule that there can be no right without a remedy.[30]

Thus, the Declaration recognizes that when a government destroys human rights and all other remedies have failed, the people are "compelled to have recourse, as a last resort, to rebellion against tyranny and oppression." Since "everyone has the right to an effective remedy," the people necessarily have the right to possess and use arms to resist tyranny, if arms use is the only remaining "effective remedy."[31]

The Anglo-American legal tradition supports the right to armed resistance among the "general principles of law recognized by civilized nations." For example, the U.S. Supreme Court noted that the right to arms, like the right to peaceably assemble, is not created by positive law, but rather derives "'from those laws whose authority is acknowledged by civilized man throughout the world.' It is found wherever civilization exists."[32]

William Blackstone's *Commentaries* on the common law, published in 1765, are by far the most influential legal treatise ever published, regarded as the foundation of the common law throughout the English-speaking world and in the one-third of the globe where British law ruled. The *Commentaries* are part of the common-law heritage of any present or former British colony or member of the Commonwealth of Nations.

In the explanation of human rights under the common law, Blackstone first described the three primary rights: personal security, personal liberty, and private property. He then explained the five "auxiliary rights" that protected the primary rights:

> The fifth and last auxiliary right of the subject, that I shall at present mention, is that of having arms for their defence suitable to their condition and degree, and such as are allowed by law . . . and it is indeed a public allowance under due restrictions, of the natural right of resistance and self preservation, when the sanctions of society and laws are found insufficient to restrain the violence of oppression.[33]

When a government is perpetrating genocide—"when the sanctions of society and laws are found insufficient to restrain the violence of oppression"—that is exactly when people most need—and have a fundamental human right to possess—"arms for their defence."

MORE U.N. GUN CONTROL, MORE GENOCIDE

Holocaust historian Abram L. Sachar observes that "the difference between resistance and submission depends very largely upon who was in possession of the arms that back up the will to do or die."[34] He is hardly alone. In 1967, the International Society for the Prevention of Crime held a Congress in Paris on the prevention of genocide. The Congress concluded that,

> defensive measures are the most effective means for the prevention of genocide. Not all aggression is criminal. A defense reaction is for the human race what the wind is for navigation—the result depends on the direction. The most moral violence is that used in legitimate self-defense, the most sacred judicial institution.[35]

I believe that it is time to make "Never Again!" a reality, and not just a slogan. Half a century after the international community made the Genocide

Convention into binding international law, overt genocide is being perpetrated in half a dozen countries in Africa. As with every other genocide in the last half-century, the U.N. refused to take meaningful action to stop it.

Philosophy professor Samuel Wheeler observes:

> It is hard to see how a United Nations interested in the safety of persons rather than nations could hold that disarming the citizenry is a good idea. In none of the deadly sequence of genocides and citizen-slaughters that have characterized the Third World in the eighties and nineties have ordinary citizens been better off for having been helpless before the assaults of government agents.... It is hard to avoid the conclusion that the United Nations initiative [of disarmament] is concerned with the interests of nation-states rather than the interests of people. It would be unkind to speculate about the post-colonial attitudes that block consideration of the possibility of directly arming the citizens of the turbulent regions of Africa and Asia that have been the locus of recent genocides.[36]

If you follow the U.N.'s plan to ban civilian firearms ownership, then you eliminate the most effective deterrent to genocide. As the ECOWAS Protocol makes clear, a total ban on civilian gun ownership is the goal of the U.N., as such a ban is being imposed on West Africa right now—making sure that victims of genocide and Islamist mob violence will be defenseless.

Civilians with light arms cannot necessarily overthrow a well-entrenched and well-armed regime, but even the most powerful governments find it very difficult to perpetrate genocide against armed populations. The historical record is very clear about how very rare it is for genocide to be attempted—let alone succeed—against an armed populace. If every family on this planet owned a good-quality rifle, genocide would be on the path to extinction.

It would be difficult to find an organization whose work has facilitated government mass murder of more people, in more diverse locations around the world, than the U.N. has in the last decade and a half. If the U.N.'s global gun prohibition campaign succeeds, genocide will become even more common.

After Kopel, Gallant, and Eisen published an article about the genocide in Bosnia, an American soldier sent them an e-mail, which Dave Kopel shared with me. That serviceman wrote:

> In 1999 I spent a year with the peacekeeping mission in Bosnia. I was stationed in the former "safe" area Gorazde. I learned a lot about that war and how the civilians were massacred. One day we were discussing guns and private ownership. In response to the statement that the U.N. believes only the police and military should have guns, a Bosnian exasperatedly asked: "Who do you think slaughtered everyone?"[37]

CHAPTER 10

The U.N. and Terrorism:
A Blood and Money Trail

The actions of the United Nations regarding terrorism run the gamut from useless to deadly: it denounces U.S. antiterrorism efforts, while at the same time it foments terrorism and contributes direct financial and material support for terrorism in the Middle East. U.N. officials mouth the right words about terrorism, but the world body virtually does nothing concrete to combat escalating violence.

Several governments that are state sponsors of terrorism are U.N. members in good standing. The U.S. State Department has officially named six such governments: Iran, Syria, Libya, North Korea, Sudan, and Cuba.[1]

Syria has the longest record as a named state sponsor of terrorism—since 1979. Sudan is the most recent nation, so designated in 1993. Yet whether a regime has been a notorious sponsor of terrorism for more than a decade or for a quarter-century does not matter to the U.N. Criminal; terrorist regimes are treated like any member state, granted seats and sometimes leading roles on U.N. committees and commissions dealing with terrorism, human rights, and Middle East issues. Notably, terrorist states have repeatedly been members of the Security Council.[2]

At the U.N., the terrorist coalition is so strong that it can block meaningful action against terrorism. Often, the coalition is able to use the U.N.—especially in the Middle East—to propagandize in its favor and to provide funding directly and indirectly. The terrorists-in-good-standing at the U.N. are often supported by other member states—including China, Russia, and many of the Arab and African states.

Since U.S. taxpayers provide 22 percent of the U.N.'s budget, vast amounts of American tax money collected from people like you and me have been used by the U.N. to pay for suicide bombers, for schools that incite children to become terrorists, and for a relentless stream of hate propaganda.

U.N. MONEY FOR OSAMA BIN LADEN

A few weeks after the September 11, 2001, attacks, the British Broadcasting Corporation announced: "A BBC investigation has revealed that the United Nations funded the work of a charity believed by the United States to be a front organization for Osama Bin Laden."[3] The charity was the Muwafaq (Arabic for "blessed relief") Foundation, located in Sudan, to which the U.N. donation was made in 1997. The Sudanese government was then (and is now) a notorious state sponsor of terrorism and an ongoing genocide perpetrator. Yet the U.N. apparently had little interest in checking the bona fides of the government-approved "charity" operating out of the same nation that had harbored Osama bin Laden until 1996.[4]

The U.S. Treasury Department explained that the Muwafaq "charity" was used as a front by Saudi Arabian businessmen to deliver money to bin Laden.[5] In November 2001, the Treasury Department stated:

> The Muwafaq Foundation provided logistical and financial support for a *mujahidin* battalion in Bosnia. The Foundation also operated in Sudan, Somalia, and Pakistan, among other places. A number of individuals employed by or otherwise associated with the Muwafaq Foundation have connections to various terrorist organizations. . . . The Muwafaq Foundation also provided support to Hamas and the Abu Sayyaf Organization in the Philippines. . . . The Muwafaq Foundation also employed or served as cover for Islamic extremists connected with the military activities of Makhtab Al-Khidamat (MK) [a group that later merged into al-Qaeda]. . . . A number of NGOs, formerly associated with the MK, including Muwafaq, also merged with al-Qaeda.[6]

The BBC reported that Charles Shoebridge, a retired British antiterrorism intelligence officer, said that the U.N. was in a good position to have looked into the credentials of the charities to which it gave money. "You would have thought that an organisation like the U.N. would have access to a certain amount of information from its constituent members' intelligence services," he added.[7]

"The fact that the U.N. has been so easily duped will no doubt cause great unease within the international community," concluded the BBC report. "Not only would it have allowed terrorists to masquerade under a cloak of decency—it actually provided hard cash with which they could fund their cause."[8]

The BBC's prediction turned out to be incorrect. The "international community"—at least the international community that runs the U.N.—kept up business as usual. Which is to say, the U.N. kept on funding terrorism.

The amount that the U.N. gave to bin Laden wasn't much, at least by the U.N.'s profligate standards for spending other people's money. The Sudanese "charities" got $1.4 million, and the BBC investigator apparently did not discover how much of that money was delivered to bin Laden's charity. We do know that the 1997 gift came at a time when al-Qaeda was hurting for money. One of al-Qaeda's top employees quit in 1996, because he was only being paid $500 a month.[9]

But the money that the U.N. gave Osama bin Laden is a pittance compared to its funding of some other terrorists.

OIL-FOR-TERRORISM

The largest financial program in U.N. history, the Iraqi Oil-for-Food program, was corrupted right from its start in late 1996, with U.N. knowledge and acquiescence. Upon taking office as secretary-general on January 1, 1997, Kofi Annan announced a "reform," which consolidated the two small U.N. programs related to Oil-for-Food. (One program had been for sanctions; the other program for trade allowed under the Oil-for-Food exemption to the sanctions.) The two programs were merged into a massive and permanent Office for Iraqi Programmes, which Annan made part of the Office of the Secretariat. The effect was to allow Annan to grow the program, under his control, to enormous size, and to limit the Security Council merely to reviewing the dissimulating reports he provided every six months.

From the beginning, Saddam Hussein lined his pockets with money intended to help poor people in Iraq and used the money to finance his military and secret police. Moreover, he used the money to stow away cash and weapons for the terrorists now determined to overthrow the democratically elected government of Iraq, murder Iraqi civilians by the thousands, and kill American and other coalition soldiers.

In January 2006, the *Weekly Standard*'s Stephen Hayes reported on Hussein's government documents that had been seized and translated. They show that Saddam's government—which, remember, was being funded by U.N. corruption—trained 2,000 terrorists every year at Iraqi bases.[10]

Although the U.N. has continued to obstruct Congressional investigations into the Oil-for-Food program, corruption ran all the way to the top—to the son of Secretary General Kofi Annan, and to the man, Benon Sevan, whom Annan appointed to run the ill-gotten program. (Sevan has fled to Cyprus, which has no extradition treaty with the U.S.) We also know that Saddam used his U.N. revenue to pass out huge bribes to high-ranking officials in the French and Russian governments. The Volcker Commission investigation found that both Kofi Annan and Deputy Secretary-General Louise Fréchette (a leader of the U.N. antigun campaign and the direct supervisor of Benon Sevan) were "informed of the issue of kickbacks, but remained passive."[11]

Now that some of the Oil-for-Food documents have been made public, we understand that it was impossible to expect that the U.N. would ever authorize force against Saddam—even though he flouted seventeen Security Council resolutions demanding proof that he had disarmed and that he allow unhindered U.N. inspections. Thanks to the corrupt program set up by Kofi Annan, Saddam bribed the U.N. itself, and bribed permanent members of the Security Council, who threatened to veto any resolution approving the use of force. After the coalition liberated Iraq, Kofi Annan sniffed that the U.S.-led invasion was "illegal," because it was not authorized in advance by the U.N.[12]

Annan's sniping about the "illegality" of the liberation of Iraq was delivered in September 2004, in a transparent attempt to influence U.S. public opinion in favor of Massachusetts Senator John Kerry, the antigun extremist who wanted to subject U.S. policies to what he called the "global test."

The week before the election, the U.N. launched an "October surprise." Mohammad ElBaradei, the Egyptian head of the U.N.'s International Atomic Energy Agency, told the *New York Times* that 350 tons of explosives had gone missing from the Al Qaaqaa munitions depot in Iraq. The media jumped on the story, and the Kerry campaign launched ads on the missing explosives so quickly that it was difficult to believe that Kerry and the media (and perhaps the U.N.) were not working in coordination.

ElBaradei's wild claims were quickly disproven, but it was not the first time, nor the last, that the U.N. would attempt to interfere with America's right to choose how to defend itself in the war on terror.

WORLD BANK

Two major multinational institutions enable developed nations to make economic development loans and grants to the Third World: the International Monetary Fund (IMF) and the World Bank. The IMF is not part of the U.N., but the World Bank is. Funding from these institutions (in other words, funding from taxpayers in countries such as the U.S.) often does much more harm than good, since corrupt third-world governments use the funding to enrich themselves and to strengthen their grip on national power.[13]

Three weeks after the September 11, 2001 attacks, a Heritage Foundation paper titled "Stop Subsidizing Terrorism," detailed IMF and World Bank support of terrorist governments.[14] Of the countries that the U.S. named as state sponsors of terrorism, Iran has received $625 million from the IMF and World Bank (even though it is a wealthy, oil-rich country), Syria has received $265 million, and Sudan $1.8 billion. When ruled by the Taliban, Afghanistan received $230 million.[15] The governing "Articles of Agreement do not allow those institutions to prohibit lending to countries that undermine international peace and stability by supporting foreign terrorist organizations," Heritage noted.

Citing public documents covering 1998–99, the Heritage Foundation also pointed out that other U.N. agencies had given millions of dollars to terrorist regimes. The Office of the U.N. High Commissioner for Refugees gave money to Libya and Iran, while the U.N. Relief and Works Agency for Palestine Refugees in the Near East gave to Syria.

The World Bank also provides funding to terrorist training centers through "investments" (that is, donations) to several Palestinian universities, all of which have official student chapters of the terrorist organization Hamas.[16] These student chapters have been, and will continue to be, the training grounds for the next generation of terrorists and their propagandists.[17]

At Al-Najah University, a World Bank beneficiary, the student chapter of Hamas celebrated the terrorist bombing of a Sbarro pizzeria in Israel by constructing a mock pizza parlor and filling it with images of severed body parts.[18]

The World Bank does not seem to mind glorifying terrorists. One of its projects was paying for the "development of the Dalal Mughrabi Street" in Gaza. Dalal Mughrabi was a terrorist for the Palestine Liberation Organization who hijacked a bus in 1978, and murdered thirty-six Israelis and American photographer Gail Rubin.[19]

FOOD, STARVATION AND U.N. CELEBRATION OF DICTATORS

Robert Mugabe, the Marxist tyrant of Zimbabwe, has stolen elections, destroyed free press, squelched the judiciary, and his regime is engaged in a campaign of genocide against the people of Zimbabwe by starving them to death.[20] In 2005, he bulldozed huge zones of the capital city of Harare where many opponents of his regime lived, leaving hundreds of thousands of destitute victims homeless and starving.

Mugabe destroyed Zimbabwe's food economy by confiscating land from white farmers, which he gave to his political cronies under the specious pretext of "land reform." Mugabe has long carried out a gun-control program to ensure that no one can resist his tyranny and genocide.

So how did the U.N. Food and Agriculture Organization (FAO) celebrate its sixtieth anniversary on October 17, 2005? By inviting Robert Mugabe to come to the celebration in Rome. Since Mugabe was on U.N. business, he was allowed to ignore a European Union (E.U.) ban on his travel. Mugabe delivered a speech on his "land reform" program before a U.N. organization that is supposed to be *fighting*, not causing, world hunger.

At the anniversary celebration, the FAO also bestowed its Agricola Medal on Brazil's notoriously corrupt President Lula da Silva, who a week later would lose his campaign to outlaw gun ownership in Brazil, and who also advocates a global U.N. tax on guns.

But when it comes to legitimizing terrorists, and undermining democratic nations' resistance to terrorism, the FAO has to take a back seat to Jean Ziegler, the U.N. Special Rapporteur on the right to food.[21] Ziegler is a Swiss socialist politician who uses his U.N. position to push extremist anti-American policies.

According to the FAO, there are seventeen countries that suffer from man-made (i.e., government-caused) food emergencies. Ziegler has mildly criticized two: Sudan (which is carrying out genocide) and Ethiopia.[22] Fifteen other countries perpetrating death by starvation have never been the subject of a critical word from Ziegler: Burundi, Central African Republic, Chad, Democratic Republic of the Congo, Republic of the Congo, Cote d'Ivoire, Eritrea, Guinea, Haiti, Liberia, Russian Federation (Chechnya), Sierra Leone, Somalia, Tanzania, and Uganda.

Ziegler reserves much harsher language for the U.S., which he calls an "imperialist dictatorship," and attacks President George W. Bush as "the Pinochet [the former dictator of Chile] who sits in the White House."[23]

After September 11, Ziegler made the preposterous claim than U.S. military action against the Taliban would cause "apocalyptic" results, which would lead to "the end for the Afghan nation." [24] Ziegler would also claim that the coalition liberation of Iraq violated the food rights of Iraqis.[25] An actual violation of Iraqi rights was the theft by Saddam Hussein's regime and its U.N. accomplices of Oil-for-Food money intended to pay for food for Iraqi civilians. Ziegler has never complained about this well-documented violation of rights.

Ziegler is also a huge fan of Cuban tyrant Fidel Castro, a state sponsor of terrorism, and claims that the U.S. economic embargo of Cuba is "genocide." Ignored is Castro's corrupt control of the Cuban economy, which he has used to make himself one of the richest men in the world. Ziegler is not alone at the U.N. in his admiration of Cuba's Marxist dictatorship. Recently, for only the second time in history, movie crews were allowed inside the U.N. General Assembly, when Kofi Annan authorized the filming of "Che," which glorifies Che Guevara. According to the Free Society

Project's Truth Recovery Archive, Guevara, while commander of Castro's Cabana prison from 1957 to 1959, ordered and often personally executed more than 200 Cubans.[26]

On December 21, 1988, the Libyan dictator Moammar Khadaffi launched what was then the deadliest attack in history against American civilians. His agents blew up Pan Am flight 103, murdering 189 Americans, and 81 people from 20 other countries. The next year Ziegler participated in the founding of the Moammar Khadaffi Human Rights Prize.[27] In 2002, Ziegler himself won the Moammar Khadaffi Human Rights Prize.[28] He shared the prize with Holocaust denier Roger Garaudy. Two years later, while serving as the U.N.'s Special Rapporteur, Ziegler helped found the explicitly anti-American magazine *L'Empire*, which denounces the war on terror.[29]

HEZBOLLAH

As our nation engages terrorists around the world, U.N. "peacekeepers" are actually working side-by-side with the Hezbollah, a Lebanese Islamic terrorist group that used truck bombs to kill 241 marines in their barracks in Lebanon in 1983. Hezbollah also kidnapped and tortured to death Marine Colonel William R. Higgins and the CIA station chief in Beirut, William Buckley.

The U.S. State Department states that Hezbollah (Arabic for Party of God) is responsible for two bombings of the U.S. Embassy in Beruit, the kidnapping of over thirty westerners, and hijacking TWA flight 847 (Athens to Rome) in 1985. Hezbollah has been designated as a terrorist organization not only by the U.S., but also by the E.U. and many democratic governments.

At the level of rhetoric, U.N. Secretary-General Kofi Annan is a staunch opponent of terrorism.[30] Yet when the U.N. Security Council was considering a 2005 resolution to tell Syria to remove its troops from Lebanon, Annan was asked whether Hezbollah should be disarmed.[31] Annan answered: "We need to recognize that they are a force in society that one will have to factor in as we implement the resolution."[32] The Security Council did adopt Resolution 1559, which ordered Syria out of

Lebanon, and ordered that Hezbollah be disarmed. Yet the secretary-general's special envoy to Lebanon, Terje Roed-Larsen, acknowledged that disarming Hezbullah was not part of his "action agenda."[33]

The announcement of the secretary-general and his special envoy that Hezbollah—even when armed in violation of a Security Council resolution and when engaged in terrorism—is entitled to consideration is hardly consistent with Annan's generalities about terrorism, such as: "It should be clearly stated, by all possible moral and political authorities, that terrorism is unacceptable under any circumstances, and in any culture."[34] Except sometimes.

Early in 2005, Annan sent his special envoy Lakhdar Brahimi to attend the funeral of Rafik Hariri, the former Lebanese prime minister who was assassinated because he spoke out against Syria's colonization of Lebanon. While in Lebanon, the U.N.'s special envoy also met with the head of Hezbollah, Sheikh Mohamed Hussein Fadlallah—a man whom diplomats from the U.S. and other freedom-loving countries resolutely refuse to dignify with an official diplomatic visit.[35]

The Security Council ordered an investigation of the assassination of Hariri. When the report was completed, Annan ordered that portions be blacked out before being released to the public. Those portions showed—when the full report was leaked—that the trail of responsibility for the assassination stretched all the way to the brother-in-law of Syrian tyrant Bashir Assad.

U.N. INTERIM FORCE IN LEBANON

In 1982, Israel invaded Lebanon, in order to stop attacks on Israel from Hezbollah and PLO bases there. In 1990, Israel withdrew from Lebanon, in compliance with Security Council Resolution 425. The U.N. deployed peacekeepers—the U.N. Interim Force in Lebanon (UNFIL)—to prevent incursions from one nation into another. Yet in practice, UNFIL has turned into an ally of Hezbollah and an active enemy of Israel.

The so-called peacekeepers of UNFIL do not interdict Hezbollah terrorist attacks on northern Israel.[36] Instead, UNFIL allows Hezbollah to take up positions that are adjacent to the UNFIL peacekeepers.[37] Moreover,

UNFIL has established a permanent dialogue with the terrorist organization.[38] As one Israeli leader summarized, "The U.N. is in fact collaborating with a terrorist organization."[39]

UNFIL's most notorious collaboration with terrorists involved the kidnapping and murder of three Israeli soldiers, and the subsequent cover-up. On October 7, 2000, Hezbollah terrorists entered Israel, attacked three Israeli soldiers on Mount Dov, and abducted them to Lebanon. The kidnapping was witnessed by several dozen UNFIL soldiers who stood idle.[40] One of the soldier witnesses described the kidnapping: the terrorists set off an explosive that stunned the Israeli soldiers. Clad in U.N. uniforms, the terrorists called out, "Come, come, we'll help you."

It appears that at least four of the UNFIL peacekeepers, all from India, received bribes from Hezbollah in order to assist the kidnapping by helping them get to the kidnapping spot and find the Israeli soldiers.[41] Some of the bribery involved alcohol and Lebanese women.[42]

But there is evidence of far greater payments by Hezbollah to the UNFIL Indian brigade, including hundreds of thousands of dollars for assistance in the kidnapping and cover-up.[43] The U.N. cover-up began almost immediately.

The Beruit *Daily Star* reported the story as told by a former officer of the Observer Group Lebanon (OGL), which is part of the U.N. Truce Supervision Organization (UNTSO):

> A few hours after the kidnapping, UNTSO learned that two abandoned cars had been discovered. One was a white Nissan Pathfinder with fake U.N. insignia; it had hit an embankment because it was being driven so fast that the driver missed a turn. The other was a Range Rover; it was missing a tire rim, and was still running when it was discovered.[44]

Rather than using the very recently abandoned vehicles as clues to rescue the kidnap victims, the U.N. initiated a cover-up. Eighteen hours after the kidnapping, a team of OGL and the Indian UNFIL began a videotaped removal of the contents of the cars.[45]

The UNTSO officer told the *Daily Star* that the U.N. ordered its personnel to destroy all photographs and written reports about the incident.[46]

Did the U.N. provide the Israelis with the automobile contents, or the videotape, both of which might have helped the Israelis rescue the kidnap victims? Of course not.

Israel found out about the videotape, and demanded that the U.N. let Israeli investigators see it. Kofi Annan and his special envoy first denied that any videotape existed, but nine months after the kidnapping, on July 6, 2001, the U.N. admitted that it had the videotape. Annan ordered an internal U.N. report, which was led by U.N. Undersecretary-General Joseph Connor. (Connor was later implicated in the Oil-for-Food scam.) The report revealed that the U.N. had two additional videotapes, one containing still photographs from the kidnapping itself.

Even after admitting the existence of the first videotape, Annan refused to allow Israel to view it, claiming that doing so would undermine U.N. neutrality. The U.S. House of Representatives thought differently. On July 30, 2001, it passed, on a 411 to 4 vote, a resolution urging the U.N. to allow Israel to see the videotape.[47] Annan relented, but only under the condition that the tape be edited so as to hide the faces of the Hezbollah perpetrators.[48]

On January 29, 2004, the bodies of the murdered Israelis were returned to Israel by Hezbollah, as part of a prisoner exchange.

U.N. ASSISTS TERRORIST CONCEALMENT

On May 11, 2004, a cameraman from the Reuters news agency filmed armed Palestinian terrorists entering a U.N. ambulance. After murdering six Israeli soldiers in Gaza, they fled in the ambulance.[49]

The U.N. first denied that the incident had ever taken place, then retreated, claiming that the U.N.-employed ambulance driver had been forced to comply with the terrorists' demands for transportation. That claim was undercut by the fact that the driver did not make any report of his supposed abduction until the videotape was made public.

This U.N. deceit was hardly unprecedented. In August 2002, a Hamas "activist" named Nidal abd al-Fattah Abdallah Nazzal, employed by U.N. Relief and Works Agency (UNRWA) as an ambulance driver, was arrested. He confessed that he had hauled weapons and explosives in ambulances belonging to the UNRWA.[50] Arrested that same month was a senior

UNRWA official, Nahd Rashid Ahmad Atallah. Using an official UNRWA car that was supposed to be delivering food, he transported armed terrorists to perpetrate their crimes. He also used his car to transport a twelve-kilogram explosive.[51]

Such terrorist techniques for killing Israelis have been exported to Iraq, where ambulances are used as cover for carrying out attacks on U.S. troops and on Iraqi civilians.[52]

U.N. DEVELOPMENT PROGRAMME

From 1999 through January 2005, the head of the U.N. Development Programme (UNDP) was Mark Malloch Brown. He left the UNDP because he was promoted to Kofi Annan's chief of staff—a perch from which he has denounced the U.S. as an "ungainly giant."

It should come as no surprise that Brown rents a house from George Soros in Westchester County, New York, and has served on several of Soros's advisory groups. One hand washes the other, and Soros—the kingpin of the global gun-ban movement—has given millions of dollars to Brown's UNDP, via his Open Society Institute.[53]

The UNDP has been an active funder of terrorists. In 1999, the UNDP was one of the top five international donors to the Taliban regime in Afghanistan.[54]

Documents captured in 2003 and 2004 also reveal that the UNDP has been funding Hamas. The money was funneled through two phony charities, the Tulkarm Charity Committee and the Jenin District Committee for Charitable Funds.[55] The latter had already been identified to the UNDP as a Hamas front by the Office of the Coordinator of the Activities of the Israel Defense Forces; the Israelis provided evidence that the deputy director of the "charity" was part of an elite Hamas terrorist unit known as the Izz ad-Din al-Qassam Brigades. The UNDP's special representative in Jerusalem, Timothy Rothermel, rejected the request to stop funding Hamas.[56]

In the summer of 2005, Ariel Sharon's Israeli government unilaterally renounced all control over Gaza, forcibly evicting Israeli settlers. It would have been a good occasion for the UNDP, which lavishes vast sums on Palestinians, to encourage optimism about a peaceful coexistence with

Israel. Instead, the UNDP provided funds to the Palestinian Authority (PA) for production of thousands of bumper stickers, banners, posters, and mugs that proclaimed "Gaza Today. The West Bank and Jerusalem Tomorrow." The materials carried the U.N. symbol, and included the words, "Paid for by the U.N. Development Program.[57] The withdrawal involved no PA negotiations, [58] but, as one critic observed, the U.N. message was "The *intifada* worked. That's contextually what this message is saying."[59]

UNRWA: THE MOTHER OF TERRORISM

If the U.N. Relief and Works Agency for Palestine Refugees in the Near East (UNRWA) were a private organization, the fair application of existing U.S. law would result in UNRWA being classified as a Foreign Terrorist Organization (FTO) by the U.S. State Department, and its assets frozen by all governments committed to fighting terrorism. Briefly put, an organization is "engaged in terrorist activity" if it knowingly transfers funds to terrorists, knowingly allows its facilities to be used for terrorism, or provides other material support to terrorists.[60]

To be sure, UNRWA is not an *exclusively* terrorist organization in the sense that al-Qaeda is. Al-Qaeda has no activities other than terrorism and terrorist propaganda.

UNRWA, however, willingly accepts large sums of money from known terrorist finance organizations and knowingly distributes large sums of money to them. Its property is used for terrorism, including bomb making, and it knowingly finances massive amounts of hate propaganda designed to incite terrorism. A great deal of UNRWA's material support for terrorism is given to Hamas, which is itself designated an FTO by the U.S. government.[61]

UNRWA: FUNDED LARGELY BY U.S. TAXPAYERS

As the largest donors to the UNRWA, U.S. taxpayers pay about a third of UNRWA's budget, giving the organization more than $100 million per year.[62] Since 1950, U.S. taxpayers have given UNRWA over $2.5 billion, roughly a third of its total spending.[63] Saudi Arabia, Kuwait, and the smaller Gulf States contribute a combined total of about 2 percent of UNRWA's budget. Other

Arab nations such as Libya, Egypt, and Syria—which constantly profess concern for the well-being of the Palestinians—contribute little or nothing.[64]

UNRWA also receives substantial terrorist funding—making it apparently the only U.N. agency that not only gives money to terrorists, but also gets money from them. According to the U.S. Department of the Treasury, a "charity" known as the Islamic African Relief Agency (IARA) transferred millions of dollars to Osama bin Laden's terrorist networks. In October 2004, Treasury froze IARA's assets. IARA's energetic head, Mubarak Hamed, has been charged with raising $5 million for bin Laden in just a single fundraising swing through the Middle East in 2000. One of IARA's subsidiaries, the Islamic American Relief Agency, gave UNRWA $510,000.[65]

Another UNRWA donor—of $5,076,000—is the Islamic Development Bank, which also created the Al Aqsa Fund. This Fund has been declared by the U.S. Treasury Department to be a Specially Designated Global Terrorist (SDGT) entity, because it funnels money from donors in the Persian Gulf to the terrorist organization Hamas.[66]

In UNRWA's public records, you will find something called the "Saudi Committee," which has given UNRWA $1,640,000. The reported name is a deceptive condensation of the Saudi Arabia Committee for Support of the Intifada Al Quds. (*Al Quds* is the Arabic name for Jerusalem.) The Saudi Committee is believed to contribute funds for Hamas suicide bombing.[67]

The government of Syria, designated by the U.S. State Department as a state sponsor of terror, has created an organization called the Syrian Arab Popular Committee. It sponsors rallies in Syria and Lebanon demanding the extermination of Israel. The committee has also given $3,538,276 to UNRWA .[68]

Why is UNRWA such an appealing, and willing, recipient of terrorist funding? Part of the answer goes back to UNRWA's creation in 1949 to help settle Palestinian refugees who fled Israel after five Arab nations (with substantial Palestinian military support) started and lost a war to destroy Israel in 1948-1949.[69] The expectation was that once UNRWA helped solve the Palestinian refugee problem, the agency would cease to exist.[70] Accordingly, UNRWA developed a bureaucratic imperative which virtually ordained that refugees would never resettle. More than fifty-six years after UNRWA was created, refugees are still living in UNRWA's camps—the only refugee population in the world whose status has persisted for more than half a century.

The creation of UNRWA has turned out to be a catastrophe. The Palestinians are the people who have been most victimized by UNRWA, although the Israelis have also suffered immensely. Because the suffering of Palestinians has been used so effectively by terrorists to build support for attacks on the U.S., Americans are also victims of UNRWA.

URWA'S FINANCIAL AID TO HAMAS

Hamas (an acronym for "Islamic Resistance Movement") has been designated an FTO by the U.S. State Department. It shocked the world in January 2006 by winning a clear majority in the Palestinian parliament, pushing aside the Fatah party which directed Palestinian politics for four decades. The terrorist designation is richly deserved. Hamas has launched hundreds of terrorist attacks, including many of the most infamous suicide bomb attacks.[71]

Where does Hamas get its money? A great deal of the terrorist money comes from UNRWA—and, therefore, from U.S. taxpayers. UNRWA's relationship with Hamas is so notorious that Congress enacted a specific requirement that UNRWA screen out beneficiaries (including UNRWA employees) who are members of Hamas or other terrorist organizations, or who have received terrorist training. *Only* if UNRWA performs such screening is UNWRA eligible for U.S. foreign aid.[72]

When the U.S. government's General Accounting Office (GAO) asked UNRWA if it was performing the required screening, UNRWA admitted that it was not.[73] The then-head of URNWA, Commissioner-General Peter Hansen, told the Canadian Broadcasting Corporation (CBC): "I am sure that there are Hamas members on the UNRWA payroll, and I don't see that as a crime."[74] It may not be a crime, according to the U.N., but it is illegal under U.S. law for UNRWA to receive U.S. aid, until UNRWA stops knowingly employing Hamas.

UNRWA is so blatantly contemptuous of the U.S. requirements that when six houses were accidentally "destroyed during bomb-making activities," UNRWA declared that there was insufficient evidence to cut the families off from UNRWA benefits.[75]

UNRWA allows its staff to openly participate in terrorist organizations, including Hamas. As one Israeli official observed, "As long as UNRWA employees are members of Fatah, Hamas, or PFLP [Popular Front for the Liberation of Palestine], they are going to pursue the interests of their party within the framework of their job. . . . Who's going to check up on them to see that they don't? UNRWA? They are UNRWA."[76]

Indeed, Hamas openly controls the UNRWA employees' union, including the executive council. UNRWA employees are so pro-Hamas that the Hamas candidates won 90 percent of the vote in the union elections and have won every UNRWA union election since 1990.[77] UNRWA Commissioner-General Hansen has admitted that Hamas runs the UNRWA union.[78] Hamas members are required to pay a portion of their salaries to Hamas, and thus UNRWA salaries provide a substantial portion of Hamas's revenue.[79]

The GAO, in an investigation of UNRWA, pointed to more cases in which UNRWA engaged in terrorist activity:

- A UNRWA employee convicted of throwing firebombs at a public bus.

- A UNRWA employee who was a member of Islamic Jihad and was convicted of possession of explosives. Islamic Jihad has been designated an FTO by the U.S. State Department.

- A UNRWA employee who was a member of Hamas and was convicted of supplying chemicals to a bomb maker.

Between 2001 and 2004, seven UNRWA employees were convicted of participation in terrorist activities.[80] Nevertheless, UNRWA brazenly lies about its role in terrorism. UNRWA Commissioner-General Peter Hansen told the GAO that, "UNRWA has no evidence that would justify denying beneficiaries relief or humanitarian aid owning [sic] to terrorism."[81] What Hansen's doublespeak really means is that even when the evidence is undeniable—such as bomb makers accidentally blowing up their own houses—UNRWA pretends that the evidence does not exist, and continues to give money to known terrorists.

UNRWA also acts as an FTO, under the standards of U.S. law, by providing safe houses to terrorists. In 2002, Hamas terrorists murdered twenty-nine people at a hotel in the town of Netanya. Israel finally decided to take action against the terrorist bases—the UNRWA camps where terrorists concealed themselves in the civilian population.

The most notorious of these camps was Jenin, near Israel's border. Two weeks after September 11, 2001, the head of Tanzim (a terrorist subdivision of Yassir Arafat's Fatah) was informed that:

> Of all the districts, Jenin boasts the greatest number of fighters from Fatah and other Islamic national factions. The refugee camp is rightly considered to be the center of events and the operational headquarters of all the factions in the Jenin area—as the other side calls it, a hornets' nest. The Jenin refugee camp is remarkable for the large number of fighting men taking initiatives in the cause of our people. . . . It is little wonder, therefore, that Jenin is known as the capital of the suicide martyrs.[82]

Jenin was hardly UNRWA's only major terrorist base, and the seizure of the UNRWA camps has revealed massive evidence—including documents and weapons—of UNRWA's material support for terrorism. UNRWA, however, claims that it has no control over its own camps, because is has no "police force, no intelligence apparatus and no mandate to report on political and military activities."[83] This is nonsense. UNRWA claims "official" ownership of the camps, and precisely demarcates their boundaries and buildings. When the owner of a house in one of the camps dies, he cannot bequeath the house to his children. As one UNRWA official put it, "This is not his property, it's our property."[84]

UNRWA PROTERRORISM EDUCATION

UNRWA runs a massive school system, including 266 schools with 242,000 students just in the West Bank and Gaza. UNRWA schools are used as bomb-making centers, as terrorist hideouts, as ammunition depots for terrorists, as offices for terrorist organizations, and for "youth clubs" that are actually terrorist cells.[85]

When Commissioner-General Hansen spoke at a 2004 conference at the Van Leer Jerusalem Institute, he was questioned about UNRWA camps serving as terrorist bases. Hansen asserted that the claims were "made up" in order "to delegitimize" UNRWA. "There hasn't been a single case documented," he declared. When Hansen said the word "terrorism," he used finger quotes.[86]

The claim that there has not been "a single case documented" is an outrageous lie, since several UNRWA employees have been convicted of terrorism, massive terrorist weapons caches have been found in UNRWA camps, and UNRWA camps openly and frequently conduct terrorist recruitment indoctrination.[87]

But the essence of his answer was the finger quotes around "terrorism." Quite plainly, Hansen rejects the idea that what UNRWA, Hamas, and related groups do is terrorism. The definitional problem is not unique to Hansen (who left UNRWA in March 2005).[88] Rather it is endemic at the U.N., and it is the core reason why the world body has refused to fight global terrorism.

ANTITERRORISM TREATY

At the verbal level, the U.N. may appear tough on terrorism, having adopted many different antiterrorism U.N. treaties and conventions. But although there is the 1997 International Convention for the Suppression of Terrorist Bombing, UNRWA houses and schools serve as terrorist bomb-making centers. Although there is the 1999 International Convention for the Suppression of the Financing of Terrorism, the World Bank and other U.N. entities finance state sponsors of terrorism and terrorist organizations such as Hamas. Although there is the 2005 International Convention Against Nuclear Terrorism, which supplements the 1970 Treaty on the Non-Proliferation of Nuclear Weapons, responsible U.N. agencies have done nothing meaningful to prevent the terrorist states of Iran and North Korea from attempting to build nuclear weapons, just as they did nothing to stop Saddam Hussein's nuclear program in the 1970s and 1980s.

There are U.N. treaties against hijacking, against violence at airports, against violence toward diplomats, against hostage taking, and against interference with maritime navigation. Nonetheless, the U.N. has for more than three decades honored the late Yassir Arafat and his terrorist PLO—the man and the group that invented the modern practice of terrorist airplane hijacking, who murdered numerous diplomats, kidnapped countless hostages, and hijacked the *Achille Lauro* cruise ship.

Nor has the U.N.'s tough talk about terrorism led to meaningful action. In 1999, Security Council Resolution 1267 created a sanctions committee that was supposed to name governments that assisted al-Qaeda and the Taliban financially, failed to freeze their assets, or allowed them to use the state's territory.[89] The committee has never been able to agree to name any government that violated Resolution 1267.[90]

On September 28, 2001, Security Council Resolution 1373 ordered all states to combat terrorism. The Resolution created a Counter-Terrorism Committee (CTC), which was supposed to receive mandatory reports from states about their antiterrorism measures. Yet the CTC has never named any state sponsor or terrorism, nor has it named any individual or group as terrorist.[91]

In 2005, Kofi Annan urged the U.N. to adopt a comprehensive anti-terrorism treaty. Sometimes called "the mother of all treaties," it was supposed to provide a wide-ranging global program against terrorism.[92] However, all 191 U.N. members have a seat on the treaty working group,[93] which means that the state sponsors of terrorism, and their allies, are solidly represented. The effort to negotiate the treaty collapsed in December 2005, because of the absence of agreement over a definition of terrorism.[94]

Kofi Annan, to his credit, pushed for compromise language:

> Any action constitutes terrorism if it is intended to cause death or serious bodily harm to civilians or noncombatants with the purpose of intimidating a population or compelling a government or an international organization to do or abstain from doing any act. [95]

It was all for naught. Even though the U.N. has many official declarations against terrorism, the absence of a definition means that any terrorist, including terrorist states such as Syria, can simply define terrorism as something done only by their political enemies. Thus, Syria can proudly declare its opposition to all forms of terrorism.[96]

Some of the leaders of the pro-terrorist bloc have also argued that the treaty should prohibit "state terrorism."[97] State terrorism is certainly a real phenomenon, and Syria is one of its prime practitioners. However, U.N.

advocates of the "state terrorism" language in the draft treaty are not after stopping genuine state terrorism, but creating a new cudgel with which to bash the U.S. for liberating Iraq and Afghanistan, and to bash Israel for defending itself against terrorists.[98]

NUCLEAR WEAPONS FOR TERRORISTS

Imagine "a world without America." Such a world is "attainable, and surely can be achieved." This was the vision of Iranian president Mahmoud Ahmadinejad, speaking on October 26, 2005, at the World Without Zionism conference in Tehran, where he called for the extermination of Israel. His chief advisor has announced, "We have established a department that will take care of England," and "England's demise is on our agenda."[99]

Most Americans still can't pronounce Ahmadinejad's name, but almost everyone saw him on television back in 1979, as one of the ringleaders of the hostage-taking at the American embassy in Tehran. Now, he rules a theocratic tyranny that is rapidly developing the ability to engage in nuclear warfare. With Iran's long-standing ties to Hezbollah and other terrorist groups, he will soon have the means to deliver a nuclear device to a target, without the device being traceable to Iran.

The U.N. International Atomic Energy Agency (IAEA), based in Vienna and run by a thirty-five-member board of governors, is supposed to be about the business of stopping him, yet a recent member of the board of governors was Pakistan, which illegally developed its own atomic bombs and recklessly sold nuclear technology on the world black market, including to North Korea. Newly elected to the board in late 2005 are Cuba, Syria, and Belarus.

For years, the IAEA, like the European Union, has been engaged in fruitless negotiations, pleading with Iran to give up its nuclear weapons program. In September 2005, the IAEA finally admitted the obvious, and declared that Iran was violating its obligations under the Nuclear Non-Proliferation Treaty, which has been in force since 1970. Yet it took until January 2006 for the IAEA to even consider referring Iran's violation to the U.N. Security Council, even though IAEA was required by its own statute to make a referral.[100] Kofi Annan, meanwhile, worked furiously to prevent the Security Council from looking into Iran's nuclear weapons development.[101] Not that the Security Council—where Iran's friends Russia and China hold a veto—would be likely to do anything more than utter ineffectual demands.

The IAEA's inaction regarding the Iranian nuclear weapons program is reminiscent of its prior inaction about the Iraqi nuclear weapons. In the late 1970s, Saddam Hussein began developing a nuclear weapons program (under the pretext of building a civilian nuclear power industry in the oil-rich nation). The IAEA did nothing, and ultimately Israel ended the program by bombing the Osirik nuclear reactor in 1981.

Saddam was persistent. By 1991, as the IAEA would later admit, he was within twelve to eighteen months of being able to build a nuclear weapon.[102] Losing the Gulf War proved a big setback to his plans. He was still trying, apparently unsuccessfully, when he was finally deposed in 2003.

In regard to Iranian nuclear terrorism—as with so many terrorism and genocide issues—the U.N. declares that it is the only entity with the legitimate right to authorize forceful action. Then, by refusing to authorize forceful action, it in effect gives the terrorists and genocidaires limitless freedom to carry out their evil plans.

FIGHTING WESTERN ATTEMPTS TO FIGHT TERROR

After the July 2005 terrorist attacks on London, the British government announced plans to use its existing legal powers to deport resident foreigners who encouraged or glorified terrorism. The U.N. promptly objected.

Manfred Nowak, the U.N. Commission on Human Rights' Special Rapporteur on torture, threatened to have Britain brought up before the U.N. General Assembly for human rights violations. Nowak's argument was that some of the deported terrorist inciters might be tortured in the country to which they would be deported, notwithstanding assurance from the recipient country.[103]

The U.N. is also against killing terrorists. Consider Abdel Aziz al-Rantissi and Sheikh Ahmad Yassin.[104] Yassin, the head of the terrorist organization Hamas, was killed in early 2004 by the Israeli Defense Forces. He was succeeded by al-Rantissi, who promptly called for more terrorism: "The doors are wide open for attacks inside the Zionist entity."[105] He had repeatedly called for the murder of Jews "everywhere."[106]

The U.S. government named both Yassin and Rantissi as Specially Designated Global Terrorists. In 2003, the Bank of England froze al-Rantissi's assets because "the Treasury have reasonable grounds for suspecting that" al-Rantissi may "facilitate or participate in the commission of acts of terrorism . . . or may be a person who commits, facilitates or participates in such acts."[107]

Kofi Annan, however, indignantly denounced the death of Yassin: "The Secretary-General strongly condemns Israel's assassination . . . extrajudicial killings are against international law."[108] Annan likewise deplored the "assassination of al-Rantissi." [109]

Despite Annan's malicious claims, the killings of the Hamas leaders were entirely proper under international law. Hamas has declared itself to be in a state of war with Israel, and that it will never cease the war until Israel is exterminated. As Columbia Law School professor Anne Bayefsky points out:

> The international legal framework . . . could not be clearer. Rantissi was a combatant in a war. His killing was not "extrajudicial" because the legal term, by definition, applies only to individuals entitled to judicial process before being targeted. Combatants—including the unlawful combatants of Hamas who seek to make themselves indistinguishable from the civilian population—are not entitled to such prior judicial process. Futhermore, the manual on laws of armed conflict of the International Committee of the Red Cross, states that civilians who take a direct part in hostilities forfeit their immunity from attack.[110]

Nevertheless, the U.N. Human Rights Commission was so unnerved that it convened in a special sitting, and for three hours flailed at Israel for killing the terrorist masterminds, before voting 31 to 2 to condemn it.[111] Shortly thereafter, the Commission adopted another one of its resolutions, with code words urging terrorism against Israel, lauding "the legitimacy of the struggle [against] foreign occupation by all available means, including armed struggle."[112]

Civilized nations fight terrorism by preventing terrorists from entering the country, yet that too, is forbidden by the U.N. The International Court of Justice (ICJ) was established by the U.N. in 1945 to hear disputes between states. For example, if two countries have a dispute about the interpretation of a fishing treaty, they can ask the ICJ to hear the case.

The current president of the ICJ is Shi Jiuyong of China. He represents a communist dictatorship whose current interests at the U.N. include prohibiting the sale of arms (including firearms) to "non-state actors," so as to prevent Taiwan from defending itself against Chinese aggression.

After suffering years of suicide bombings and other terrorism, Israel began building a security fence to protect itself from violent attacks. Although the fence is not complete, it has already reduced terrorist attacks by 90 percent.[113]

On July 9, 2004, the ICJ ruled the security fence illegal.[114] The court acknowledged that Israel faced a problem of "violence," but it refused to describe the violence as terrorism. After the ICJ decision (which, as a matter of international law, is nonbinding and merely advisory), the General Assembly insisted by a vote of 150 to 6 that Israel remove the security fence from the West Bank.[115] The U.N. followed up in March 2005 with a two-day International Meeting on the Question of Palestine, damning Israel for building the fence.[116]

It should be noted that Spain, Turkey, Saudi Arabia, and India have also built defensive structures in disputed territories, and the U.N. has never voted to condemn those actions.

The U.N. is the place where state sponsors of terrorism applaud themselves for their opposition to terrorism. It is the place where the liberation of Afghanistan from Osama bin Laden and the Taliban can be denounced as terrorism. It is the place where the worst human rights violators in the world—tyrannical rulers of countries where there is no such thing as a fair trial—can froth with anger about the killing of terrorist commanders without a trial.

The U.N. produces enormous quantities of paper announcing its opposition to terrorism—yet produces even larger quantities of propaganda in favor of terrorism. It funds terrorists all over the world, including al-Qaeda, Fidel Castro, Hamas, Hezbollah, Islamic Jihad, Iran, North Korea, the Taliban, and Saddam Hussein. The U.N. talks to the western media about celebrating diversity and global understanding, but it collaborates with and covers up for terrorists. It actively prevents settlement of the Arab-Israeli conflict. It funds vicious hate propaganda, and allows its refugee camps and schools to be used as terrorist bases and bomb factories.

In this chapter, I have explained how the U.N. has promoted terrorism against the U.S.—by giving money to bin Laden, by giving World Bank money to governments that sponsor anti-American terrorism, and by taking up the propaganda line that American resistance to terrorism is evil.

The subsidies to anti-American terrorists, and the attempt to delegitimate America's right of self-defense, were not invented out of thin air. Rather, they were founded on decades of practice in doing the same thing—on a much larger scale—to Israel. In effect, U.N. policies aiding terrorism and demonizing resistance to terrorism have been perfected in their use against Israel, and are now in the early stages of being deployed against the U.S.

There is another lesson too. During the 1930s, far too many people in Britain, France, the U.S., and other democracies failed to realize that what Hitler was doing to the German Jews was in fact a direct attack on their own personal security. What tyrants and terrorists do to minority groups often foreshadow what will be done to larger groups. Aggressors first go after the victims who seem to be the easier targets, and then work their way up to other targets. U.N.-sponsored aggression against the Jews and Israel has, in fact, led to U.N.-sponsored aggression against America. As Harvard's Ruth Wisse explains:

> A society's deflection of energy to anti-Semitism is a sign of its political demoralization; the more it whips up frenzy against the Jews, the more it requires going to war to release that frenzy. The rise of anti-Semitism at the U.N. correlates with the rise of the politics of resentment against what the Jews represent—an open and democratic society, the ethic of competition and individual freedom.[117]

No one agrees with every Israeli policy—or with every U.S. policy for that matter. Both nations thrive as contentious democratic societies, where citizens are free to express their disagreements on all sorts of issues.

But Israel is the canary in the coal mine, and there is a direct link between the U.N.'s long-standing assistance to terrorist war on Israel and the U.N.'s more recent assistance of terrorist war on the U.S.

If you think that unresolved tensions between Israel and the Arabs are part of the cause of global terrorism today, then consider which global organization has done the most to cause, rather than solve, those problems.

When the U.N. should take firm action against terrorism—as in the

International Atomic Energy Agency's duty to prevent terrorist Iran from building nuclear weapons to attack the U.S., Israel, and England—it dithers and lets the terrorists move forward.

SELF-DEFENSE IS NOT A PRIVILEGE

The ultimate conflict of our times—a conflict that the U.N.'s pro-terrorism actions force us to confront directly—is between civilization and barbarism. We know the Second Amendment protects our right to self-defense—including self-defense against tyrants and terrorists. This right was not invented by the American Founders, but instead has roots that are as old as civilization itself. Ancient Greece and Rome recognized the right. The right has been expounded by Jewish scholars studying the Torah and Talmud, and by Christian scholars explaining self-defense as part of the natural law that God inscribes on every human heart. It is a right extolled by Confucius and by the great Taoist philosophers of ancient China. And it is a right recognized for many centuries by the great scholars of legitimate (and antiterrorist) Islamic law.

Against this vision of civilization is the barbaric principle of the U.N. and its proxies such as IANSA that self-defense is a privilege that the government can and should take away. If the U.N. can take away anyone's legitimate self-defense rights, it can take away everyone's. And, indeed, it is trying to do precisely that—to prohibit you from owning any firearm for personal and national protection.

As a moral issue, it doesn't matter whether an innocent victim is attacked by a lone criminal, by disorganized gangs of predators (as in New Orleans after Hurricane Katrina), by organized criminals kidnapping girls for sex slavery (as in Cambodia or Albania), by U.N.-funded terrorists, or by a terroristic, genocidal government. The innocent have a right to own firearms to defend themselves anywhere and everywhere.

It is this right that the U.N. and its terrorist allies are working aggressively to destroy, and the National Rifle Association vows to fight them every step of the way.

CHAPTER 11

Don't Trust Direct Democracy

F irst lesson is don't trust direct democracy," said Rubem Fernandes.[1] At a United Nations forum, Lessons from the Brazilian Referendum, that country's self-appointed gun-ban czar shows an arrogant contempt for a free people.

That disdain for democracy by the likes of Fernandes's group Viva Rio is the core reason Brazilian citizens made world history by rejecting a total ban on civilian sales of firearms and ammunition in October 2005. In voting down the firearms prohibition by a 63 percent margin, 100 million voters chose for themselves a right that is universally rejected by the U.N. disarmament cadres. To the simple question "should the sale of firearms and ammunition be banned in Brazil," they answered with a resounding "NO."

In his remarks, Fernandes told assembled U.N. officials, World Council of Churches delegates, and representatives of a host of gun-control NGOs in New York, "The notion of rights came up. . . . The debate on rights was new to Brazil. . . . The notion of rights was new, it grew."

"'I have a right to a gun;' this was an argument that started weak and grew. . . . The debate on rights rose as a very profound matter."[2] Fernandes said that putting the question to the very people he would disarm was a mistake: "First lesson is don't trust direct democracy." This was a sentiment echoed in private conversations with other gun-ban advocates who were in an ugly, I-told-you-so mood.

Days before Brazilians went to the polls on October 23, 2005, the global gun-ban movement was electrified with a certainty that the world's first nationwide "civil disarmament" plebiscite would provide a huge payoff for their years of massive investments of time and money in propaganda campaigns and grassroots organizing.

The international and domestic forces arrayed to bring about the firearms and ammunition ban included a complex web of global gun-confiscation groups, official U.N. entities, private billionaires, foreign governments, leftist international church groups, the Brazilian government, and much of the country's entertainment industry. All of this was stage-managed by a radical social engine called Viva Rio, and by the International Action Network on Small Arms (IANSA), which describes itself as "the organization officially designated by the U.N Department of Disarmament Affairs (DDA) to coordinate civil society involvement to the U.N. small arms process."[3]

IANSA head Rebecca Peters told the *Washington Post*, "If the ban is passed, then I definitely expect other countries to try the same thing." [4] Before the historic vote, IANSA was ecstatic in its prediction: "Brazilians will be able to vote in a radical referendum that is without precedent in the world . . . *for IANSA members in Brazil, the referendum is a huge opportunity and the culmination of years of campaigning.* . . . Opinion polls show that 60 to 80% of Brazilians favour a prohibition on gun sales to civilians . . . a message that the majority of people do not believe that having guns in their communities makes them safer."[5]

In virtually all of the world press, there was a premature sense of celebration over the impending ban.

In an October 13, 2005, opinion piece titled "Follow Brazilian lead and close the arms industry," Terry Crawford-Browne, the head of a South African gun-control group called Economists Allied for Arms Reduction, predicted the ban would pass in a four-to-one landslide. "The yes vote is being supported by a broad civil society coalition," Crawford-Browne wrote. "Churches, schools and universities are rallying around in solidarity that disarmament provides people with the greatest security."[6]

"Significantly," he wrote, "it is in the poor areas—the *favalas*—where this sentiment is strongest. Gangsters have in the past terrorized the residents with guns, and the people have responded that they intend to take control of their own lives." As for middle-class gun owners, he predicted a yes vote "with the realization that guns are often taken from their owners and used against them."

On the day of the voting in Brazil, the *Sunday Herald* in Scotland told its readers, "MORE than 122 million Brazilians will make history today by voting in the world's first national referendum on the sale of guns. . . ."[7]

Brazil made history all right. And the vote was stunning in its breadth and depth. But it was a vote for freedom, not repression. The overwhelming pro-ban victory IANSA's Peters was predicting for the future of her whole civil disarmament movement was in fact, a defeat on a cosmic level.

In a lengthy December 2005 interview in NRA's magazine, *America's 1st Freedom*,[8] Luciano Rossi, who was among the prime movers in the winning "No ban" campaign, provided an analysis of the vote—perhaps the only such breakdown published in the U.S. Rossi is the managing director of the firearms firm that has borne his family name for well over a century.

The ban did not win anywhere, he said, not in any city, state, or with any segment of the population. The poor people—the slum dwellers whose vote had been seen as a given and who were the object of millions in targeted expenditures—voted to defeat the ban.

"Maybe 40% of the 100 million people who went for voting that Sunday, maybe 40% know only how to write their own names. And we won with them. It was amazing."

The vote against the ban won in all twenty-six states of the country. As for urban areas where the poor were expected to do as they were told by government propagandists, Rossi said the victory was "the stuff of history. . . . In Rio, where all the criminals, the gangs, the banditos supported the ban . . . 64% said 'no!'

"Some cities were 99%," Rossi said. "And the state in the north where the 'no' won by the smallest percentage, we won by 55%. I think if the campaign had lasted for one more week, it would be an even bigger victory all over the country—like 85%."

This was a true example of the most basic democratic process at work where the will of the people was expressed. It was the people versus the iron will of a cabal of self-appointed international civil disarmament groups not elected by anyone anywhere.

Indeed, this was history in the making, but it was history that was briefly rationalized, quickly forgotten, and even erased in many quarters. The reaction from U.S. antigun groups was virtual silence. They had not a word to say. But they—and particularly IANSA—were directly a party to the defeat.[9] Among the North American groups listed as IANSA members are the Brady Campaign, the Million Mom March, the Coalition to Stop Gun Violence, Join Together, and the HELP Network.

The same silence marked the response of the government of Brazil. It had invested massive effort and treasure in pressing for the ban. Politicians wanted the referendum to disappear, much like Soviet Union leaders who were airbrushed out of historic photographs. For the politicians in Brazil who supported the ban, there is good reason for silence: fear.

"There is no doubt that those people lost a lot of credibility, people who joined the ban, and number one was the president [Luiz Inácio] Lula," Rossi said.

"We have to thank him that he was the propaganda boy of the other side. For sure, he lost a lot of credibility with this try of taking rights away. And below him, just about every senator, congressman who got engaged on the pro-ban has been burned. I don't know how many will lose elections next year, but probably a lot of them."

While the global firearms-confiscation crowd would rather forget its crushing defeat, gun owners everywhere must study what happened in Brazil. That victory, that resonance with ordinary citizens of the world who understood that they possess a basic human right to own firearms, must be studied, amplified, and replicated.

Had the vote gone the other way, the media would have endlessly analyzed the issue, and proponents of the ban would be trumpeting it with every breath. It would be major news well into the future. The defeat, however, left the world press stunned and angry. The international media was desperate for excuses.

"Many in Brazil and abroad had hoped that a yes-vote on the referendum would make the world's fifth-largest nation an example to the many other countries where gun use is out of control, especially the U.S.," whined the indie-media Web site www.corpwatch.com.[10]

The *Khaleej Times* in Dubai, United Arab Emirates, was typical, saying, "Yet it is hard to justify the overwhelming opposition to gun sales ban. *It only goes to show that majority is not necessarily always right.*"[11]

That editorial rant continued, "It is believed that it is not so much that Brazilian voters' belief in the so-called right to own guns but their opposition to the extremely unpopular government of President Luiz Inácio Lula da Silva and its policies could have undermined the proposed ban . . . the proposed ban had wide support from human rights groups and the clergy before campaigning on the referendum began."

That was the same excuse offered in many U.S. publications. The big lie repeated and repeated was that the huge majority against the ban was nothing more than a vote against the Lula government.

The *Japan Times* tried a different spin:

> Last Sunday in Brazil, a country with the second-highest rate of gun deaths on the planet, almost two-thirds of Brazilians voted against a total ban on the sale of firearms. Explain that.
>
> Part of the answer was a ruthless media campaign by the local gun lobby that exploited the free television time both sides are granted in Brazilian referendums. . . . They translated reams of propaganda from the National Rifle Association in the U.S. and pumped it out over the air unaltered, with the result that millions of Brazilians now believe they have a constitutional right to bear arms. (They don't.)[12]

This theme was echoed in many media outlets as well—the failure of the gun-ban referendum in Brazil was, they opined, the National Rifle Association's fault. While NRA has been aggressive in fighting the global metastasizing of gun control, and has a presence at the U.N., the assertion that the victory in Brazil hinged on NRA was overblown and diversionary to say the least.

In terms of protecting freedom in nations under attack from the likes of George Soros, Rebecca Peters, and their army of radical political carpet-baggers, something far more significant and far more remarkable happened in Brazil. The threat of the ban was the catalyst for an indigenous grassroots movement to protect what liberty the people had left. The truth is, the campaign against the ban was totally homegrown. It was purely the hard work of Brazilians telling other Brazilians the truth about what the ban would mean for their future.

Brazil was a remarkable turning point, and Brazilians who told the world what they stood for and what the gun-ban crowd stood for are due all of the credit. Above all, ordinary Brazilians saw the same light that was lit in 1776. Rights. Liberty. Freedom. Self-protection. Protection of family.

What the organizers of the brilliant "No" campaign did take from NRA is what we hope all other such movements take—something all American gun owners would be more than willing to give: our love of freedom. And that love of freedom is what the gun-ban crowd fears the most worldwide.

In "Gunning For the World," a think-piece that contained a handful of thoughtful views of what happened in Brazil, author David Morton concluded:

"The number of civilians in Brazil who legally own a gun is estimated to be only about 2 million. In other words, some 59 million Brazilians voted to preserve a prerogative the vast majority of them will never enjoy."[13]

That thought was a critical key to what really happened in Brazil. In all of the brief media lip-biting and blame-laying, almost no one went to the source of the winning campaign. No one except the editors at *America's 1st Freedom* asked Luciano Rossi how the victory came about. He explained in the December 2005 issue:

At the beginning, when the subject of the referendum started to get hot, 40 days before the voting day, everybody was very much believing that with the strong lobby of network television, together with the government, would be strong enough to bring the victory to their side. Their target vote was mainly among the poor population which in Brazil, is by far the largest block.

Every side of the 'yes' and the 'no' had 10 minutes every day on television to explain its ideas—time that is given each side by the government. (Allotted for 20 days leading up to two days before the actual voting.)

So for our side, we developed a campaign that was designed to clarify what was really being decided. We made it very clear to the most simple people in Brazil, that what was in consideration was that voting "yes" to the ban means everybody will lose forever the right to buy a legal firearm.

We said that we know that most of you don't have a firearm, don't now want to have a firearm, but by voting no, you are at least having the possibility of someday, if you want to buy a firearm, you can.

In 20 days, it changed the whole debate. The people started really understanding what game was being played against them. It was fantastic, it was historical stuff that happened in Brazil.

The mainstream media in Brazil was worked hard by Viva Rio and its axis. And also the U.N. directly in the form of UNESCO.

A year before the official campaigns for and against the referendum were allowed to begin, UNESCO, through the U.N. International Programme for the Development of Communication, provided significant funding to influence the outcome of the vote through a grant that "aims at increasing the quality and quantity of coverage . . . in the lead-up to the 2005 gun-ban referendum. . . ." Among the specifics was a zealous core of organized and trained "women from affected communities to build capacity for media advocacy and develop skills for working with journalists from all media. . . ."[14]

The recipient of this largess was Viva Rio, which the UNESCO funding documents said, "coordinates national and regional campaigns, including a women's disarmament campaign called 'Choose Gun Free! It's Your Weapon or Me,' and other projects and research programmes on disarmament in Brazil. . . . News and information websites developed and hosted by Viva Rio will facilitate networking and communications. . . ."

As for the Viva Rio's arguments, its English Web site reveals a single-minded goal: "to reform permissive and inefficient legislation on arms control, seeking to end civilian use of firearms."[15] Among its disarmament efforts were "Public awareness campaigns on the need for civil disarmament [in order that] 'honest citizens' and their families do not become victims of their own guns in accidents or do not fall victim to armed assailants if they try to defend themselves with a gun."

For the beleaguered Brazilian population—the victims of real criminal violence—the notion of seeking reconciliation with criminal predators was absurd. What Rossi and his allies offered made far better sense: the right to choose to exercise the basic human right to own a gun for self-defense. "Our argument was very well-focused. What will be the next right the government will take from you? It was like giving an electrical discharge on the people, to really wake up."[16]

In addition to recognizing the issue of gun ownership as a basic and universal human right, Rossi said that honest, law-abiding people began to realize that they were being punished for the acts of violent criminals.

"We started putting out our arguments, and saying, 'Look, the government is saying that the crime rate in Brazil is your fault—the fault of the law-abiding population!"

Remarkably, the truth of just who was committing violence was often spelled out in the media, but with a total disconnect between criminals and the honest citizens who would pay the price of disarmament.

In its hand-wringing about the defeat, corpwatch.com inadvertently made that point, saying, "Most of the gun-related violence has its roots in the cocaine trafficking."[17] Quoting a Dutch social worker in Rio, the article said, "And today gangsters have even more sophisticated weapons, such as laser-guided weapons they use to shoot police helicopters out of the sky. . . . When quantities of these inexpensive and readily available weapons enter Brazil and get into the wrong hands at the wrong time, they transform criminal activities and gang rivalries into major wars; they turn minor, often domestic, incidents into massacres; change tranquil societies into battlegrounds; and undercut efforts for peace and reconciliation."

Another tenuous argument that Brazilian voters may have found totally specious was that legal guns are a danger because they may be stolen and used by criminals. A Viva Rio propaganda piece titled "Brazil: Most crime guns start out legally" is typical:

In Brazil, most of the crime guns seized by police were once legally owned, according to a report from the government of Rio de Janeiro state (Brazil), released on 3 October 2005.

The findings disprove claims by the Brazilian gun lobby that the illegal gun trade is responsible for most gun crime in Rio de Janeiro, which suffers higher rates of gun violence than many war-torn regions.[18]

From the get-go in Brazil that was a theme of the civil disarmament crowd: if only we take guns from honest people, criminals will no longer be criminals. Like all gun control, at a local level, national level, or on a global scale, there is a universal failure of the gun-ban crowd to recognize any difference between good and evil—between honest citizen and criminal predator. But ordinary people—including the vast majority of Brazilians—understand the difference between good and evil, and they are the victims of evil every day.

Blaming law-abiding gun owners for the acts of real criminals was, Rossi explained, "like a punch on the face of the population, because the government was insisting that the high rate of murders in Brazil was being caused by people who had legal firearms. The pro-ban propaganda hid the truth about the murder rate which is one of the highest in the world—most of the killing is between gangs and drug dealers."

In addition to the radio and television campaign waged by the antiban forces, Rossi said a key news story helped change the political dynamic. It was something never revealed in the U.S. media.

"The outlaws from the slums in Rio de Janeiro, the drug dealers that control the slums 100%, it came up in the news that they were financing the pro-ban campaign. The banditos were financing it in the slums! Everybody got very angry, and said look, 'If the banditos are supporting the ban, something is wrong, you know?'"

GUNS BANS AND SOAP OPERAS

Where the antiban side was limited to government allotted time, gun-ban forces had massive additional help from Brazil's Global television network and its soap operas, which net huge audiences, especially among Brazil's poor. Rossi explained:

> The government was 100% sure that they could present distortion statistics, they could use artists of the soap operas. Because in Brazil, the population loves soap operas. There are three every day, different time between 6 o'clock at night and 9 o'clock at night, three different soap operas that have 65% of the televisions tuned on the Global Network television. This year, Global Television created fictional situations on their soap operas to start establishing on the brains of the people that firearms in the hands of legal guys were dangerous.

In fact, the use of soap opera stars and other entertainment and sports figures had been critical to enacting the 2003 law that brought the referendum into being. A story in the *Guardian* (London)—covering a protest march in Rio demanding passage of the "The Statute of Disarmament"—admired the effectiveness of daily dramatized propaganda:

The protest had been heavily promoted in the soap opera 'Women in Love.' For weeks, the show's characters have talked about the march and their presence guaranteed a large turnout despite the weather.

The popular soap opera, which threads together the stories of several women, has hit hard on the issue of gun violence in recent weeks. A scene where a character was killed by a stray bullet was front-page news last month, eclipsing many real killings.

But according to Rossi, that constant media propaganda and the enlistment of big television and movie stars in the ban campaign backfired: "The ban propaganda started very heavily with celebrities like 80% of the programs of television and then, like on day 10, when 50% of the days were done, they started collecting their polls; they were losing like crazy. And they just banned the celebrities. They just put those people away," he said.

Of all of the facts that came out in NRA's interviews with Rossi, a stunner was the cost: the equivalent of 200 million U.S. dollars for the first-ever national referendum. Brazil is a relatively poor nation. But the real shock was something never mentioned anywhere in the U.S. media—the actual number of firearms that would have been subject to a ban on sales. Rossi said:

> The whole country will spend about $80 million this year to buy all the apparel and the equipment for the police. And they spend $200 million on the referendum to ban the sale of under 2000 units a year! That's the number of guns allowed as legal sales. Two thousand. For 180 million people. It's unbelievable. . . . That's the total legal civilian sales in Brazil. Everything. Shotguns. Rifles. Revolvers. It's almost a zero market already because, the new law that came into effect two years ago is so restrictive.

THE STATUTE OF DISARMAMENT

So what was this new law that so discouraged legal commerce in firearms for Brazilian citizens? The Statute of Disarmament was adopted at the end of 2003 after a long and shrill campaign by a host of global pressure groups.[19] These players included direct U.N. entities like UNESCO, a collection of U.N. gun-ban NGOs like IANSA, and, directly and indirectly, the governments of Canada and the United Kingdom, among others. (As its host nation, the U.K. provides abundant financial support for IANSA.)

Bear in mind that for years, law-abiding Brazilian gun owners have lived under very strict laws. They were limited as to the caliber of handguns—nothing larger than .38 caliber. They were limited to no more than fifty rounds of ammo a year. And they were limited in the number of firearms and types they could own.

There is never an end to the demands of the world gun-ban crowd. Rebecca Peters is fond of saying that the law merely "regulates" firearms, but in truth, for many poorer Brazilians, the new law disarmed them or caused them to secretly fade into the ranks of good people that the likes of Peters can now call "gun criminals."

The Statute of Disarmament created a draconian system of universal firearms registration and gun owner licensing, all compounded with exorbitant fees beyond the reach of a majority of Brazilians.

To get a license to continue owning a firearm under the law, an ordinary citizen has to prove psychological fitness; undergo a background check in which even having ever been sued in civil court is a disqualifier; must prove legal employment; and must provide "proof of technical capacity" to handle firearms. And he or she must present an approved reason to own a gun. All of this involves a complex bureaucracy of government and court officials at the federal, state, and military levels. Getting a license takes months. Additionally, it is unlawful for a citizen to openly carry a firearm for any reason.

Under the Statute of Disarmament, registration fees and reregistration fees alone made compliance impossible for millions of law-abiding Brazilian gun owners. Those fees amount to one-third of average family incomes in Brazil's rural states. And there was no grandfather clause to allow continued legal possession of firearms owned prior to the law's enactment.

The law further requires that guns seized by police be destroyed within forty-eight hours. Millions of legally owned guns, mostly common sporting arms, became "illicit small arms"—the U.N. term for contraband.

Amidst those global entities were the indigenous forces in Brazil: the federal government, and, at the center of it all, Viva Rio. Campaigning on fear of violent crime—which indeed was rampant in urban Brazil—this confederation brought harsh strictures on law-abiding Brazilians that, for many, made continued ownership of firearms impossible.

A self-serving study created by Viva Rio claimed there are 15.5 million firearms in the hands of Brazilian citizens, and that 8.7 million of them are not registered and are therefore illegal.[20] For Brazilians fearful that continued gun ownership would make them criminals, the government created an amnesty period during which they could give up their guns and receive between $50 and $150 compensation, regardless of actual value. After that, firearms possession without registration and licensing became a no-bail criminal offense.

Unlike other firearm confiscation schemes in Canada, Australia, or England, this one was not aimed at any particular type of demonized firearm. No "assault weapons" or "Saturday Night Specials." This was directed at all guns—any guns in private hands.

The amnesty period in Brazil was accompanied by a political orgy of gun burnings and crushings, with confiscation advocates joyously participating. According to the Canadian group Project Ploughshares:

> [T]he State Government of Rio, Brazil, in partnership with the NGO Viva Rio, organised the public destruction of 4,158 firearms . . . crushed with a steam roller. Three hundred rifles and shotguns were also destroyed in a pyre. This 'Flame of Peace' was the first arms destruction by this method to take place in South America, and is a method favoured by the United Nations due to its strong anti-violence symbolism.[21]

For peaceable Brazilian gun owners, seeing their seized personal firearms go up in smoke had become a reality. For gun-ban groups pressing their war against individual freedom worldwide, Brazil had become paradise.

For its part, IANSA took a share of the credit, saying it "coordinated the third Week of Action Against Small Arms . . . with International Gun Destruction Day," and featured an event in Brazil where "6,500 illegal firearms confiscated by police were destroyed by Viva Rio, the Brazilian Army, and the Rio state government."[22]

This frontal attack on freedom was achievable only with generous financial assistance from the global disarmament community and propaganda from those who control the airwaves in Brazil. The massive gun collection and destruction program would receive a UNESCO prize in the Human Rights and Peace Culture category.[23]

In terms of the rats' nest of connections between activist gun-ban funders and participants in the Brazil gun-control free-for-all leading up to and including the referendum, look no farther than IANSA, Viva Rio, and the World Council of Churches (WCC), which was totally immersed in the internal affairs of Brazil.

The "Summary Report on the WCC's Microdisarmament Efforts 2000-2001," provides just a glimpse at the complexity of the political and funding network.[24] I won't attempt to map these entangled relationships; let the WCC paint the picture:

> The WCC is a founding member of the International Action Network on Small Arms (IANSA), which it described as working to co-ordinate activities and campaigning by bringing together human rights organisations, foreign policy think tanks, gun control groups, development and humanitarian relief agencies, victim support groups, and local community and public health groups. IANSA has a range of objectives to reduce the demand for small arms by civilians.

The WCC is an active IANSA partner and is making its particular contribution through facilitating the formation of the Ecumenical Network on Small Arms (ENSA). It is also a member of the Geneva Action Network on Small Arms (GANSA), a working group of the NGO Committee for Disarmament, of which WCC is a board member.

Under a section titled "Capacity-building," the report says, "In the development of the Ecumenical Network on Small Arms, seed funding was provided," by what it calls "the Microdisarmament Fund," to Viva Rio, Brazil, for "[t]he nationwide campaign, 'Enough, I Want Peace' (*Basta! Eu Quera Paz*) . . . particularly networking in community centres, as well as *training of partners in a large scale gun collection and destruction initiative.*" (Emphasis added.)

VIVA RIO

So there is a circle. This is global political and funding inbreeding on a colossal scale. Viva Rio, which rose from humble socialist activist beginnings in the early 1990s, has become a combination crypto-political party and quasi-government body, bloated by international foundation largess and funding from foreign governments.

By its own description the NGO says, "Viva Rio is funded by the public sector (Federal, State and Municipal governments), the private sector (national private companies and multinational corporate organisations), foreign government development agencies (e.g., DFID of the U.K. government and DFAIT of the Canadian government), donor foundations (e.g., Ford Foundation), NGOs (e.g., Save the Children Sweden) and international agencies (e.g., UNESCO and UNICEF)."[25]

Viva Rio is also largely self-sufficient, funded by its own banking and venture-capital operations, which amount to profit centers based on an amalgam of socialism and capitalism. The only comparison to this party-state-business marriage is Communist China.

An article published by another NGO called South North Network Cultures and Development touted Viva Rio as "fully autonomous . . . It gets state and municipality subsidies and is increasingly self-sufficient thanks to its own profit-generating activities, e.g., the insurance brokers company, the microcredit bank, etc. Business is sponsoring its activities. . . . 'Viva Rio' is a brilliant example of a lively social and cultural movement engendered by civil society. . . . In this sense, it is a deeply democratic movement. Yet it is not reduced to US-inspired democracy, based on individualism. . . ."[26]

So what are Viva Rio's origins, and how did it become so powerful in the global civil disarmament movement? A 2004 analysis of how Viva Rio came into being may also go a long way to explaining why Brazilians overwhelmingly voted "NO" on the gun-ban referendum.

Adele Kirsten, the former director of Gun Free South Africa (another IASNA partner), has attempted to explain the inception and growth of various national gun-ban movements including Viva Rio. Kirsten is a close associate of Rebecca Peters and a self-proclaimed "non-violent, social justice activist." She describes the origins of civil disarmament movements in

Brazil and Australia as being similar, having been born out of what she called "defining moments"—mass killings.

"[G]un massacres in Australia and Brazil . . . acted as internal stimuli for social mobilisation in the fight against gun violence," she says.[27] But her attempt to connect the dots between the Port Arthur massacre in Australia and Brazil is truly bizarre. On one hand, the Australian government's 1997 confiscation and destruction of 700,000 long guns that had been the lawful property of law-abiding Aussies came a year after a lone gunman, a sociopath, murdered thirty-five vacationers at Port Arthur, Tasmania.

On the other hand, the creation of Viva Rio and its ultimate rise as the center of the civil disarmament movement in Brazil, according to Kirsten, involved a 1993 massacre in which "eight street children were gunned down by police on the steps of the Candeleria church in central Rio de Janeiro."

Innocent vacationers senselessly murdered by a lone sociopath, children murdered on church steps by agents of the state—only a gun prohibitionist would see a parallel. And only a gun prohibitionist would think that you can prevent such atrocities by stripping away the means of self-defense from potential victims.

As seen by the repressive confiscation of firearms from law-abiding citizens—be they in Australia, Brazil, or England—the only way to enforce the "end to civilian use of firearms" is through the threat of government force or with the actual brutal application of police power.

Kirsten explains that in its newfound role of being an agent for civil disarmament in Brazil, Viva Rio discovered its initial forays into gun control "were critical in building the relationship with the state." (Emphasis added.)

This is the same state that Kirsten said had such recent history of brutality and fear. And that relationship between Viva Rio and the state—formerly the instrument of repression and "gun massacres"—provides massive funding for Viva Rio for a diversity of activities. And it provides a connection with corporate funding, and funding from foreign governments and U.N. entities. Kirsten says that with the advent of IANSA, Vivo Rio took on a global aspect with respect to disarming the civilian populations of the world.

As it gathered power—as a campaigner for government disarmament of law-abiding Brazilians—Viva Rio, now with full assistance and support from IANSA and its other partners, embarked on a massive organizing, networking, and propaganda campaign to impose draconian gun controls on Brazilians.

Again, in her telling of history, Kirsten says:

In 1999, Viva Rio organized the '*Rio, Abaixe essa Arma*' (Rio, Put that Gun Down) campaign to mobilise support for a change in firearms legislation. Over a million signatures were collected in support of a law banning the commerce of small arms in Brazil. This focus on firearms and the strengthening of legislation and arms control management systems has remained central in subsequent campaigns.

Not coincidentally, this was a time when a conference of global gun-ban groups met in Rio. The U.N. Non-Governmental Liaison Service (NGLS) November 1999 newsletter noted, "Among other activities, Viva Rio has mobilized a network of 1,815 public schools, or nearly one and a half million school children and teachers, in its campaign to control small arms in the country."[28] As for direct U.N. support, the newsletter announced that:

[t]he campaign has received the support of the United Nations Educational, Scientific and Cultural Organization (UNESCO), which is sponsoring the initiative within the framework of actions taken to mark the year 2000 as International Year for Culture and Peace.

In addition to calling for government legislation to ban small arms, Viva Rio is also encouraging citizens in Rio de Janeiro to hand in their weapons. A network of church organizations has been set up in the city where citizens can turn in their guns, which are immediately destroyed by trained personnel.

Again returning to Kirsten's history of the growth of Viva Rio, she fast forwards to September 2003, "when 50,000 people, including Brazil's Minister of Justice, the Secretary of Public Security, the Governor of Rio, and other representatives of government joined community associations, civil society organisations, actors and singers, religious leaders and students on the famous Copacabana beach to march for a gun free Brazil. This public display of support was timed to coincide with a decision in Congress regarding sweeping reforms to the country's gun legislation."

Kirsten's analysis ignores a whole other dynamic to the complex of "actors" revolving around Viva Rio and confiscatory gun control. There is a moral disconnect—a kind of resonant dissonance—in all of this, which is also reflected by Amnesty International's involvement in the Brazil gun ban. Amnesty International's online newsletter, *The Wire*, declared: "On Mother's Day, 13 May 2001, the Brazilian non-governmental organization (NGO) Viva Rio launched a campaign under the slogan '*Arma Nao! Ela Ou Eu*' ('Choose gun-free! It's your weapon or me'). Their aim was to bring together women from all sections of Brazilian society to force the men of Brazil to give up their guns."[29]

But the rest of the story had little to do with an argument that the women of Brazil didn't buy into after all. What it did have to do with was the sociopathic split personality that marks what I call "humanitarian tyranny."

Amnesty said, "Urban violence in Brazil is endemic, and there is no doubt that Brazilian society lives in fear. Those living in poor urban communities are trapped in a no-man's land between the violence of criminal gangs, who commit serious crimes including torture and killings, and that of the state response to them. The police forces . . . resort to brutal, ad hoc solutions and human rights violations in the absence of a coherent approach to public security issues."

Juxtapose that thought with what Amnesty says next: "Viva Rio is working with the poorest communities of Rio de Janeiro to find practical local solutions to the problems of gun crime. Initiatives include working with the local police to set up a system for storing and recording guns that are seized, with the aim of tracing the source of the guns and ensuring that they are not reintroduced into the community."

This is absolutely schizophrenic. On one hand the state—the police—are brutal human rights violators. On the other hand, all that is forgiven when it comes to disarming ordinary civilians. The organs of the state—what Kirsten calls the "agents of political repression [that] were known for their use of torture and human rights abuses"—morph into partners when it comes to "microdisarmament" or civil disarmament, creating a "civil society" by taking firearms from law-abiding people.

Neither Amnesty, nor anyone in the phony international human rights community ever made the connection. When it comes to gun control, they always ally with the "oppressors." These people are evil. They celebrate the loss of the most important human right of all—armed self-protection by decent men and women.

Although obtusely unintended by Kirsten or by Amnesty, the emphasis on what they describe as a long history of repression by police—especially recent history still fresh in the minds of many Brazilians—could not have been lost on voters, especially the poor, who most likely are victims of brutal repression.

The failed referendum was supposed to have been the crown jewel for world "microdisarmament." It was no coincidence that Rio was the host for a meeting where the gun-ban crowd made real their intentions with respect to world citizens anywhere who had the temerity to freely possess and use firearms.

As part of the lead up to the concerted U.N. effort in 2006 to press an international treaty to disarm civilians worldwide, a meeting of gun-ban NGOs was held in Rio de Janeiro in March 2005, just seven months before the Brazilian plebiscite. With the theme being how to end or suppress private possession of firearms, any group or individual in support of civilian ownership of arms was specifically excluded. This is U.N. democracy at work.

A key paper presented at that March 2005 meeting was a manifesto against gun ownership in the United States.[30]

Titled "The regulation of civilian ownership and use of small arms," the document declared that the "U.S. public holds one-third of the global gun arsenal: an estimated 234 million guns" and claimed that "the permissive and massive legal market for small arms in the U.S. is a major source of illicit firearms throughout the western hemisphere."

Chief among its recommendations was that global "awareness raising campaigns could help all societies move from a culture of 'rights' for weapons owners to one of 'responsibility' for ensuring that society is not harmed with their weapons."

"A culture of rights." That is precisely what the Brazilian people realized that they had in their grasp. After decades of oppressive government, they saw the light of real freedom.

But there is another point made in this manifesto against basic human rights, as part of its conclusion: "Along with weapons collection, however, it is critically important that appropriate regulatory regimes be implemented *to establish norms of non-possession. . . .*"

"Norms of non-possession." In U.N.-speak, that means making possession "abnormal." It means making peaceable private ownership and use of firearms an aberration. It means propagandizing a generation or two of children to associate nothing good with firearms. It is a kind of brainwashing for citizens who seek only to exercise a basic human right.

It is everything that was rejected by Brazilians who stood up to Viva Rio and its U.N. fellow travelers and loudly proclaimed, "We trust direct democracy."

CHAPTER 12

U.N. and the Internet

Just as there is a powerful movement to "control" private ownership of firearms out of existence using the tendrils of the United Nations, there is an equally dangerous effort to "control" the most modern means that free people have ever possessed to express the political ideals needed to preserve or gain their liberty—the Internet.

And the Internet, the most effective tool of communication since the invention of the printing press, is solely an American creation, born as an integral part of our national defense. We share it with the world as the most open avenue for free expression and the exchange of ideas ever created. It reflects the principles contained in America's unique First Amendment. It also serves to protect what is becoming recognized as a most basic human right for all peaceable peoples—the individual right to own and use firearms.

But the Internet, as Americans know it and use it, is in extreme danger, especially if a future U.S. government believes its control should be "internationalized" and run by the powers that are moving to control the U.N. When you think of global Internet control, think global gun control. They are the same thing—the taking of individual freedom by international despots.

A few headlines tell a powerful story about what could someday happen to American's First Amendment rights—and our Second Amendment rights—if we ever elect a president and a Congress that would relinquish control of the net.

"U.N. to Control Use of Internet?"[1] . . . "E.U. Wants Shared Control of Internet"[2] . . . "China Again Tightens Control of Online News and

Information"³ . . . "China charges U.S. monopolizes the Internet, seeks global control"⁴ . . . .

The article that goes with that last headline, published by *The World Herald Tribune*, reported that China's U.N. ambassador demands international Internet control:

> Sha Zukang told a U.N. conference that controls should be multilateral, transparent and democratic, with the full involvement of governments, the private sector, civil society and international organizations.
>
> "It should ensure an equitable distribution of resources, facilitate access for all and ensure a stable and secure functioning," he said at the conference on Internet governance.
>
> Sha said China opposes the "monopolization" of the Internet by one state, a reference to the United States, which ultimately controls the digital medium.

China? Democratic? Transparent? Let's try to inject a little reality here. For a feel of what life would be like for Americans were the Internet in the hands of a U.N. body controlled by the likes of China, look no further than the laws and regulations that nation uses to repress its own people's speech on the Internet.

A remarkable white paper, *Freedom of Expression and the Internet in China: A Human Rights Watch Backgrounder*, says that "as of January 2001, sending 'secret' or 'reactionary' materials over the Internet became a capital crime."⁵

Human Rights Watch (HRW) says that the People's Republic of China (PRC), through its Ministry of Public Security, issued a series of decrees including "Regulations for the Safety Protection of Computer Information Systems," requiring that "all Internet users register with a police bureau in their neighborhood within thirty days of signing up with an ISP. Police stations in provinces and cities followed up on this almost immediately. They also set up computer investigation units."⁶

As Tom Malinowski, HRW's Washington Advocacy Director, points out:

> [T]he stakes here are much greater than the future of freedom in China. China is already exporting technology for monitoring the

Internet to other repressive governments—Zimbabwe, for example. And such governments in every part of the world are now watching to see if China can bend Internet providers to its will. If China succeeds, other countries will insist on the same degree of compliance, and the companies will have no standing to refuse them. We will have two Internets, one for open societies, and one for closed societies. The whole vision of a world wide web, which breaks down barriers and empowers people to shape their destiny, will be gone. Instead, in the 21st Century, we will have a virtual Iron Curtain dividing the democratic and undemocratic worlds.[7]

Of all the amazing technological developments I have seen in my lifetime, I would have to say that the creation and growth of the Internet has had the most profound effect on the dissemination of knowledge and the sharing of ideas. With a relatively small investment of money and training, someone in a cabin a hundred miles from the nearest town can search the world's most prestigious libraries or communicate instantly with individuals on the other side of the world. As the U.S. Supreme Court has noted, "Through the use of chat rooms, any person with a phone line can become a town crier with a voice that resonates farther than it could from any soapbox."[8]

In the same instant, we can express our views and convince others to share our ideas and ideals. And just as the ability to print and disseminate the written word changed the political face of the medieval world, so has the Internet opened a whole new means of political discussion in our time. As Americans accustomed to our freedom of speech, we see this development as positive—an opportunity to consider any political notion or to promote any idea.

But to a tyrant or a demagogue, nothing could be more threatening than the free exchange of ideas. Nothing could be more dangerous than the notion that governments exist at the sufferance of their citizens. That an individual can better choose how to live and take care of family and community than a bureaucratic behemoth such as the U.N., for example, simply does not compute. The deep-seated urge to control how people live or what they think is basic—from the most petty dictator to the most bloated bureaucracy.

We have seen how the desire to manipulate information and ideas works, even in the United States. Can we count on the national media for a factual accounting of issues relating to our Second Amendment rights? Virtually never. When did you read or hear anything fair or factual about firearms rights or about the Second Amendment or NRA in the national media? The Internet has changed that.

Anyone who wants to examine all aspects of an issue can do so freely, without what former NBC news anchor Tom Brokaw called a "gate-keeper"—a network filter to politically cleanse raw information. But that information is available on the Internet. How threatening this freedom must be to those accustomed to presenting their own opinion as fact, and manipulating fact to support their own opinion. To be challenged by a well-informed audience—dangerous!

Most of the people in the world cannot begin to imagine the freedom that we have here. And we have a hard time imagining what it would be like *not* to have that freedom. Envision this. You are sitting at your computer, ready to take action against a gun ban pending before Congress, a ban the media says will likely become law. First, you do what you always do, seek the most up-to-date and accurate facts and information. Your local newspaper says the gun ban will be a great benefit to society. The national media is touting it. You want access to the truth so you can convince your friends and neighbors to contact their senators and congressmen.

You type in the URL for the National Rifle Association—www.nra.org—and you get an error message: "Host not found." Then you type the Web address of a civil liberties think tank—a known, proven source for accurate information and analysis—and you find yourself looking at a screen saying, "content blocked."

You can access the Violence Policy Center and the Brady Campaign. No problem. But every pro-gun site is blocked or filtered. Nothing is coming into your in-box from any of the pro-Second Amendment online news-letters you always get. Nothing from your state association. Their sites are blocked as well.

So you send an e-mail to your congressman and U.S. senators telling them about the Internet blackout and urging them to vote against the gun-ban legislation, and, you copy the e-mail to friends and family and cowork-ers who care about First Amendment rights as a shield for the Second

Amendment. Your e-mails are blocked. Your urgent political speech falls into a cyber trashcan, while the voices of those hyping the bans on speech and gun ownership sail through. Your in-box fills with returned mail, with cover messages listing the "Postmaster" at the address of your Internet Service Provider (ISP) saying, "Action: failed" or "Status: Permanent failure—no additional status information available."

As a hedge, you consider sending your congressional letters through the U.S. Postal Service—but the bill is up for floor action in three days, and you know your message of opposition won't arrive in time because federal mail screening to counter active terrorism threats causes weeks or months of delays in delivery to Congress.

You try again to reach the site of your activist state association, and you get a new error message: "ACCESS FORBIDDEN BY THE UNITED NATIONS INTERNET GOVERNANCE AUTHORITY. Your attempted access has been recorded."

You go to another pro-gun site, and it is there, but wait a minute—the headline on the main page says they *support* the gun ban. The site has been hacked, the original content dumped and fraudulent material added.

CHINA CENSORS THE INTERNET

All of these things—all of this censorship, including replacing site content—are already worldwide realities for millions of people today. A chilling account of Internet repression—including some of the error messages I cite—was recently published in *The* (London) *Independent*. Author Daniel Howden writes:

> China remains the benchmark in censorship. Beijing has cajoled major U.S. players such as Google, Microsoft and Yahoo into adapting their sites and services to suit the censors. A Chinese web surfer typing the word [sic] "democracy" or "freedom" or "human rights" into their server will probably receive an error message announcing: "This item contains forbidden speech."[9]

Howden quotes Brad Adams, Asia director of Human Rights Watch saying, "when companies like Yahoo!, Microsoft, and Google decide to put profits from their Chinese operations over the free exchange of information, they are helping to kill that dream."

China's rapidly growing technological skill, in league with greedy big business, gives the government the means to track and control Internet use. China has been particularly outspoken in its goal of controlling the flow of "dangerous" ideas. Its U.N. Ambassador Sha Zukang in March 2005 told a U.N. Conference:

> It is of crucial importance to conduct research on establishing a mul-
> tilateral governance mechanism that is more rational and just and
> more conducive to the Internet development in a direction of stable,
> secure and responsible functioning and more conducive to the con-
> tinuous technological innovation.[10]

At this same moment, China closed 47,000 Internet cafes. "The cafes closed in the crackdown had been 'admitting minors and engaged in dissemina-tion of harmful cultural information,' the Communist Party newspaper *People's Daily* said on its Web site."[11]

Equally disturbing was a report that aired on Radio Free Europe:

> [R]epresentatives of a group of social investment funds meeting in
> San Francisco drew attention to another issue that Beijing would pre-
> fer not to see in the media, namely the role of Western Internet com-
> panies in allegedly helping the Chinese Communist Party suppress
> free speech and political activism at home.
>
> The investor [sic] group and Reporters Without Borders charged
> that firms including Yahoo, Cisco, Microsoft, and Google face risks in
> "collaborating to suppress freedom of opinion and expression." The
> critics called attention to a case in which Yahoo reportedly provided
> information about one Chinese journalist's e-mails that enabled the
> authorities to send him to jail.[12]

The following was filed earlier in 2005 by the same Radio Free Europe reporter:

> On 16 June, state media reported that the Beijing Security Service
> Corporation, which is run by the police, is setting up a new Beijing

Internet Security Service and is looking for 4,000 recruits to staff it. About 800 of them will go to Internet cafes throughout the city and most of the rest to various other Internet-related businesses. Among their duties will be to "delete all kinds of harmful information" as a part of a drive that is reportedly being extended to other cities as well.[13]

And in a January 17, 2006, editorial, *The New York Times* said:

Microsoft has silenced a well-known blogger in China for committing journalism. At the Chinese government's request, the company closed the blog of Zhao Jing on Dec. 30 after he criticized the government's firing of the editors at a progressive newspaper. Microsoft, which also acknowledges that its MSN Internet portal in China censors searches and blogs, is far from alone. Recently Yahoo admitted that it had helped China sentence a dissident to 10 years in prison by identifying him as the sender of a banned e-mail message.

Even as Internet use explodes in China, Beijing is cracking down on free expression, and Western technology firms are leaping to help. The companies block access to political Web sites, censor content, provide filtering equipment to the government and snitch on users. Companies argue that they must follow local laws, but they are also eager to ingratiate themselves with a government that controls access to the Chinese market.[14]

Indeed, bloggers do not escape Chinese government censorship, either. "Web sites and portals must now 'give priority' to news and opinion material that have already appeared in the state-run print media. This seemingly puts a stop not only to freewheeling, opinion-driven blogging but also to the use of the Internet to break and develop news stories that the official media have not reported. The *Los Angeles Times* observed . . . that the new rules could be interpreted broadly enough to enable the authorities to punish anyone who sends friends an e-mail describing a local riot."[15]

Expanding Internet censorship from an internal function to an international reality is a short step. Obviously, our free exchange of ideas is anathema to countries such as China. The notion of using a U.N. bureaucracy to gain greater control over the free dissemination of thought among their citizens is very attractive.

"In my opinion, freedom of speech seems to be a politically sensitive issue. A lot of policy matters are behind it," observed Houlin Zhao, the man who wants to control the greatest forum for free expression in history. As a director of the U.N.'s International Telecommunication Union (ITU) and a former senior Chinese government official, Zhao is a leader in the world body's effort to supplant the U.S. government in the supervision of the Internet.[16]

China, of course, is not the only U.N. member determined to control the free flow of information on the Internet. Take Syria, for example:

> Today the Syrian government relies on a host of repressive laws and extralegal measures to suppress Syrians' right to access and disseminate information freely online. It censors the Internet—as it does all media—with a free hand. It monitors and censors written and electronic correspondence. The government has detained people for expressing their opinions or reporting information online, and even for forwarding political jokes by e-mail. Syrian bloggers and human rights activists told Human Rights Watch that plainclothes security officers maintain a close watch over Internet cafes.[17]

How about Cuba? The group Reporters Without Borders reports that under dictator Fidel Castro's iron fist,

> Internet use is very restricted and under tight surveillance. Access is only possible with government permission and equipment is rationed. [A] Cuban who wants to log on to it or use public access points must have official permission and give a "valid reason" for wanting to and sign a contract listing restrictions. . . .[18]

CONSPIRACY AGAINST THE FREE FLOW OF INFORMATION

The U.N. World Summit of Information Society (WSIS) was held in mid-November 2005 in Tunis, Tunisia. It was a follow-up of a meeting held in Geneva, Switzerland, under the aegis of the U.N.'s ITU. The Tunis meeting was one of a series of U.N. events in which participants discussed a variety of difficulties affecting worldwide use of the Internet—from practical problems such as SPAM, cyber crime, and securing the Internet against terrorism, to Internet access in third-world countries. At the same time, the WSIS provided a platform for attacks on U.S. stewardship over the Internet.

And, in what seems like some kind of a U.N. in-joke, not only is the ITU headed by a representative from Communist China, the U.N. WSIS was held in an especially repressive country, Tunisia. None of this was lost on New Zealand journalist Gwynne Dyer, who noted:

> The scenes in Tunis itself reinforce the notion that this conference is really a conspiracy against the free flow of information.
>
> Tunisian police rough journalists up outside the conference centre, and an alternative "Citizens' Symposium on the Information Society" finds its reservations for hotel meeting rooms mysteriously canceled.
>
> Seven leading Tunisian figures including the head of the Union of Tunisian Journalists are on hunger strike to demand greater freedom of speech in their own country while the world's attention is temporarily turned their way.[19]

Another concerned journalist, Rohan Jayasekera, who is a Toronto-based Internet expert, noted with justifiable alarm:

> In the run up the 16–18 November conference Christophe Boltanski, a journalist with the Paris daily *Liberation,* was tear-gassed, beaten and stabbed in Tunis under the eyes of police who later refused to log his assault. The attack occurred less than 24 hours after *Liberation* ran Boltanski's story on how plain-clothes police had beaten human rights activists in the weeks before WSIS.[20]

Much closer to home, former Delaware governor Pete du Pont wrote in the *Wall Street Opinion Journal*:

> [W]hen the U.S. attends those IGF [Internet Governance Forum] meetings, our representative will surely be reminded of the repeated

advice Tony Mauro, the Supreme Court correspondent for *The American Lawyer*, recalls receiving from Europeans at a run-up meeting of the U.N. Internet group in Budapest three years ago. *Do not invoke the First Amendment in Internet discussions, he was told, for it is viewed as a sign of U.S. arrogance.*

If the U.N. establishment believes free speech is arrogance, we can be confident that U.N. control of the Internet would be calamitous.[21]

Perhaps the most outrageous critic of U.S. maintenance of the Internet was Robert Mugabe, the dictator of Zimbabwe. Bitter, jealous, and oozing paranoid suspicion, he illustrates the fear in the heart of every tyrant. The U.N. actually seems to give credence to this racist lunatic. Judge for yourself—here is Mugabe in his own words:

> Yes, we seek equal access to information and the control of communication technologies whose genesis in fact lies in the quest for global hegemony and dominance on the part of rich and powerful nations of the north. The ICTs [Information and Communications Technologies] that we seek to control and manage collectively are spin-offs from the same industries that gave us the awesome weapons that are now being used for the conquest, destruction and occupation of our nations. The ICTs by which we hope to build information societies are the same platforms for high-tech espionage, the same platforms and technologies through which virulent propaganda and misinformation are peddled to de-legitimise our just struggles against vestigial colonialism, indeed to weaken national cohesion and efforts at forging a broad Third World front against what patently is a dangerous imperial world order led by warrior states and kingdoms.

Mugabe then offers his two cents' worth on the war against terrorism in Iraq:

> [M]y country Zimbabwe continues to be a victim of such aggression, with both the United Kingdom and United States using ICT superiority to challenge our sovereignty through hostile and malicious broadcasts calculated to foment instability and destroy the state

through divisions. Our voice has been strangled and our quest to redeem a just and natural right has been criminalized. Today we are very clear. Beneath the rhetoric of free press and transparency is the iniquity of hegemony. The quest for an information society should not be at the expense of our efforts towards building sovereign national societies."[22]

ICANN AND THE INTERNET

A great deal of spleen from anti-American U.N. members has been directed at supposed U.S. control of the Internet. This ire is directed at a nonprofit organization in Marina Del Rey, Calif., called ICANN—the Internet Corporation for Assigned Names and Numbers. ICANN regulates top-level domain names such as ".com" and ".org." It determines what companies run the thirteen "root servers," the computers that hold the master list of all Web addresses worldwide.

ICANN works under a memorandum of understanding (MOU) with the U.S. Commerce Department, which "plays no role in the internal governance or day-to-day operations of the organization."[23] As the Internet has grown into a worldwide entity, eight of its thirteen root servers are located outside the U.S. It is, in practice, an international organization.

However, the fact that a U.S. nonprofit corporation controls the domain names and addresses for the Internet is threatening to some of the more repressive or anti-American countries in the world. This issue was debated—but not resolved—at the U.N.'s Tunis summit. After no final decisions were reached, there was an agreement to have a further, nonbinding summit in Athens, Greece, during the summer of 2006.

The Athens meeting will supposedly provide a forum for further discussion of Internet issues, but its determinations will have no binding force of law. Meetings and jawboning are the obvious products of the U.N.—but, as in meetings on the control of small arms, bureaucratic hot air can eventually lead to concrete results. Envision the U.N.'s International Action Network on Small Arms—IANSA—vetting your computer for "dangerous" speech.

In the face of international pressure to relinquish U.S. control of the Internet, the Bush administration firmly stated at the end of June 2005 that the management of root directories and domain names by ICANN would remain a U.S function. Michael D. Gallagher, assistant secretary at the National Telecommunications and Information Administration said:

> The United States Government intends to preserve the security and stability of the Internet's Domain Name and Addressing System (DNS). Given the Internet's importance to the world's economy, it is essential that the underlying DNS of the Internet remain stable and secure. As such, the United States is committed to taking no action that would have the potential to adversely impact the effective and efficient operation of the DNS and will therefore maintain its historic role in authorizing changes or modifications to the authoritative root zone file." [24]

Speaking at a press conference at the Tunis Summit, Ambassador David Gross, of the U.S. Department of State, expressed Bush administration support for the agreement that would, for the time being, leave the management of domain names to ICANN:

> It [the agreement] reaffirms the importance of technology and particularly the Internet to the world. . . . It focuses and refocuses and reaffirms the importance of the free flow of information. . . . It reaffirms the importance of technology and particularly the Internet to the world. It preserves the unique role of the United States government in assuring the reliability and stability of the Internet." [25]

And in the same press conference, Michael Gallagher pointed out that "the Internet itself is not controlled by any single government; it is not controlled by any single person. It is a manifestation of the creativity and the genius of the world spirit." [26]

Ambassador Gross also made an important point, saying that the Internet has prospered

> largely because governments have not played a dominant role; but rather, private enterprise and very importantly, individuals have done that. It has allowed for innovation, it has allowed for changes, both in

terms of the network itself, and the applications, the sorts of software that run over the Internet. And that freedom to innovate is very, very important.[27]

In a pointed rebuke of regimes that stifle free speech on the Internet, John Marburger, White House Office of Science and Technology Policy director told the Tunis Summit:

Phase I of this Summit produced a Declaration of Principles that was our shared focus on the ability of all peoples to access information through the reaffirmation of their right of freedom of opinion and expression.

It is vital that the Internet remain a neutral medium open to all in order to realize that access for our citizens. It is the role of governments to ensure that this freedom of expression is available to its citizens and not to stand in the way of people seeking to send and receive information across the Internet. . . . The legacy of WSIS should be an environment that nourishes the growth of the Internet not only as a vehicle of commerce, but also as an extraordinary vehicle for freedom and personal expression.[28]

The possibility of the Internet being controlled by the U.N., or any other international entity, has evoked a strong response by Congressional leaders. A sense of the Senate resolution introduced by Norm Coleman (R-MN) unanimously passed the Senate on November 18, 2005, and upheld the United States' current role in overseeing the governance of the Internet. Senator Coleman said:

The Internet has flourished under the supervision and market-based policies of the United States.

This resolution makes clear the determination of the Senate to oppose any attempt by the United Nations or any other international group to control or politicize the Internet now or in the future. The potential risks to our economy, security, and freedom of expression are too profound to allow the World Wide Web to be governed by the U.N. or any other international entity.

The senator went on to say:

> The resolution supports the four governance principles articulated by the Bush administration on June 30, 2005. These are:
>
> Preservation of the security and stability of the Internet domain name and addressing system (DNS).
>
> Recognition of the legitimate interest of governments in managing their own country code top-level domains.
>
> Support for the Internet Corporation for Assigned Names and Numbers (ICANN) as the appropriate technical manager of the Internet DNS.
>
> Participation in continuing dialogue on Internet governance in multiple existing fora, with continued support for marked-based approaches toward, and private sector leadership of, its further evolution."[29]

Senator Coleman also said the dispute is not over. "It has been put on hold, but it is not dead."[30]

On the House side, Rep. John Doolittle, (R-CA) introduced H. Con. Res. 268. The resolution, which also expressed the sense of the House that the U.S. should not relinquish control of the Internet to the U.N., passed 423 to zero. A press release from Representative Doolittle noted:

> The United States invented the Internet and it has been our gift to the world, paid for by our taxpayers. The U.N.'s desire to take that gift as a means of increasing its power must be stopped.
>
> If the U.N. were to be successful in its efforts to control the Internet, countries where human rights records range from questionable to criminal could be put in charge of determining what is and is not allowed to appear online. For example, we need only look back to 2003 when the U.N. decided that Libya, a country frequently condemned by human rights groups, was the U.N.'s choice to head its Human Rights Commission.[31]

Not too long ago, I heard some badly educated pundit referring to "First Amendment Rights worldwide." After I stopped laughing, I realized that we are so accustomed to free speech and a free press that the idea that these freedoms truly do not exist worldwide sneaks in under our radar. Our Bill of Rights is a uniquely American document, and a threat to dictators and bureaucratic busybodies alike.

Were the U.N. to control the most important means of communications in history, you can bet globalist billionaire George Soros and Rebecca Peters would be silencing all Internet access by those who oppose their world vision of a global gun ban. The Internet is still safely in the proper hands for now, but this fight, like the global efforts to disarm Americans, will never go away.

And neither will our duty to protect the sanctity of the First Amendment with the vigor equal to our defense of the Second Amendment. We had better not underestimate the monumental patience of international organizations like the United Nations. All of the seemingly useless summits and committees, the endless busywork of meetings and "programmes," can eventually bear fruit—and result in the loss of our God-given rights.

Epilogue

Stripped bare of cheap drama and shrill emotion, the right to keep and bear arms in defense of self, family, and country is ultimately self-evident. Reduced to its essence, our Second Amendment avows profound respect for human freedom, worth, and self-destiny.

But two centuries after the Second Amendment was codified into our culture, the United Nations declares that this civil liberty is a cause of the world's gun problems. In turn, it claims unspoken jurisdiction over sovereign American citizens by crafting a treaty that calls us to surrender our firearm freedom to their global thugocracy and accept whatever lesser standard of freedom—if any—the U.N. deems appropriate.

Indeed, so insistent and insulting is the U.N. mandate that it chose to conduct its largest ever global gun ban conference on U.S. soil on the Fourth of July, 2006.

The global gun ban treaty is, then, a ticking time bomb—just a gavel-slam away from becoming the law of our land once enough sympathetic politicians occupy the White House and the U.S. Senate. Which may be very soon.

In these pages, I have shown that the U.N. anti-gun axis is no sideshow struggling on a shoestring. It is a global collective of five hundred member organizations from a hundred nations, well funded through a maze of countries, grants, foundations, and benefactors. Their proclaimed mission is to endow themselves with global control of all firearms, long guns or hand guns, civilian or military, legal or illegal, everywhere, for everyone.

Yes, that means you.

They don't stop there. If you study the words of those who advocate global gun control, you will find sweeping police powers offensive not just to the right to keep and bear arms, but to the entire Bill of Rights. You will find that you are subject to record-keeping, oversight, inspections, supervision, tracking, and tracing. You will read about surveillance, documentation, verification, paper trails, and massive data banks for new global agencies and international data centers where your privacy is on display.

But what you will *not* find are any provisions by which oppressed people may be liberated from tyrants and dictators. You will not find the barest mention of anyone's rights to self-defense, to privacy, to property, to due process, or protection of personal freedoms of any kind. Nor will you find demands for arrest, prosecution, conviction, and mandatory sentencing or imprisonment of illicit traffickers or gunrunners.

Such gaping omissions expose the U.N. mission for what it is: a powerful reemergence of the socialist imaginings of the twentieth century. Fantasies that prey upon citizens who fall for social engineering, like students on campus, journalists in media, the intellectuals in think tanks, self-important U.N. leaders, and insulated billionaires with too much time and money on their hands.

The U.N. is a gang of governments led by unelected elitists who think they know better how to live our lives, how to spend our money, how to educate our children, and how to protect our homes. People who believe that, if they could just be in charge, they could make our lives perfect.

How perfect are their peoples' lives? None of the one hundred countries backing the U.N. gun ban allows its citizens the individual freedoms guaranteed to Americans in our treasured Bill of Rights. On the contrary, most of those countries openly flaunt the institutionalized anti-American sentiment so pervasive at the U.N.

What's more, the U.N. counts among its "members in good standing" nearly fifty dictatorships and at least six states that sponsor terrorism. Combined, these "members in good standing" of the U.N. have murdered more than 100 million of their own citizens in the past century. That's four times more than died in their wars.

The U.N. proves that among the world's police are its worst offenders. Member countries are notorious for corruption, greed, scandal, and butchery.

The Sudan—the only country that still allows slavery—is in charge of the U.N. Human Rights Commission. Human rights gladiators Libya and Cuba are seated members.

The U.N. was blind to mass murder by Pol Pot in Cambodia, a U.N. member. The U.N. famously ignored genocide in member state Rwanda, where nearly one million people were slaughtered—not by guns but with machetes. Yet your Second Amendment rights make the world a more dangerous place?

The U.N. presided over the Oil-for-Food debacle, where billions of dollars vanished into the pockets of insiders. As this book goes to press, U.N. staffers are under investigation for a sex-for-food ring in West Africa, drug trafficking in Cambodia, sex slaves in the Balkans, extortion in Kenya, and food program fraud in South Africa. And that's just for starters.

Why should the United Nations, with its shocking record of inaction, failure, and corruption, be given supremacy over any honest man or woman on the globe? We can no more leave our freedom in the hands of freedom's enemies than drop off our child at Molester's Daycare.

Still, too many fall for the U.N.'s bargain: If you will surrender your right to own a firearm to the new Global Godmother, you will be safer.

But wait. If you study nations where the gun banners had their way, you'll not only decline the bet, you'll condemn the gambler. The people of Australia, England, Canada, South Africa—and others who voluntarily turned over their guns—now enjoy far *less* safety in return for their freedom.

The promise of "you'll gain security if you'll give up this liberty" is precisely the bargain our forefathers rejected. America must reject it again and forever, especially in the form of foreign intervention.

So we are at a crossroads. This is America's cultural war gone global. With every sun that sets, our planet is growing not more free but less free, as more and more nations cave to the pressures of the U.N. and international gun prohibitionists.

The United States is the last standing truly free nation, offering every law-abiding human the greatest measure of freedom mankind has ever experienced.

The Bill of Rights is why that's so. The Bill of Rights is not ours to possess or revise. It is only ours to enjoy, to preserve, and then to bequeath. In their absence, we must speak out for the visionaries who founded our great nation in the belief, among others, that law-abiding people have the right to be armed.

So let the roar of our voices be heard by all nations, United or not: If you cannot respect our Bill of Rights, you'd best keep your hands off it.

Neither the United Nations nor any other foreign influence may claim jurisdiction to meddle with the freedoms guaranteed by our Bill of Rights, endowed by our Creator, and are the birthright of all humankind.

Notes

Introduction

1. William Jefferson Clinton, *My Life* (New York: Random House, 2004), 928.
2. UN Conference on Illicit Trade in Small Arms and Light Weapons in All Its Aspects, statement by John R. Bolton, United States Under Secretary of State for Arms Control and International Security Affairs (Plenary, New York, July 9, 2001), cited on http://canberra.usembassy.gov/hyper/2001/0709/epf103.htm.
3. Lawrence Auster, "Global Gun Controllers Surrender to U.S.," *NewsMax*, July 24, 2001, http://www.newsmax.com/archives/articles/2001/7/24/111205.shtml.
4. David Kopel, "U.N. Out of North America: The Small Arms Conference and the Second Amendment," Nationalreview.com, August 9, 2001, cited on www.freerepublic.com/forum/a3b72cc7a49a3.htm.
5. Auster, "Global Gun Controllers Surrender to U.S."
6. Ibid.
7. UN Conference on the Illicit Trade in Small Arms and Light Weapons in All Its Aspects, "A Programme of Action," http://disarmament.un.org:8080/update/jun2001/article2.htm.
8. *Great U.N. Gun Debate*, DVD (National Rifle Association, 2005).
9. Brooks Tigner, "EU Builds Strategy Against Small Arms," DefenseNews.com (October 24, 2005), http://www.defensenews.com/story.php?F=1155112&C=landwar.
10. Ibid.
11. Eric Green, "Meeting Aims to Combat Illicit Arms Trafficking in the Americas," news release prepared by the Department of State, October 7, 2005, cited on http://usinfo.state.gov/xarchives/display.html?p=washfile english&y=2005&m=October&x=20051007122742AEneerG0.3076898&t=livefeeds/wf-latest.html.
12. Kelly Hearn, "As Brazil Votes to Ban Guns, NRA Joins the Fight," *Nation*, October 21, 2005, http://www.thenation.com/doc/20051107/hearn.
13. Monte Reel, "Brazilians Reject Measure To Ban Sale of Firearms," *Washington Post*, October 24, 2005, http://www.washingtonpost.com/wp-dyn/content/article/2005/10/23/AR2005102300394_pf.html.
14. "Fix It Or Scrap It," *Economist*, January 14, 2006, 17.
15. Winston Churchill, "The Sinews of Peace" (speech, Westminster College, Fulton, Missouri, March 5, 1946), cited on http://www.hpol.org/churchill/.

Chapter One: Global Repression

1. *The Great U.N. Gun Debate*, DVD (London: King's College, Starcast Productions, Ltd., 2004.

2. Ibid.
3. Ibid.
4. Ibid.
5. Ibid.
6. Ibid.
7. Ibid.
8. Ibid.
9. David B. Kopel, "Bypassing U.S. Voters," *National Review Online*, August 3, 2001, http://www.nationalreview.com/kopel/kopel080301.shtml (accessed January 29, 2006).
10. Ibid.
11. Julie Lewis, "Gun-ho Diplomacy," *The Bulletin*, March 28, 2000, 42.
12. Rebecca Peters, "Turn in the Guns," *Sydney Herald*, April 26, 1997.
13. Ibid.
14. David Gonzalez, "Gun Makers, and a Culture, on Trial," *New York Times*, February 3, 1991.
15. Samantha Lee and Rebecca Peters, "Handguns, Deadly Loophole in Control," *Newcastle Herald*, April 30, 2001.
16. "Compensation for the Surrender of Prohibited Firearms," *Australian Shooters Journal*, September 1996.
17. *The Great U.N. Gun Debate*
18. Ibid.
19. Ibid.
20. C. Sutton, H. Gilmore, and Simon Kent, "He Could Have Been Stopped: Bungling Let the World's Worst Killer Go Free," *Sydney Sun-Herald*, May 5, 1996.
21. Adele Kirsten, "The Roll of Social Movements in Gun Control: An International Comparison Between South Africa, Brazil and Australia," Centre for Civil Society Research Report No. 21.
22. Ibid.
23. Julie Lewis, "Gun-ho Diplomacy," *The Bulletin*, March 28, 2000.
    Rebecca Peters and Roland Browne, "Australia's New Gun Control Philosophy: Public Health is Paramount," *The Drawing Board: An Australian Review of Public Affairs*, vol. 1, no. 2 (University of Sydney School of Economics and Political Science) (November 2000).
24. Ibid.
25. Ibid.
26. Ibid.
27. Ibid.
28. Ibid.
29. Erwin Dahinden, Julie Dahlitz, and Nadia Fischer, eds., "Common Elements in Firearms and Ammunition Control Legislation: A Framework for the Strengthening of Regulations," *Small Arms and Light Weapons: Legal Aspects of National and International Regulations*, vol. 4, *Arms Control and Disarmament Law* (Geneva: United Nations), 139–141.
30. e.g., "Arms Control: Critics of the Law to Curb Gun-related Crimes Say That It Attempts to Disarm Law-abiding Citizens While Leaving Criminals Armed," *Guardian* (Johannesburg, South Africa), January 7, 2005, 6.
31. Joseph A. Klein, *Global Deception: The U.N.'s Stealth Assault on America's Freedom* (Los Angeles: World Ahead Publishing, 2005), 131.
32. Ibid.

33. The Samuel Rubin Foundation's donees include International Association of Lawyers Against Nuclear Arms, the Women's International Link for Peace, the Hague Appeal for Peace, Institute for Pacific Studies, and Americans for Peace Now. John Gizzi, "The Anti-War Movement Arsenal: Center for National Security Studies, Center for Defense Information, Center for International Policy," *Organization Trend* (Capital Research Center: June 2004). Also, Public Media Center, Tides Foundation & Tides Center (a major antigun donor), Trauma Foundation (also involved in anti-gun work), Preamble Center, Winrock Int'l Institute for Agricultural Development, Institute for Agriculture and Trade Policy, Essential Information.

34. "Institute for Policy Studies," DiscovertheNetworks.org: A Guide to the Political Left, http://www.discoverthenetworks.org/groupProfile.asp?grpid=6991.

35. http://www.iansa.org/campaigns_events/index.htm.

36. http://www.smallarmssurvey.org/index.html.

37. http://www.hdcentre.org/?aid=2.

38. http://www.hdcentre.org/?aid=125.

39. http://www.hdcentre.org/datastore/Small%20arms/Rio_Chair_summary.pdf.

40. http://www.iansa.org/regions/europe/documents/eucommission_on_small_arms_control.pdf.

41. http://www.fosda.org/resource/ecowas_protocol.htm/.

42. http://disarmament.un.org/cab/orgs/Nairobi%20Secretariat/NairobiProtocol.pdf.

43. http://www.oas.org/main/main/asp?sLang=E&sLink=http:www.oas.org/juridico/english/treaties.htlm.

44. http://www.osce.org/item/13550.html.

45. http://www.iss.co.za/AF/RegOrg/unity_to_union/pdfs/sadc/3Protocol_on_Firearms.pdf.

46. Katharine Q. Steele, "National Rifle Association Is Turning to World Stage to Fight Gun Control," *New York Times*, April 2, 1999.

47. http://www.wfsa.net.

48. Stefan Halper, "51. The United Nations," *Cato Handbook for Congress: 105th Congress* (Washington, D.C.: Cato Institute, 1999).

49. Derek Miller, et al., "Regulation of Civilian Possession of Small Arms and Light Weapons," *International Alert Briefing 16* (2002), 12.

50. William Godnick, *Tackling the Illicit Trade in Small Arms and Light Weapons* (London: British American Security Information Council, 2002), 13.

51. Miller, *Regulation of Civilian Possession of Small Arms*, 5.

CHAPTER TWO: U.N. Disarmament Agenda

1. Edward J. Laurence, "Addressing the Negative Consequences of Light Weapons Trafficking: Opportunities for Transparency and Restraint," *Lethal Commerce: The Global Trade in Small Arms and Light Weapons*, eds. Jeffrey Boutwell, Michael T. Klare, and Laura Reed (Cambridge, Mass.: American Academy of Arts and Sciences, 1995), 149.

2. UNIDIR, *Curbing Illicit Trafficking in Small Arms and Sensitive Technologies: An Action Oriented Agenda* (Geneva).

   Don Brandt, *A Deadly Pandemic: Small Arms and Light Weapons* (World Vision)

   Jeffrey Boutwell, Michael T. Klare, and Laura Reed, *Lethal Commerce: The Global Trade in Small Arms and Light Weapons* (Cambridge, Mass.: American Academy of Arts and Sciences, 1995).

NOTES

Lora Lumpe, ed., *Running Guns: The Global Black Market in Small Arms* (New York: Zed Books, 2000).

Jayantha Dhanapala, et al., *Small Arms Control: Old Weapons, New Issues* (Geneva: UNIDIR, 1999).

Glenn Oosthuysen, *Small Arms Proliferation and Control in Southern Africa* (SAIIA Southern Africa Press, 1996).

Swiss Small Arms Survey, *Small Arms Survey 2001: Profiling the Problem* (New York: Oxford University Press, 2001).

Swiss Small Arms Survey, *Small Arms Survey 2002: Counting the Cost* (New York: Oxford University Press, 2002).

Swiss Small Arms Survey, *Small Arms Survey 2003: Development Denied* (New York: Oxford University Press, 2003).

Swiss Small Arms Survey, *Small Arms Survey 2004: Rights at Risk* (New York: Oxford University Press, 2004).

Michael Renner, *Small Arms, Big Impact: The Next Challenge in Disarmament* (World Watch, 1997).

Virginia Gamba, *Society under Siege: Crime, Violence and Illegal Weapons* (Institute for Security Studies, 1997).

Binalakshmi Nepram, *South Asia's Fractured Frontier: Armed Conflict, Narcotics and Small Arms Proliferation in India's North East* (New Delhi: Mittal Publications).

Erwin Dahinden, Julie Dahlitz & Nadia Fischer, eds., *Small Arms & Light Weapons—Legal Aspects of National & International Regulation* (United Nations, probably 2002).

Curbing Illicit Trafficking in Small Arms and Sensitive Technologies: An Action-oriented Agenda, ISBN: 9290451270.

United Nations, *Disarmament Study Series: Small Arms*, ISBN: 9211422337.

United Nations, *Small Arms Problem in Central Asia: the Features and Implications*, ISBN: 9290451343.

United Nations, *Disarmament and Conflict Resolution Project: Small Arms Management and Peacekeeping in Southern Africa*, ISBN: 9290451122.

United Nations International Study on Firearm Regulation, ISBN: 9211301904.

David Capie, *Under the Gun—The Small Arms Trade in the Pacific* (Victoria University Press and Department of Internal Affairs, 2003).

UNIDIR, *The Scope and Implications of a Tracing Mechanism for SALW* (2003).

S. Meek & N. Stott, *Destroying Surplus Weapons: An Assessment of Experience in South Africa and Lesotho* (2003).

The Handbook of Best Practices on Small Arms and Light Weapons, (Austria: Organization for Security and Co-operation in Europe (OSCE) 2003).

David Capie, *Small Arms Production and Transfers in Southeast Asia*, (Strategic and Defence Studies Centre, Australian National University, 2002).

Debbie Hiller & Brian Wood, *Shattered Lives—The Case for Tough International Arms Control* (London: Amnesty International & Oxfam International, 2003), ISBN 0 85598 5224.

Emily Schroeder and Lauren Newhouse, *Gender and Small Arms—Moving into the Mainstream* (Institute for Security Studies, October 2004).

Nicolas Florquin and Shelly O'Neill Stoneman, *"A House Isn't A Home Without a Gun": SALW Survey of Montenegro* (South Eastern Europe Clearinghouse for the Control of Small Arms and Light Weapons, July 2004).

Notes

Suzette R. Grillot, Shelly O. Stoneman, Hans Risser, and Wolf-Christian Paes, *A Fragile Peace—Guns and Security in Post-Conflict Macedonia,* a report commissioned by UNDP (copublished with Bonn International Center for Conversion and South Eastern Europe Clearinghouse for the Control of Small Arms and Light Weapons, 2004).

Disposal of Surplus Small Arms: A Survey of Policies and Practices in OSCE countries (copublished with South Eastern Europe Clearinghouse for the Control of Small Arms and Light Weapons, Saferworld, and the British American Security Information Council).

Chandré Gould and Guy Lamb, eds., *Hide and Seek: Taking Account of Small Arms in Southern Africa* (Institute for Security Studies, October 2004).

Cate Buchanan and Mereille Widmer, *Putting Guns in Their Place—a resource pack for two years of action by humanitarian agencies* (Centre for Humanitarian Dialogue, October 2004).

Edward Mogire, *A Preliminary Examination of the Linkages between Refugees and Small Arms* (Bonn International Center for Conversion, Germany, 2004).

Swiss Small Arms Survey, *Firearm Related Violence in Brazil,* (copublished with the Pan-American Health Organization and the World Health Organization).

Wendy Cukier, *Global Gun Epidemic: From Saturday Night Specials to AK47s* (Praeger, Canada: Forthcoming, 2005).

3. Cukier, *Global Gun Epidemic.*
4. Kirsten, "The Roll of Social Movements in Gun Control.
5. United Nations, Press Release UNIS/CP/346, May 12, 1997.
6. United Nations, Secretary General, *Supplement to an Agenda for Peace: Position Paper on the Secretary-General on the Occasion of the Fiftieth Anniversary of the United Nations,* S/1995/1 (1995), section D., paragraphs 60–65.
7. Swadesh Rana, *Small Arms and Intra-State Conflict* (New York: United Nations Publications, 1995).
8. Most Americans have no idea how extensive U.N. structure is. The U.N. has three headquarters; in addition to the New York headquarters there is a huge facility in Vienna and similarly sized headquarters in Geneva. The Geneva HQ is located in the old Palis de Nations, which itself was the building that housed the League of Nations.
9. Kyodo News Service (Tokyo), "Parents of Japanese Boy Killed in U.S. Appeal for Gun Control," 2002.
10. Walter Mondale (speech, National Press Club), as transcribed in Video Monitoring Services of America, September 6, 1996, 6.
11. A/RES/50/70 B. By the end of 2005, there were almost thirty U.N. General Assembly resolutions.
12. Special Assistant to the Minister of Foreign Affairs.
13. http://www.miis.edu/gsips-faculty.html?id=35.
14. Boutwell, et al., *Lethal Commerce: The Global Trade in Small Arms and Light Weapons.*
15. Raymond Bonner, "U.N. Panel May Approve Limit on Guns Despite N.R.A. Pleas," *New York Times,* April 30, 1998.
16. Definition 1 is from the 1997 "Report of the Panel of Government Experts on Small Arms" paragraph 24: "Small arms and light weapons range from clubs. . . . The small arms and light weapons which are of the main concern for the purposes of the present report are those which are manufactured to military specifications for use as lethal instruments of war."

Definition #2 is from the 1997 "Report of the Panel of Government Experts on Small Arms," paragraphs 25 and 26: "Broadly speaking, small arms are those weapons designed for personal use, and light weapons are those designed for use by several persons serving as a crew."

Based on this broad definition and on an assessment of weapons actually used in conflicts being dealt with by the United Nations, the weapons addressed in the present report are categorized as follows:

1. Revolvers and self-loading pistols
2. Rifles and carbines
3. Sub-machine guns
4. Assault rifles
5. Light machine guns (Description continues with heavy machine guns, grenade launchers, etc.) Paragraph 26.

Definition 3 is from the 1997 "Report of the Panel of Government Experts on Small Arms," paragraph 28: "In conflicts dealt with by the United Nations, non-military weapons not manufactured to military specifications, such as hunting firearms and homemade weapons, have been used in violent conflicts, terrorism, and the intentional harming of civilian populations. In such cases, and where such weapons are used and accumulated in numbers that endanger the security and political stability of a State, the Panel considered them relevant for the purposes of this report.[8]" (Endnote 8 describes home-made weapons that can be constructed out of readily available material with little skill.)

Definition 4 is from the "Report of the Group of Government Experts on Small Arms," paragraphs 129 and 130: "The scope of the International Conference will be the illicit trade in small arms and light weapons in all its aspects." (Paragraph 129)

In this context, the primary focus of attention should be on small arms and light weapons that are manufactured to military specifications (see endnote 5). Other types of firearms used in conflicts may, however, also have to be considered in dealing with the problems in the most effected regions of the world. (Paragraph 130)

Definition 5 is from the "Report of the Group of Government Experts on Small Arms," endnote 5: "The Group followed the practice of the previous Panel of Governmental Experts on Small Arms in its definitions of small arms and light weapons. Broadly speaking, small arms are those weapons designed for personal use and light weapons are those designed for use by several persons serving as a crew. The category of small arms includes revolvers and self-loading pistols, rifles and carbines, sub-machine guns, assault rifles and light machine guns."

These definitions are overly broad on two counts. First they refer to and include, somewhat convolutedly, to civilian firearms such as hunting rifles (Definition 3). More importantly, they rely on the broad, undefined term "manufactured to military specifications." This is generally thought to mean military design.

If the term were interpreted as merely being manufactured to certain standards of increased durability or tolerances it would be unworkably narrow. For example, an M–16 manufactured by a regular producer under a government contract would be within the definition, but a copy of the same firearms, made in an illegal workshop, would not be within the definition.

17. United Nations, A/54/258, 122.
18. United Nations, draft Programme of Action, Third Session, March 19–20, 2001,

Preparatory Committee for the United Nations Conference on the Illicit Trade in Small Arms and Light Weapons in All Its Aspects, A/CONF.192/PC/L.4/ Rev 1, February 2, 2001.
19. This is a deadly, yet subtle, combination of legalese and diplomatic terminology.
20. Hereafter cited as Article and paragraph "II/2" for example.
21. Association Nationale de defense des Tireurs, Amateurs et Collectionners d'armes (ANTAC) France.

> Associazione Nazionale Produttori Armi e Munizioni (ANPAM). Italy.
> British Shooting Sports Council (BSSC) United Kingdom.
> Canadian Institute for Legislative Action (CILA) Canada.
> Fair Trade Group (FAIR) United States.
> Federation of European Societies of Arms Collectors (FESAC) The Netherlands.
> Forum Waffenrecht (FW) Germany.
> International Ammunition Association, Inc. (IAA) United States.
> National Rifle Association of America–Institute on Legislative Action (NRA-

ILA) United States.

> Safari Club International (SCI) United States.
> Single Action Shooting Society (SASS) United States.
> South Africa Gun Owners' Association (SAGA) South Africa.
> Sporting Clays of America (SCA) United States.
> Sporting Shooters' Association of Australia (SSAA) Australia.
> World Forum on the Future of Sports Shooting Activities (WFSA) Belgium.

22. Full text of the presentations at http://disarmament.un.org/cab/smallarms/ngospeakers.htm.
23. United Nations, A/CONF.169/L.8, Rev. 1.
24. United Nations, A/CONF.169/11.
25. Yomiuri Shimben, reprinted in *Daily News* (Ketchikan, AK), quoted in *Gun Week*, October 20, 1995.
26. United Nations, Economic and Social Council, Resolutions 1995/27.
27. United Nations, Economic and Social Council, E/CN.15/1998/L.6/Rev. 1.
28. United Nations, Economic and Social Council, E/CN.15/1998/4, 4–7.
29. United Nations, General Assembly, resolution, A/55/383/Add.2, (2001),11.
30. Ibid, 10.
31. Under the U.N., charter states do have the right of self-defense. Unfortunately, this is not usually interpreted as the right of self-defense for individuals themselves.
32. The Chinese broach no criticism of their policies from the U.N., especially on "human rights" issues. See Joseph Kahn, "China Disputes U.N. Envoy On Widespread Use of Torture," *The New York Times*, December 7, 2005, A5.
33. United Nations, A/55/383/Add.2, 11.
34. Ibid, 5–6.

CHAPTER THREE: Demonizing Lawful Gun Owners
1. United Nations, Press Briefing on Small Arms Conference, July 5, 2001, http://www.un.org/News/briefings/docs/2001/SmallArmsConfBrf.doc.html; Edith M. Lederer, "U.N. Investigating Whether E-Mails From U.S. Gun Enthusiasts a Security Threat," Associated Press, July 5, 2001; Dave Kopel, "Score One for Bush: A U.N. Conference Concludes Without Too Much Permanent Damage," *National Review Online*, July 30, 2001, http://www.nationalreview.com/kopel/kopel073001.shtml.

2. United Nations Department of Public Information in cooperation with the Department for Disarmament Affairs, "Setting The Record Straight: UN Conference On The Illicit Trade In Small Arms And Light Weapons in All Its Aspects (New York, July 2001), 9–20, http://www.un.org/Depts/dda/CAB/smallarms/ facts.htm.

3. Dave Kopel, Paul Gallant, and Joanne D. Eisen, "Jamaican War Zone: An Island of Intoxicative Beauty? Try Again, Mon," *National Review Online,* October 30, 2000, http://www.nationalreview.com/kopel/kopel103000.shtml.

4. Preparatory Committee for the United Nations Conference on the Illicit Trade in Small Arms and Light Weapons in All Its Aspects, second session, January 8–19, 2000, "Working paper by the Chairman of the Preparatory Committee. Draft Programme of Action, January 9, 2001," sect. 6(f).

5. Canadian War Museum, "Temporary Exhibitions: The Art of Peacemaking," April 26, 2001, http://web.archive.org/web/20041113095142/; http://www.civilization. ca/cwm/ihuman/cwmhumeng.html.

6. Ad Hoc Committee on the Elaboration of a Convention Against Transnational Organized Crime, *Revised Draft Protocol Against the Illicit Manufacturing of and Trafficking in Firearms, Their Parts and Components and Ammunition, Supplementing the United Nations Convention against Transnational Organized Crime, Twelfth session, Vienna, 26 February–2 March 2001,* December 18, 2000, A/AC.254/4/Add.2/ Rev.6.

7. Peter Lock, "Pervasive Illicit Small Arms Availability: A Global Threat," European Institute for Crime Prevention and Control, affiliated with the United Nations; HEUNI Paper No. 14 (Helsinki, 1999), 27. (The "affiliated with the United Nations" phrase appears as part of the group's name on the title page of this document.)

8. Kopel, "Score One for Bush."

9. "Report of the Panel of Government Experts on Small Arms," A/52/298 (August 27, 1997), paragraph 26, http://www.smallarmsnet.org/docs/saun13.pdf.

10. Swiss Small Arms Survey, *Small Arms Survey 2001* (New York: Oxford Univ. Pr., 2001), http://www.smallarmssurvey.org/publications/yb_2001.htm.

11. John Hughes-Wilson & Adrian Wilkinson, "Safe and Efficient Small Arms Collection and Destruction Programmes: A Proposal for Practical Technical Measures," United Nations Disarmament Programme (May 2001), 16, paragraph 4.1.2, http://www.undp.org/bcpr/smallarms/docs/sa_prac_meas.pdf:

    "It may be possible to start a programme of weapon registration as a first step towards the physical collection phase.... The advantage to the local community is that they can retain their weapons until they feel that the security environment is sufficiently safe to allow for weapons surrender.... Assurances must be provided, and met, that the process of registration will not lead to *immediate* weapons seizures by security forces." (Emphasis added.)

12. "Conference On Small Arms Set To Convene At Headquarters, 9–20 July," Press Release, DC/2782 (July 5, 2001), http://www.un.org/News/Press/docs/2001/dc 2782.doc.htm.

13. Of course smokeless powder never explodes; it deflagrates.

14. Kopel, "Score One for Bush.

15. Ibid.

16. The Laogai Research Foundation provides extensive information on human rights abuses in China, including on China's system of *de facto* slave labor, http://www. laogai.org/.

17. Lock, "Pervasive Illicit Small Arms Availability"

18. Kofi A. Annan, "Small Arms, Big Problems," *International Herald Tribune* July 10, 2001, http://disarmament.un.org/cab/smallarms/sg.htm.
19. The ICBL's website is http://www.icbl.org/.
20. Annan, "Small Arms."
21. Kopel, "Score One."
22. Kopel, Gallant, and Eisen, "Does the Right to Bear Arms Impede or Promote Economic Development?" 23. In a letter to the *New York Times* answering a *Times* editorial criticizing the U.S. for not allowing the conference to be used as a tool to disarm civilians, Whittlesey elaborated: "The highest priority of freedom-loving people is liberty, even more than peace. The small arms you demonize often protect men, women and children from tyranny, brutality and even the genocide too frequently perpetrated by governments and police forces. The world's numerous dictators would be delighted to stem the flow of small arms to indigenous freedom fighters and civilians alike to minimize any resistance.

    "The right of individual self-defense in the face of criminal intimidation and government aggression is a deeply held belief of the American people dating back to 1776, when small arms in the hands of private individuals were the means used to secure liberty and independence."
23. Faith Whittlesey, "Small Arms in a Big, Brutal World," *New York Times*, July 13, 2001, A20.
24. UN Conference on Illicit Trade in Small Arms and Light Weapons in All Its Aspects, statement by John R. Bolton, United States Under Secretary of State for Arms Control and International Security Affairs (Plenary, New York, July 9, 2001), http://usinfo.state.gov/topical/pol/arms/stories/01070902.htm.
25. David B. Kopel, Paul Gallant, and Joanne D. Eisen, "Firearms Possession by 'Non-State Actors': the Question of Sovereignty," *Texas Law Review of Law and Politics*, vol. 8 (2004), 373, http://www.davekopel.com/2a/LawRev/Non-state-actors.pdf.
26. Ibid.
27. Declaration of Independence (1776), paragraph 2.
28. *Mandel v. Mitchell*, 325 F. Supp. 620, 629 (E.D.N.Y., 1971).

CHAPTER FOUR: Choking Off the Second Amendment
1. Patrick F. Fagan, "How U.N. Conventions on Women's and Children's Rights Undermine Family, Religion, and Sovereignty: Supplemental Material: Quotations from CRC and CEDAW Committees of the United Nations" Heritage Foundation Backgrounder, no. 1409 (Washington, D.C., February 5, 2001), http://www.heritage.org/Research/InternationalOrganizations/BG1407.cfm.
2. *Diplomat Charges U.N. Committee With Misuse of U.N. Documents, C-Fam (Catholic Family and Human Rights Institute)* (July 27, 2001), http://www.c-fam.org/FAX/Volume_4/faxv4n32.html.
3. *Reid v. Covert* (1957): "No agreement with a foreign nation can confer power on Congress, or on any other branch of Government, which is free from the restraints of the Constitution".
4. Phyllis Schlafly, "Can Globalism Amend Our Constitution?" August 11, 2003.
5. *Knight v. Florida*, 528 U.S. 990, 993-99 (1999) (Breyer, J., dissenting from denial of certiorari).
6. *Gratz v. Bollinger*, 123 S. Ct. 2411, 2442, 2445 (2003) (Ginsburg, J., dissenting); *Grutter v. Bollinger*, 123 S. Ct. 2325, 2347 (2003) (Ginsburg, J., concurring).
7. Ruth Bader Ginsburg, "Looking Beyond Our Borders: The Value of a

Comparative Perspective in Constitutional Adjudication," *Idaho Law Review*, vol. 40 (2003), 8.

8. Joseph Bruce Alonso, "The Second Amendment and Global Gun Control," *Journal on Firearms & Public Policy*, vol. 15 (2003), 1–33. The article is based on a paper that won first place in the NRA Civil Rights Legal Defense Fund student lawyer essay contest in 2002.

9. Frye, "Small Arms," 42; Barbara Frye, "Progress report on the prevention of human rights violations committed with small arms and light weapons," E/CN.4/Sub.2/2004/37 (2004), paragraph 58, http://www1.umn.edu/humanrts/demo/smallarms2004-2.html; Barbara Frye, "Specific Human Rights Issues," United Nations Economic and Social Council, Human Rights Commission, Sub-Commission on the Promotion of Human Rights, E/CN.4/Sub.2/2003/29 (June 25, 2003), paragraphs 36 and 47. The theory is that the state is culpable for criminal violence due to failure to exercise "due diligence" in preventing crime.

10. Frye, "Small Arms," 44; Frye, "Progress report," paragraph 22, http://www1.umn.edu/humanrts/demo/smallarms2004-2.html.

11. The International Criminal Court, based in The Hague in the Netherlands, is not formally part of the United Nations, but was created as a result of United Nations initiative in the 1990s. Defendants before the international criminal court are deprived of many of the due process protections of the U.S. Constitution. There is no jury trial and no right to a speedy trial. The prosecution has a right to appeal acquittals, and during the appeal, the defendant remains incarcerated. Judges and prosecutors are drawn from a variety of nations, including dictatorships with no respect for due process. A person sentenced by the ICC may be sent to a prison anywhere in the world. Non-government organizations may suggest that a prosecutor bring charges against a particular defendant. The U.S. has not currently joined the ICC system, but the only objection lodged by the U.S. government is concern that American soldiers could be tried as war criminals; if the ICC waived jurisdiction over American soldiers, then presumably the U.S. would join. Many of the people prosecuted by the ICC have been genuine war criminals or genocidaires. Nevertheless, there is good reason to be concerned about American citizens being brought within the ICC net.

12. See U.N. History chapter.

13. Frye, "Progress report," paragraph 58.

CHAPTER FIVE: Congress and the Second Amendment

1. Act of July 16, 1866, 14 Stat. 173, 176.

2. The significance of the Freedmen's Bureau Act to the Fourteenth Amendment is recognized in the following: A. Amar, *The Bill of Rights and the Fourteenth Amendment*, 101 Yale L.J. 1193, 1245 n.228 (April 1992); M. Curtis, *No State Shall Abridge: The Fourteenth Amendment and the Bill of Rights* (1986); H. Flack, *The Adoption of the Fourteenth Amendment* 17 (1908). The definitive book on the subject is Stephen P. Halbrook, *Freedmen, the Fourteenth Amendment, and the Right to Bear Arms, 1866–1876* (Westport, Conn.: Praeger Publishers, 1998). *See also* Nelson Lund, "Outsider Voices on Guns and the Constitution," 17 *Constitutional Commentary*, No. 3, 701 (2000).

3. *Cong. Globe*, 39th Cong., 1st sess., January 5, 1866, 129.

4. P. Foner and G. Walker, eds., 2 *Proceedings of the Black State Conventions, 1840-1865*, 302 (1980).

Notes

5. *Cong. Globe*, 39th Cong., 1st sess., January 22, 1866, 337.

6. *Cong. Globe*, 39th Cong., 1st sess., January 29, 1866, 512.

7. Ibid at 517.

8. *Cong. Globe*, 39th Cong., 1st sess., February 1, 1866, 585.

9. *Cong. Globe*, 39th Cong., 1st sess., February 5, 1866, 654.

10. Ibid.

11. Ibid., 657

12. Exec. Doc. No. 70, 39th Cong., 1st sess., 1866, 233, 236 (emphasis in original).

13. *Cong. Globe*, 39th Cong., 1st sess., March 9, 1866, 1292.

14. *Cong. Globe*, 39th Cong., 1st sess., February 6, 1866, 585.

15. *Cong. Globe*, 39th Cong., 1st sess., February 8, 1866, 748.

16. Ibid., 743.

17. Ibid., 748.

18. *Cong. Globe*, 39th Cong., 1st sess., February 9, 1866, 775.

19. Ibid., 1292 (emphasis added).

20. *Cong. Globe*, 39th Cong., 1st sess., February 17, 1866, 908–09.

21. *The Loyal Georgian* (Augusta: February. 3, 1866), 1, col. 2.

22. Ibid., 2, col. 2.

23. Ibid., 3, col. 4.

24. *Cong. Globe*, 39th Cong., 1st sess., February 19, 1866, 916.

25. *Cong. Globe*, 39th Cong., 1st sess., February 20, 1866, 936.

26. Ibid., 941.

27. Ibid., 943.

28. *Cong. Globe*, 39th Cong., 1st sess., March 7, 1866, 1238.

29. *Cong. Globe*, 39th Cong., 1st sess., June 26, 1866, 3412.

30. *Cong. Globe*, 39th Cong., 1st sess., March 9, 1866, 1291.

31. Ibid., 1292.

32. Ibid.

33. *Cong. Globe*, 39th Cong., 1st sess., February 2, 1866, 606, (Senate); March 13, 1866, 1367 (House).

34. *Cong. Globe*, 39th Cong., 1st sess., March 27, 1866, 1679.

35. *Cong. Globe*, 39th Cong., 1st sess., April 4, 1866, 1757.

36. Ibid., quoting Kent's *Commentaries*.

37. *Cong. Globe*, 39th Cong., 1st sess., April 6, 1866, 1809,.

38. "The Civil Rights Bill in the Senate," *New York Evening Post*, April 7, 1866, 2.

39. *Cong. Globe*, 39th Cong., 1st sess., April 9, 1866, 1861.

40. 14 Stat. 27 (1866) (emphasis added).

41. *See* 42 U.S.C. § (1981).

42. *Cong. Globe*, 39th Cong., 1st sess., May 22, 1866, 2743.

43. *Cong. Globe*, 39th Cong., 1st sess., June 26, 1866, 3412.

44. *Cong. Globe*, 39th Cong., 1st sess., May 10, 1866, 2545.

45. *Cong. Globe*, 39th Cong., 1st sess., May 23, 1866, 2765.

46. Ibid.

47. Ibid., 2766.

48. *Cong. Globe*, 39th Cong., 1st sess., May 23, 1866, 2773.

49. Ibid.

50. Ibid., 2774.

51. Ibid., 2775.

52. Ibid., 2878.

NOTES

53. Ibid.

54. *Cong. Globe*, 39th Cong., 1st sess., June 8, 1866, 3042.

55. *Cong. Globe*, 39th Cong., 1st sess., June 13, 1866, 3149.

56. *Cong. Globe*, 39th Cong., 1st sess., June 17, 1866, 3210.

57. *Cong. Globe*, 39th Cong., 1st sess., June 26, 1866, 3412.

58. Ibid.

59. Ibid.

60. Ibid.

61. *Cong. Globe*, 39th Cong., 1st sess., July 2, 1866, 3524.

62. *Cong. Globe*, 39th Cong., 1st sess., July 3, 1866, 3562.

63. *Cong. Globe*, 39th Cong., 1st sess., July 16, 1866, 3849.

64. Ibid., 3850.

65. Ibid., 3842.

66. 14 Stat. 173 (1866).

67. Ibid., 176–77.

68. P.L. 274, 77th Cong., 1st sess., Ch. 445, 55 Stat., pt. 1, 742, October 16, 1941 (emphasis added).

69. *New York Times*, November 11, 1938, 1.

70. Ibid., 4.

71. *New York Times*, November 4, 1939, 5.

72. *New York Times*, July 1, 1940, 3.

73. *New York Times*, July 2, 1940, 4.

74. *New York Times*, September 5, 1940, 17.

75. *New York Times*, January 4, 1941, 7.

76. *United States v. Miller*, Brief for the United States, 15.

77. *United States v. Miller*, 307 U.S. 174, 178 (1939).

78. Letter reprinted in *Cong. Rec.*, 77th Cong., 1st sess., May 2, 1941, A2072.

79. House Committee on Military Affairs, 77th Cong., 1st sess., S. 1579, To Authorize the President of the United States, July 31, 1941, 18.

80. House Committee on Military Affairs, Rept. No. 1120 [to accompany S. 1579], 77th Cong., 1st Sess., August 4, 1941, 1.

81. Ibid., 2. The Report should have said "Amendment 2" instead of "section 2."

82. 87 Cong. Rec., 77th Cong., 1st sess., August 5, 1941, 6778.

83. Ibid.

84. *Cong. Globe*, 39th Cong., 1st sess., August 6, 1941), 6811.

85. Ibid.

86. Ibid.

87. *Cong. Globe*, 39th Cong., 1st sess., August 13, 1941, 7097.

88. Ibid., 7098.

89. Ibid.

90. Ibid., 7100.

91. Ibid., 7100–7101.

92. Ibid., 7101.

93. Ibid., 7101.

94. Ibid.

95. Ibid.

96. Ibid., 7102.

97. Ibid.

98. Ibid., 7103.

99. 87 Cong. Rec., 77th Cong., 1st Sess., 7164 (August 13, 1941).

100. Rpt. No. 1214, Conference Report [to accompany S. 1579], 77th Cong., 1st sess., September 25, 1941. 2.

101. P.L. 274, 77th Cong., 1st Sess., Ch. 445, 55 Stat., pt. 1, October 16, 1941, 742.

102. Senate Judiciary Committee, Subcommittee to Investigate Juvenile Delinquency, 90th Cong., 2nd sess., 1968, 56.

103. Ibid., 479, 481.

104. §1(b), P.L. 99-308, 100 Stat. 449, May 19, 1986.

105. Senate Judiciary Committee, *The Right to Keep and Bear Arms: Report of the Subcommittee on the Constitution,* 97th Cong., 2nd sess., 1982, 12. In addition, two other scholarly studies were inserted into the legislative record in support of Congress's finding during Senate debate. D. Caplan, *Restoring the Balance: The Second Amendment Revisited,* 5 Fordham Urban L.J. 31, 1976, reprinted in 131 Cong. Rec. S8692, June 24, 1985; S. Halbrook, *To Keep and Bear Their Private Arms: The Adoption of the Second Amendment, 1787–1791,* 10 N. Ky. L. Rev.13, 1982, reprinted in 131 Cong. Rec. S9105, July 9, 1985.

106. 18 U.S.C. §926(a).

107. 18 U.S.C. §926A.

108. 131 Cong. Rec. S9114, July 9, 1985.

109. 132 Cong. Rec. H1695, April 9, 1986.

110. P.L. 10992, 119 Stat. 2095, October 26, 2005.

111. Ibid., § 2.

112. Ibid., § 2(a)(3).

113. Ibid., § 2(a)(4).

114. Ibid., § 2(a)(5).

115. Ibid., § 2(a)(6).

116. Ibid., § 2(a)(7).

117. Ibid., § 2(a)(8).

118. Ibid., § 2(b)(1).

119. Ibid., § 2(b)(2) (3).

120. Ibid., § 2(b)(4).

121. Ibid., § 2(b)(5).

122. Ibid., § 3.

123. 151 Cong. Rec. S9374, S9378, July 29, 2005.

124. Ibid., S9394.

125. Ibid., S9385.

126. Ibid., S9396.

127. 151 Cong. Rec. H8996, October 20, 2005.

128. Ibid., H906-07.

129. Ibid., H9009.

130. Ibid., H9010.

CHAPTER SIX: U.N. Gun Prohibition

1. Measures included the Royal Ordinance of January 27, 1920, Royal Ordinance of July 8, 1927, Royal Ordinance of April 26, 1929, and Royal Ordinance of July 1, 1935. The most comprehensive was Royal Ordinance No. 55 of March 28, 1938, which provided for a licensing system. Royal Ordinance No. 55 was expanded on May 29, 1953. Jay Simkin, Aaron Zelman, and Alan M. Rice, *Lethal Laws* (Milwaukee: Jews for the Preservation of Firearms Ownership, 1994), 305.

NOTES

2. See Genocide chapter for data.

3. See Genocide chapter for data.

4. These were the Cambodian People's Armed Forces (CPAF), the National Army of Democratic Kampuchea (NADK, the armed forces of the PDK or Khmer Rouge), the Armée Nationale pour un Kampuchea Indépendent (ANKI), and the Khmer People's National Liberation Armed Forces (KPNLAF).

5. Formally, the "Agreements on a Comprehensive Political Settlement of the Cambodian Conflict."

6. U.N. Security Council Res. 745 (1992) established UNTAC, which became operational on March 15 of that year. S.C. Res. 745, U.N. SCOR (1992), http://www.un.org/documents/sc/res/1992/scres92.htm. UNTAC consisted of four distinct components: The Military Component, The Electoral Component, the Civil Administration Component, and the Repatriation Component.

7. Jianwei Wang, *Managing Arms In Peace Processes: Cambodia* (U.N. Institute for Disarmament Research 1996), 35, Table 1.

8. Wang, 34.

9. Decaying consent is defined by the U.N. as "a pulling back from willingness to abide by an agreement because circumstances are not working out as hoped or envisioned." Donald C. F. Daniel, "Is There a Middle Option in Peace Support Operations? Implications for Crisis Containment and Disarmament," *Managing Arms in Peace Processes: The Issues* (U.N. Institute for Disarmament Research, 1996), 60.

10. David R. Meddings and Stephanie M. O'Connor, "Circumstances Around Weapon Injury in Cambodia after Departure of a Peacekeeping Force: Prospective Cohort Study," *British Medical Journal*, vol. 319 (1999), 412–13. Meddings and O'Connor used data from the International Committee of the Red Cross-supported Mongkol Borei hospital in northwestern Cambodia. Land mine and other weapon injuries, in addition to firearm injuries, were included in the study. Approximately one-third of the victims were injured in noncombat situations, and of that category, civilian intentional firearm-related injuries comprised the largest category.

11. Ibid., 412.The authors found: "30% of weapon injuries occurred in contexts other than interfactional combat. Most commonly, these were firearm injuries inflicted intentionally on civilians. Civilians accounted for 71% of those with non-combat injuries, 42% of those with combat-related injuries, and 51% of those with weapon injuries of either type. . . . The incidence of weapon injuries remained high when the disarmament component of a peacekeeping operation achieved only limited success. Furthermore, injuries occurring outside the context of inter-factional combat accounted for a substantial proportion of all weapon injuries, were experienced disproportionately by civilians, and were most likely to entail the intentional use of a firearm against a civilian."

12. Wang, 75–76: "[T]here would be a three-week grace period to allow people either to surrender their weapons or to get their papers in order. Gun holders were supposed to surrender their arms at the local UNTAC, CIVPOL, or military contingent where they would be given a receipt for their weapon and would face no legal action. Those who wished to retain their weapons could apply to the police force or the relevant authorities for a firearm license."

13. Sitra Sivaraman, "Violent Crime Thrives in Wounded Society," *Inter Press Service*, August 25, 1998, quoting Mouen Chhean Nariddh: "While the world focuses on the human rights and political situation in Cambodia, silent but steady violent crime is emerging as one of the country's biggest killers.".

14. "U.N. Ban Starts in Cambodia," *BBC News,* April 7, 1999.
15. Ibid.
16. United Nations, *United Nations Conference on the Illicit Trade in Small Arms, Small Arms Conference Hears Call For Stepped-Up Control Of Illicit Trade: But Several States Insist on Right to Acquire Arms for Security Purposes,* DC/2787, 3rd meeting (July 10, 2001). http://www.un.org/News/Press/docs/2001/dc2787.doc.htm.
17. Ibid.
18. Swiss Small Arms Survey, *Small Arms Survey 2002* (New York: Oxford University Press), 296; Working Group for Weapons Reduction (WGWR), *Small Arms Reduction and Management,* http://www.ngoforum.org.kh/Development/Docs/ngo_2002/36.htm.
19. Bertil Lintner, "Drugs and Politics," *Far East Economic Review,* February 7, 2002; Craig Skehan, "Thais Run Huge Arms Trade," *Sydney Morning Herald,* August 14, 1999. "Smuggling is largely controlled by corrupt military officers".
20. For example, there is the *Protocol to Prevent, Suppress and Punish Trafficking in Persons, Especially Women and Children, Supplementing the United Nations Convention Against Transnational Organized Crime,* G.A. Res. 25, Annex II, U.N. GAOR, 55th sess., Supp. No. 49, at 60, U.N. Doc. A/45/49 (2001).
21. Bonn International Center for Conversion, *Help Desk for Practical Disarmament: Cambodia,* http://www.bicc.de/helpdesk/stories/cambodia.html; BBC, "U.N. Ban Starts in Cambodia." "Many Cambodians remain skeptical, saying they keep weapons precisely because they have little faith in the public institutions that are meant to maintain law and order".
22. Swiss Small Arms Survey, *Small Arms Survey 2002,* 296. The Small Arms Survey may have been naïve in concluding that most Cambodians support the weapons collection program in theory; when speaking to foreigners or in public, Cambodians may be reluctant to go on record contradicting the government. It would not be unreasonable to fear that voicing disagreement with the weapons confiscation program would be a quick way to have one's home put at the top of the list for searching by the government.
23. John Locke, *Two Treatises of Government* (1690).
24. For a detailed account of how the Khmer Rouge thoroughly disarmed the Cambodian people before beginning the genocide, and how such disarmament almost always is completed before genocide begins, see Aaron Zelman and Richard W. Stevens, *Death by "Gun Control": The Human Cost of Victim Disarmament* (2001). *See also* David B. Kopel, "Book Review: Lethal Laws," *New York Law School Journal of International and Comparative Law,* vol. 15 (1995), 355–98, http://www.davekopel.com/2A/LawRev/lethal.htm.
25. "Japan Provides Aid to Help Cambodia's Small Arms Management," *WorldSources, Inc.,* January 13, 2003, http://static.highbeam.com/x/xinhuachina/january132003/japanprovidesaidtohelpcambodiassmallarmsmanagement/index.html. This program evolved into Japan Assistance Team for Small Arms Management in Cambodia (JSAC) in April 2003. For more, see the JSAC website, http://www.bigpond.com.kh/users/adm.jsac/jsacENG.html.
26. Embassy of Japan, "Signing of Grant Contracts for the Japanese Grant Assistance for Grass-roots Projects (HUSANONE)," Japanese ODA News, March 16, 2001, http://www.bigpond.com.kh/users/eojc/pressrelease/p010315z.htm.
27. "Japan Provides Aid."
28. "Berisha and Nano: Albania's Rivals," *BBC News,* September 13, 1998,

http://news.bbc.co.uk/1/hi/world/europe/170543.stm. "An estimated 90% of Albania's population invested around $2bn in the get-rich-quick schemes, and lost the best part of their money—often their life savings—when the crisis came."

29. Georgios A. Antonopoulos, "Albanian Organized Crime: A View from Greece," *Crime & Just. Int'l*, November/December 2003, 7.

30. Support to Security Sector Reform (SSSR)—The United Nations Development Programme (UNDP), *Albania, Background*, § 1, http://www.undp.org.al/salwc/?background (last visited May 20, 2005); Afrim Krasniqi, "Demilitarizing Communities in Albania," *Choices* (December 2002), 14, http://www.undp.org/dpa/choices/2002/december/Pages14-15.pdf; Chris Smith, *Illegal Arms in Albania and European Security*, Speech at Seminar on Contemporary Arms Control and Disarmament, Geneva, Switzerland, September 16, 1998, http://www.geneva-forum.org/Reports/salw_vol1/19980916.pdf: Between January 1997 and March 1997, "an estimated 750,000–1 million light weapons were stolen from government armories (the OSCE [Organization for Security and Co-Operation in Europe] estimates a figure of 1.5 million). The state lost approximately 80 percent of its weaponry stock, in addition to 1.5 billion pieces of ammunition."

The weapons stolen during the Albanian upheaval were stored in government armories, not in civilian homes and closets; thus, the stolen weapons had been secured under what the antigun activists call "safe-storage" conditions.

The claim is often made by firearm-prohibitionists that civilian gun stocks serve as "piggy-banks" for criminals, and therefore restrictive legislation concerning civilian ownership and use of firearms is necessary to prevent criminal acquisition from civilian sources. For example, Canadian prohibitionist Wendy Cukier has stated, "Diversion of civilian held small arms also fuels the illicit supply." Wendy Cukier, "Small Arms and Light Weapons: A Public Health Approach," *Brown Journal of World Affairs*, vol. 9, no. 1 (2002), 272.

31. Jan Wahlberg, *Weapons for Development: The Economic, Social and Political Context*.

32. United Nations Development Programme, Gramsh Pilot Programme, Weapons in Exchange for Development, Progress Report (February 23, 1999).

33. U.N. Arms Control of a Different Type Gets Promising Results in Albania," Associated Press (August 31, 2002), http://209.157.64.200/focus/f-news/742498/posts.

34. Eric Roman Filipink, "SALW Issues and OSCE Field Missions: The Experience of the Presence in Albania" (Joint Azerbaijani-Swiss Workshop, June 21–22, 2001), http://www.isn.ethz.ch/pfpdc/documents/2001/06-01_baku/filipink.htm.

35. United Nations Development Programme: Albania, *SALWC 2002-2003, Results and Current Situation, Situation after 4 Aug 2002*, http://undp.org.al/salwc/?salwc.

36. UNDP Albania, *Small Arms and Light Weapons Control Project, Background*, 6, http://undp.org.al/salwc/?background.

37. Ibid.

38. Jolyon Naegele, "Albania: Weapons-Collection Program Meets with Mixed Results," Radio Free Europe/Radio Liberty (2001), http://www.rferl.org/nca/features/ 2001/10/10102001111812.asp.

39. Naegele. See also *Socio-Economic Analysis and Impact Assessment*, SALWC Project, Centre for Rural Studies, at 26, http://undp.org.al/salwc/?reports (last visited September 23, 2003). "The main reason for having a weapon is self/family protection for more than 73.7% of the respondents." The researchers explained that although many Albanians said they would be willing to disarm, "many of them

would like to keep one weapon (with the reason to protect himself and his family and business) as the others still have weapons."

40. Human Rights Watch, *Albania, Human Rights Watch World Report 2003*, http://www.hrw.org/wr2k3/europe1.html.

41. Antonopoulos, *Albanian Organized Crime*, 6.

42. Don B. Kates, "Democide and Disarmament," *SAIS Review*, vol. 23 (2003), 305, quoting Alec Wilkinson, "A Changed Vision of God," *New Yorker*, January 24, 1994, 54–55. The case of the Cambodian genocide illustrates how encouraging governments to limit small arms ownership can have terrible consequences. As the killing began, Cambodian soldiers undertook an extraordinary house-to-house search to confiscate the weapons people could have used to defend themselves. A witness recounts that the soldiers would "knock on the doors and ask the people who answered if they had any weapons. 'We are here now to protect you,' the soldiers said, 'and no one has a need for a weapon any more.' People who said that they kept no weapons were [nevertheless] forced to stand aside and allow the soldiers to look for themselves."

43. Moses and Rikha Havini, *Bougainville—The Long Struggle for Freedom.*, http://www.eco-action.org/dt/bvstory.html.

44. Parliament of Australia, Joint Standing Committee on Foreign Affairs, Defence and Trade, "History of the Bougainville Conflict," in *Bougainville: The Peace Process and Beyond*, http://www.aph.gov.au/house/committee/jfadt/bougainville/bv_chap2.htm.

45. Parliament of Australia, *Bougainville*

46. Yauka Aluambo Liria, *Bougainville Campaign Diary* (Melbourne: Indra Press, 1993), 61.

47. David B. Kopel, Paul Gallant, and Joanne D. Eisen, eds., "Firearms Possession by 'Non-State Actors': The Question of Sovereignty," *Texas Review of Law and Politics*, vol. 8, no. 2 (2004), 396, http://www.davekopel.com/2A/LawRev/Non-state-actors.pdf.

48. Plaintiffs' Complaint in class-action lawsuit by Hagens Berman LLP. The federal district court decided that it lacked jurisdiction to hear the case. *Sarei v. Rio Tinto PLC*, 221 F.Supp.2d 1116 (C.D.Cal. 2002). The case is currently on appeal to the Ninth Circuit.

49. Aziz Choudry, "Bougainville—Small Nation, Big Message," *Scoop*, November 21, 2001, http://www.scoop.co.nz/mason/archive/scoop/stories/53/29/ 200111212157.5376f317.html.

50. Parliament of Australia, *Bougainville*.

51. Liria, *Bougainville Campaign Diary*, 191.

52. Amnesty International, *Bougainville: The Forgotten Human Rights Tragedy*, ASA 34/001/1997, February 26, 1997.

53. Kofi Annan, Secretary-General to the United Nations (address, Parliament of Rwanda, Kigali, Rwanda, May 7, 1998). U.N. Press Release SG/SM/6552, AFR/56, May 6, 1998. <http://www.un.org/News/Press/docs/1998/19980506.SGSM6552.html>.

54. Liria, *Bougainville Campaign Diary*, 118–19.

55. Choudry, "Bougainville."

56. Dorothy Hunt, *Conflict in Bougainville—Part 3: Interview with Sam Kauona Sirivi*, June 30, 2000.

57. "PNG and Bougainville Seal Peace After Decade of War," *Sydney Morning Herald*, August 31, 2001, 1.

58. The Rotakas Record: Joint Bougainville Ex-combatants Agreement on Weapons Disposal, May 3, 2001, http://rspas.anu.edu.au/melanesia/PDF/Rotokas-agree-ment-Final.pdf.
59. "Kiwi's Supply Gun Lockers," *P.N.G. Post-Courier*, November 21, 2001.
60. "Kiwi's Supply Gun Lockers."
61. Damien Murphy, "Ona Refuses to Lay Down Arms," *Sydney Morning Herald*, June 11, 1999.
62. Thomas Kilala, "Bougainville Bill Clears First Hurdle," *The National*, January 24, 2002.
63. United Nations Security Council, *Report of the Secretary-General on the United Nations Political Office in Bougainville*, U.N. SCOR S/2003/345, ¶ 16 (2003), http://www.un.dk/doc/s2003345.pdf. "The predecessor of the Bougainville Peace Agreement, the Lincoln Agreement, did call for rehabilitation and reintegration, but this aspect has not kept pace with weapons disposal."); "PMG Out," *P.N.G. Post-Courier*, July 1, 2003 (promised funds for Bougainville development were not provided); "Tanis: Gov't Is Not Serious," *P.N.G. Post-Courier*, February 24, 2004. "The autonomous Bougainville government establishment grant had been used for purposes other than the one it was meant for."
64. Alpers and Twyford, 87.
65. "B'ville Restoration not Moving Ahead," *P.N.G. Post-Courier*, May 29, 2003; "Services Collapse in Bougainville," *P.N.G. Post-Courier*, May 30, 2003.
66. Art. 21, ¶ 3.
67. Art. 25.

CHAPTER SEVEN: United Nations Corruption
1. "What the U.S. Pays the U.N." Eye on the U.N., http://www.eyeontheun.org/facts.asp?1=1&p=15.
2. Annan was Assistant Secretary-General for Peacekeeping Operations from March 1992 through February 1993, Under-Secretary-General for Peacekeeping Operations from March 1993 through December 1996, and Secretary-General from January 1996 to the present.
3. Michael J. Jordan, "U.N. Tackles Sex Abuse by Troops: Changes include a new code of conduct for peacekeepers and monitors within each mission," *Christian Science Monitor*, June 21, 2005.
4. Michael J. Jordan, "Sex charges haunt U.N. forces: In places like Congo and Kosovo, peacekeepers have been accused of abusing the people they're protecting," *Christian Science Monitor*, November 26, 2004.
5. Colum Lynch, "U.N. Faces More Accusations of Sexual Misconduct: Officials Acknowledge 'Swamp' of Problems and Pledge Fixes Amid New Allegations in Africa, Haiti," *Washington Post* (March 13, 2005), A22.
6. Ibid.
7. Jordan, "U.N. Tackles Sex Abuse by Troops."
8. Ibid.
9. Kenneth Cain, Heidi Postlewait, and Andrew Thomson, *Emergency Sex and Other Desperate Measures: A True Story From Hell on Earth* (New York: Miramax Books, 2004), 70.
10. *Human Rights Before and After the Elections*, HRW Index No.: C510, May 1, 1993. See also *An Exchange on Human Rights and Peace-Keeping in Cambodia*, HRW Index No.: C514, September 1, 1993.

11. Lynch, "U.N. Faces More Accusations."

12. Editorial, "Sex and the U.N.: When Peacemakers Become Predators," *N.Y. Sun,* January 11, 2005.

13. Stewart Payne, "Teenagers 'Used for Sex by U.N. in Bosnia,'" *Daily Telegraph* (London), April 25, 2002; Kate Holt, "How the U.N. Was Forced to Tackle Stain on Its Integrity. 'The Independent' was first to reveal the scandal. Kate Holt defied threats to tell the story," *The Independent,* February 11, 2005.

14. U.S. House of Representatives, Committee on International Relations, Subcommittee on Oversight and Investigations, *The Oil-for-Food Program: The Systemic Failure of the United Nations,* 109th Cong., 1st sess., December 7, 2005, 31. [Hereinafter cited as *Systemic Failure.*]

15. Holt, "How the U.N. Was Forced to Tackle Stain on its Integrity."

16. Dore Gold, *Tower of Babble: How the United Nations has Fueled Global Chaos* (N.Y.: Three Rivers Pr., 2005), 10, citing "New Briefs," *Corrieree Della Serra,* (August 24, 2001) (U.N. Wire)(accusations about Ethiopia/Eritrea); *Inter Press Service* (July 26, 2002) (U.N. Commission of Inquiry confirms Mozambique allegations); Dominic Hipkins, "Bosnia Sex Trade Shames U.N.," *Scotland on Sunday* (February 9, 2003) (interview with Madeleine Rees, the U.N. High Commissioner for Human Rights in Bosnia, who made the charges about Bosnian child prostitution, and accused the U.N. of a cover-up).

17. Lynch, "U.N. Faces More Accusations."

18. Jordan, "U.N. Tackles Sex Abuse by Troops"; also, Jordan, "Sex Charges Haunt U.N. Forces."

19. Jordan, "Sex Charges Haunt U.N. Forces"

20. Ibid.

21. Eric Jansson, "Kosovo Raises Concern over U.N. Staff Role," *Financial Times,* September 16, 2005, http://news.ft.com/cms/s/82c34ce4-2622-11da-a4a7-00000e2511c8.html. UNMIK is the United Nations Mission in Kosovo.

22. Cain, et al., 255.

23. Cain, et al., 265–66.

24. *Systemic Failure,* 31; Editorial, "Sex and the U.N."

25. U.N. High Commissioner for Refugees, "Note for Implementing and Operational Partners by UNHCR and Save the Children-UK on Sexual Violence & Exploitation: The Experience of Refugee Children in Guinea, Liberia and Sierra Leone based on Initial Findings and Recommendations from Assessment Mission 22 October–30 November 2001," February 2002, http://www.unhcr.ch/cgi-bin/texis/vtx/partners/opendoc.pdf? See also "U.N. DR Congo Sex Abuses 'On Film,'" *BBC News,* November 23, 2004; Holt, "How the U.N. Was Forced to Tackle Stain on its Integrity."

26. U.N. High Commissioner for Refugees, "UNHCR remedial actions and preventive measures against sexual exploitation and abuse of refugees," October 22, 2002, http://www.unhcr.ch/cgi-bin/texis/vtx/news/opendoc.htm?tbl=NEWS&page=home&id=3db54e985.

27. Lynch, "U.N. Faces More Accusations."

28. U.S. Department of State, "Account Tables," http://www.state.gov/m/rm/rls/iab/2003/7809.htm; U.S. Department of State, "The Budget in Brief: Fiscal Year 2006 Budget Request," February 7, 2004.

29. Holt, "How the U.N. Was Forced to Tackle Stain on its Integrity."

30. "Crisis in the Congo: Sex Charges Roil U.N," *Fox News,* March 3, 2005.

31. Holt, "How the U.N. Was Forced to Tackle Stain on its Integrity."
32. Ibid.
33. Ibid.
34. Emily Wax, "Congo's Desperate 'One-Dollar U.N. Girls': Shunned Teens, Many Raped by Militiamen, Sell Sex to Peacekeepers," *Washington Post*, March 21, 2005, A01.
35. Brian Ross, David Scott, and Rhonda Schwartz, "U.N. Sex Crimes in Congo: Prostitution, Rapes Run Rampant," ABC News Internet Ventures, February 14, 2005. This is a transcript of an ABC News *20/20* report on the Congo.
36. Colum Lynch, "U.N. Says Its Workers Abuse Women in Congo: Report Laments a 'Significant' Incidence of Pedophilia, Prostitution and Rape," *Washington Post*, November 27, 2004, A27.
37. Colum Lynch, "U.N. Sexual Abuse Alleged in Congo: Peacekeepers Accused in Draft Report," *Washington Post*, December 16, 2004, A26.
38. Lynch, "U.N. Says Its Workers Abuse Women."
39. Ibid.; Marc Lacey, "In Congo War, Even Peacekeepers Add to Horror," *New York Times*, December 18, 2004.
40. Lynch, "U.N. Says Its Workers Abuse Women."
41. Ibid.
42. Brian Ross, "Q & A on U.N. Sex Abuse Scandal. ABC News' Chief Investigative Correspondent Responds to Your Questions," February 18, 2005, http://abcnews.go.com/2020/UnitedNations/story?id=512580&page=.
43. Ross, "Q & A on U.N. Sex Abuse Scandal."
44. Ross, et al., "U.N. Sex Crimes in Congo."
45. Editorial, "Sex and the U.N."
46. Editorial, "Sex and the U.N."
47. Editorial, "Sex and the U.N."
48. Editorial, "Sex and the U.N."; Lynch, "U.N. Sexual Abuse Alleged in Congo."
49. Editorial, "Sex and the U.N."
50. Thalif Deen, "Cash Crunch, Sex Abuse Charges Hit U.N. Peacekeeping," *Inter Press Service News Agency*, May 27, 2004.
51. Ross, "Q & A on U.N. Sex Abuse Scandal" (emphasis added).
52. Ross, et al., "U.N. Sex Crimes in Congo."
53. Lynch, "U.N. Says Its Workers Abuse Women."
54. "Comprehensive review of the whole question of peacekeeping operations in all their aspects. Letter dated 24 March 2005 from the Secretary-General to the President of the General Assembly," A/59/710, 59th sess., agenda item 77.
55. Warren Hoge, "Report Finds U.N. Isn't Moving to End Sex Abuse by Peacekeepers," *New York Times*, October 19, 2005; Abby Wisse Schachter, "The Rapes Continue," *New York Post*, October 24, 2005. See also Editorial, "The Worse U.N. Scandal," *New York Times*, October 24, 2005.
56. Evelyn Leopold, "U.N. Told It Ignored Years of Abuse by Peacekeepers," *Reuters*, May 31, 2005. "We, the member states, have refrained, from opening up this subject to public discourse over the last 60 years (because) sentiments of pride, mixed in with a deep sense of embarrassment, have often produced in us only outright denials," Zeid told the council. "And yet almost all countries that have participated in U.N. peacekeeping operations have, at one stage or another, had some reason to feel deeply ashamed over the activities of some of their peacekeepers."

Notes

57. Schachter, "The Rapes Continue."

58. Patrick Goodenough, "U.N. 'Whistleblower' Loses Job," CNSNews.com, December 15, 2004, http://www.cnsnews.com/ForeignBureaus/Archive/200412/FOR20041215b.html. The third author, Heidi Postlewait, has a contract that expires in 2006.

59. Schachter, "The Rapes Continue."

60. U.N. Security Council Resolution 687, April 3, 1991.

61. Most of the information in this section comes from U.S. House of Representatives, Committee on International Relations, Subcommittee on Oversight and Investigations, *The Oil-for-Food Program: The Systemic Failure of the United Nations*, 109th Cong., 1st sess., December 7, 2005.

62. *Systemic Failure*, 10.

63. *Systemic Failure*, 11, citing a confidential interview with a diplomat at the U.N.

64. *Systemic Failure*, 2. See also Ibid., 12–17.

65. Michael Soussen, "The Cash-for-Saddam Program," *Wall St. Journal*, March 8, 2004; Jed Babbin, *Inside the Asylum: Why the United Nations and Old Europe are Worse than You Think* (Wash., D.C.: Regnery, 2004), 24–25. See also *Systemic Failure*, 21–22, citing Rehan Mullick, Testimony before the Committee on International Relations Subcommittee on Oversight and Investigations, March 17, 2005.

66. *Systemic Failure*, 21-22.

67. Judith Miller, "Panel Pegs Illicit Iraq Earnings at $21.3 Billion," *New York Times*, November 16, 2004.

68. Claudia Rosset, "Oil-for-Terror?" *National Review*, April 18, 2004.

69. Gold, 122, citing U.S. General Accounting Office, statement of Joseph A. Christoff, Director, International Affairs and Trade, U.S. Senate, Committee on Foreign Relations, "United Nations: Observations on the Oil-for-Food Program," April 7, 2004.

70. *Systemic Failure*, 9-10, citing "Comprehensive Report of the Special Adviser to the DCI on Iraq's WMD, Section on Regime Intent, 2004," 1 (the "Duelfer Report").

71. *Systemic Failure*, 19.

72. Barbara Slavin, "Scope of Oil-for-Food Fraud 'Overwhelming,'" *USA Today*, November 18, 2005.

73. Gold, 121–22.

74. Gold, 124–25.

75. Gold, 124–25.

76. Editorial, "Kofi Annan's 'Leadership,'" *Washington Times*, April 24, 2005.

77. Editorial, "Kofi Annan's 'Leadership.'"

78. "2,000 Firms 'Paid Oil-for-Food Kickbacks,'" *Daily Telegraph* (London), October 27, 2005.

79. Slavin, "Scope of Oil-for-Food Fraud 'Overwhelming.'"

80. Editorial, "Kofi Annan's 'leadership.'"

81. Francis Harris, "U.N. Investigator Claims Annan Lied About Son's Role," *Daily Telegraph* (London), December 9, 2005.

82. Joseph A. Klein, *Global Deception: The U.N.'s Stealth Assault on America's Freedom* (Los Angeles: World Ahead Publishing, 2005), 25.

83. Harris, "U.N. Investigator."

84. "Annan Says Exoneration by Iraq Oil-for-Food Report 'Great Relief,'" *U.N. News Centre*, March 29, 2005.

85. Harris, "U.N. investigator."

247

86. Harris, "U.N. investigator."

87. *Systemic Failure*, 2–3.

88. Warren Hoge, "U.N. Looking at Charges of Fraud in Procurement," *New York Times*, January 24, 2006.

89. George Russell and Claudia Rosett, "U.N. Procurement Scandal: The Case of the Official Who Never Was," *Fox News*, December 9, 2005, http://www.foxnews.com/story/0,2933,178232,00.html.

90. Claudia Rosett, "Business as Usual: Corruption and Conflicts of Interest at the U.N." *OpinionJournal.com*, October 27, 2005, http://www.opinionjournal.com/columnists/cRosett/?id=110007463.

91. The censors in Annan's office apparently did not know about how Microsoft Word tracks edits made in a document. The *Washington Post* obtained an electronic copy of the Mehlis Report which showed the edits of Annan's staff. The document is available on the *Washington Post* website, at http://www.washingtonpost.com/wp-srv/world/syria/mehlis.report.doc.

92. "Press Conference by Secretary-General Kofi Annan at United Nations Headquarters," *United Nations*, December 14, 1998, http://www.un.org/News/Press/docs/1998/19981214.sgsm6837.r1.html, quoted in Klein, 34.

93. Stewart Stogel, "Staff Blasts Organization," *NewsMax*, June 15, 2004.

94. Peter Dennis, "The U.N., Preying on the Weak," *Washington Post* April 12, 2005, A21.

95. Paul Greenberg, "For the Record: Bill Clinton vs. History," *Jewish World Review*, June 3, 2003, http://www.jewishworldreview.com/cols/greenberg060303.asp.

96. Per Ahlmark, "U.N. Chief's Career Clouded," *Australian*, May 3, 2004, quoted in Gold, 225.

97. Goodenough, "U.N. 'Whistleblower' Loses Job."

CHAPTER EIGHT: United Nations and Genocide

1. The Convention on the Prevention and Punishment of the Crime of Genocide, 78 U.N.T.S. 277, 102 Stat. 3045, October 9, 1948 (adopted by U.N. General Assembly 1948, entered into force 1951).

2. R.J. Rummel, "Democide Since World War II," http://www.hawaii.edu/powerkills/GENOCIDE.ENCY.HTM; Tables 1–5, http://www.hawaii.edu/powerkills/POSTWWII.TAB.GIF; http://www.hawaii.edu/powerkills/WF.CHAP6.HTM; http://www.hawaii.edu/powerkills/POSTWWII.HTM.

3. Ibid.

4. Ibid.

5. Ibid.

6. Most of the information about Rwanda is from Dore Gold, *Tower of Babble: How the United Nations has Fueled Global Chaos* (N.Y.: Three Rivers Press, 2005), 137–54.

7. Jean Hatzfeld, *Machete Season: The Killers in Rwanda Speak*, trans. Linda Coverdale (N.Y.: Farrar, Straus & Giroux, 2005) (1st pub. in France, 2003), 177.

8. Hatzfeld, 179.

9. "Report of the Independent Inquiry Into the Actions of the United Nations During the 1994 Genocide in Rwanda," December 15, 1999, 6–7, http://www.un.org/Docs/journal/asp/ws.asp?m=S/1999/1257.

10. For details see Hatzfeld..

11. Hatzfeld, 91.

12. "Report of the Independent Inquiry into the Actions of the United Nations dur-

ing the 1994 Genocide in Rwanda," December 15, 1999, http://www.fas.org/man/dod-101/ops/war/docs/rwanda_report.htm.

13. Hatzfeld, 57.
14. Joseph A. Klein, *Global Deception: The U.N.'s Stealth Assault on America's Freedom* (L.A.: World Ahead Pub., 2005), 30, citing Associated Press, "Kofi Annan was Aware of Tutsis' Peril," *Pioneer Press* (May 4, 1998), http://geocities.com/CapitolHill/Lobby/4621/rwanda1.html.
15. Thalif Deen, "U.N. Declares War on Small Arms," *Asia Times,* October 1, 2002.
16. U.N. Resolution 713, September 25, 1991, http://www.cco.caltech.edu/~bosnia/natoun/unres713.html.
17. U.N. Charter, art. 51: "Nothing in the present Charter shall impair the inherent right of individual or collective self-defence if an armed attack occurs against a Member of the United Nations."
18. *Summary for the Press,* an authorized summary of the conclusions from the Epilogue of the main report *Srebrenica, a "Safe" Area—Reconstruction, Background, Consequences and Analyses of the Fall of a Safe Area.* "The promise made by U.N. general Morillon in 1993 to the people of Srebrenica that they were under the protection of the U.N. and would not be abandoned. . . . The proclamation of the zone as a safe area created an illusion of security for the population." http://www.srebrenica.nl/en/content_perssamenvatting.htm.
19. Report of the Secretary-General Pursuant to General Assembly Resolution 53/35 (1998): Srebrenica Report (November 30, 1998), http://www.haverford.edu/relg/sells/reports/Unsrebrenicareport.htm.
20. U.N. Resolution 819, S/RES/819, April 16, 1993, http://gopher.undp.org/00/undocs/scd/scouncil/s93/20.
21. *Srebrenica: A Cry from the Grave,* http://www.pbs.org/wnet/cryfromthegrave.
22. For a history of the case, which has been before the I.C.J. in various settings ever since 1993, see http://www.icj-cij.org/icjwww/ipresscom/ipress2004/ipresscom2004-37_bhy_20041208.htm.
23. *Application of the Convention on the Prevention and Punishment of the Crime of Genocide (Bosnia & Herzegovina v. Yugoslavia (Serbia and Montenegro))* (1993) I.C.J. 3 (Request for the Indication of Provisional Measures Order of April 8) [Hereinafter *Bosnia v. Yugoslavia*].
24. *Bosnia v. Yugoslavia,* 438.
25. *Bosnia v. Yugoslavia,* 439–44.
26. *Bosnia v. Yugoslavia,* 501. Craig Scott, "A Memorial for Bosnia: Framework of Legal Arguments Concerning the Lawfulness of the Maintenance of the United Nations Security Council's Arms Embargo on Bosnia and Hercegovina," *Michigan Journal of International Law* 1 (1994), 16.
27. Geraldine Coughlan, "Dutch Felt Srebrenica 'Not Worth Sacrifice,'" *BBC News,* December 6, 2002.
28. Gold, 169.
29. David Rohde, *Endgame: The Betrayal and Fall of Srebrenica* (1997), 179–80. "The 10,000 to 15,000 men gathered in ?u?njari's moonlit fields knew the stakes couldn't be any higher. Only one-third of them were armed. The first groups to leave would have the best chance of survival. The last ones would face Serb troops who could pick and choose when to ambush the Muslims they'd seen coming for days. . . . At midnight, the lead scouts in the column slipped out of the enclave. What would become known as the 'Marathon of Death' had begun." See also Mike

NOTES

O'Connor, "Bosnian Men Tell of Survival Deep in Serb Territory," *New York Times,* April 9, 1996.

30. Laura Silber and Allan Little, *Yugoslavia: Death of a Nation* (New York: Penguin, reprint ed. 1997), 345, 349–50.

31. William Drozdiak, "Milosevic to Stand Trial for Genocide," *Washington Post,* November 24, 2001.

32. Security Council Decides on Phased Lifting of Arms Embargo against Former Yugoslavia by Vote of 14 to None, with Russian Federation Abstaining, U.N. Press Release SC/6127, November 27, 1995, http://www.un.org//News/Press/docs/1995/19951122.sc6127.html.

33. Drozdiak, "Milosevic to Stand Trial for Genocide."

34. U.N. Press Release, August 2, 2001, http://www.un.org/icty/pressreal/p609-e.htm.

35. *Srebrenica: Reconstruction, Background, Consequences and Analyses of the Fall of a Safe Area, Netherlands Institute for War Documentation,* April 10, 2002, http://194.134.65.22/srebrenica.

36. Convention on the Prevention and Punishment of the Crime of Genocide, adopted by Resolution 260 (III)A of the U.N. General Assembly, December 9, 1948.

37. *American College Dictionary* (New York: Random House, 1967 ed.).

38. *Case Study: The Srebrenica Massacre* (July 1995), http://www.gendercide.org/case_srebrenica.html.

39. Report of the Secretary-General Pursuant to General Assembly Resolution 53/35 (1998) Srebrenica Report, ¶¶ 503-04, http://www.haverford.edu/relg/sells/reports/UNsrebrenicareport.htm.

40. John G. Taylor, *East Timor: The Price of Freedom* (London: Zed Books, 1999), 154.

41. Taylor, 158–60.

42. Charles Scheiner (speech, Guns Know No Borders rally, Dag Hammarskjold Plaza, New York, July 17, 2001), http://www.pcug.org.au/~wildwood/01julguns.htm.

43. Andrew Latham, "Light Weapons and Human Security—A Conceptual Overview," *Small Arms Control: Old Weapons, New Issues*, ed. Jayantha Dhanapala, et al. (U.K.: United Nations Institute for Disarmament Research, 1999), 13–14; http://www.unog.ch/unidir/.

44. Letter by James F. Dunnigan to Paul Gallant and Joanne D. Eisen (February 23, 2002), quoted in David B. Kopel, Paul Gallant, and Joanne D. Eisen, "Firearms Possession by 'Non-State Actors': The Question of Sovereignty," *Texas Review of Law and Politics*, vol. 8 (no. 2, 2004), 389.

45. Michael Wagner, "Army in the Way of Freedom," *Sydney Morning Herald,* April 29, 1999.

46. Jonathan Head, "Militia Terror in Timor," *BBC News,* July 10, 1999.

47. Head, "Militia Terror."

48. U.N. Press Release SG/SM/6966, April 23, 1999, http://srch1.un.org/plweb-cgi/fastweb?state_id=1014054694&view=unsearch&numhitsfound=1&query=SG/SM/6966&&docid=581&docdb=pr1999&dbname=web&sorting=BYRELE-VANCE&operator=adj&TemplateName=predoc.tmpl&setCookie=1.

49. U.N. Press Release SG/SM/6980, May 6, 1999, http://srch1.un.org/plweb-cgi/fastweb?state_id=1014054353&view=unsearch&numhitsfound=1&query=SG/SM/6980&&docid=671&docdb=pr1999&dbname=web&sorting=BYRELE-VANCE&operator=adj&TemplateName=predoc.tmpl&setCookie=1.

50. Kopel, et al., "Non-State Actors," 391.

51. U.N. Report of the Secretary General: Question of East Timor, S/1999/862 (August 9, 1999), http://srch1.un.org/plweb cgi/fastweb?state_id=1014 054432&view=unsearch&docrank=1&numhitsfound=5&query=S/1999/862&& docid=97&docdb=screports&dbname=web&sorting=BYRELEVANCE&operator=adj&TemplateName=predoc.tmpl&setCookie=1.

52. U.N. Resolution 1246, S/Res/1246 (June 11, 1999), http://srch1.un.org/plweb-cgi/fastweb?state_id=1014054536&view=unsearch&numhitsfound=1&query=S /RES/1246(1999)&&docid=371&docdb=scres&dbname=web&sorting=BYREL EVANCE&operator=adj&TemplateName=predoc.tmpl&setCookie=1.

53. Mark Dodd, "Fears of Bloodbath Grow as Militias Stockpile Arms," *Sydney Morning Herald,* July 16, 1999, 9.

54. According to UNAMET, 98.6 percent of registered voters did so. Taylor, 228.

55. Janine de Giovanni, "East Timor's Aftermath," *New York Times,* October 24, 1999.

56. Kopel, et al., "Non-State Actors," 392.

57. Seth Mydans, "East Timorese, First Wary, Then Jubilant, Greet U.N. Troops in Village Near Capital" *New York Times,* September 22, 1999.

58. See chapter on U.N. and the Second Amendment.

59. Barbara Frye, "Progress Report on the Prevention of Human Rights Violations Committed with Small Arms and Light Weapons," E/CN.4/Sub.2/2004/37 (2004), paragaph 50, http://www1.umn.edu/humanrts/demo/smallarms2004-2.html.

60. Paul Daley, "Falintil Resists Move to Give Up Weapons," *The Age* (Melbourne), October 6, 1999, 13.

61. Mark Dodd, "Cosgrove Sees Falintil as a Legal Police Force," *Sydney Morning Herald* (December 2, 1999), 10.

62. Mark Dodd, "Viva the Defence Force: Guerilla Veterans Join the Army," *Sydney Morning Herald* (February 2, 2001), 8.

63. http://www.un.org/peace/etimor/untaetR/reg00105E.pdf.

64. Eric Reeves, "Darfur: Genocide Before Our Eyes," in ed. Joyce Apsel, *Darfur: Genocide Before Our Eyes* (New York: Institute for the Study of Genocide, 2005), 29.

65. Alex de Wall, "Counter-Insurgency on the Cheap," *London Review of Books,* August 5, 2004, http://www.lrb.co.uk/v26/n15/waal01_.html.

66. Jay Nordlinger, "About Sudan," *National Review,* May 23, 2005, 39.

67. Scott Straus, "What's In A Name?" 84 Foreign Affairs 123 (January–February 2005); *Darfur Rising: Sudan's New Crisis,* International Crisis Group, Africa Report No. 76, March 25, 2004, http://www.crisisweb.org/home/getfile.cfm ?id=1132&tid=2550, 18–19. The SLA drew its first recruits from Fur self-defence militias that had arisen during the 1987-1989 conflict. The emergence in 2001 of a group of largely Fur and Massaleit fighters in southern and western Darfur coincided with the decision of Zaghawa young men to rebel against the government. The Zaghawa insurgents were unhappy about the government's failure to enforce the terms of a tribal peace agreement requiring nomads of Arab background to pay blood money for killing dozens of Zaghawas, including prominent tribal chiefs. The SLA grew out of this increased cooperation between the Fur, Massaleit and Zaghawa groups. "Massaleit" is spelled in a variety of ways depending on author.

68. *Targeting the Fur: Mass Killings in Darfur,* A Human Rights Watch Paper, January 21, 2005, http://hrw.org/backgrounder/africa/darfur0105/darfur0105.pdf, 6.

69. Stuart Taylor, "Genocide in Darfur: Crime without Punishment?" *National Journal,* February 21, 2005; U.S. State Department Pub. 11182 (September 2004),

http://www.state.gov/g/drl/rls/36028.htm ("The U.N. estimates the violence has affected 2.2 million of Darfur's 6 million residents.") Jonathan Karl, "The Darfur Disaster," *The Weekly Standard,* May 2, 2005; Eric Reeves, "Who is Dying?" *New Republic Online,* July 20, 2005, http://www.tnr.com/etc.mhtml?pid=2732.

70. Roger Sandall, "Can Sudan Be Saved?" *Commentary,* December 2004, 38. Although "Janjaweed" is more commonly used, "Jajaweed" is also used.

71. "Sudan 'Bombing Darfur Villages,'" *BBC News,* January 27, 2005. "The Sudanese air force has bombed villages in Darfur despite agreeing to stop using planes in the war-torn region, aid agencies say."

72. Amnesty International, *Sudan: Arming the Perpetrators of Grave Abuses in Darfur,* (November 16, 2004), ¶ 8, http://web.amnesty.org/library/index/engafr541392004. The president of the JEM, Khalil Ibrahim, stated: "About 90% of our armament comes from what we have captured from Sudanese army barracks." However, arms are readily available to them from other opposition groups.

73. *Sudan: Arming the Perpetrators of Grave Abuses in Darfur,* ¶ 4.1. See also *Sudan— Darfur in Flames: Atrocities in Western Sudan,* Human Rights Watch, vol. 15, no. 5 (April 2004), 19. "Clearly there was SLA presence in certain villages, which provides military justification for the use of force, however the use of force must be proportional . . . to the expected military gain"; *Darfur Rising: Sudan's New Crisis,* International Crisis Group, Africa Report No. 76, March 25, 2004, http://www.crisisweb.org/home/getfile.cfm?id=1132&tid=2550.

74. Straus, "What's In A Name?"

75. "New Clashes Break out in Darfur," *BBC News,* July 25, 2005. "Last week, the commander of the African Union peacekeeping force in Darfur, Festus Okonkwo, told the BBC that there had been no major attacks in the region since January and that there had also been a reduction in attacks on villages. But US aid official Andrew Natsios said this was chiefly because there were no villages left to burn down."

76. *Sudan: Arming the Perpetrators of Grave Abuses in Darfur,* ¶ 4.1.

77. *Sudan—Darfur in Flames.* The Human Rights Watch report also noted: "In yet another telling example of the government's refusal to provide security for civilians, a number of tribal leaders of the Fur, Zaghawa and Masaalit communities reportedly made repeated attempts to inform government authorities of the grave abuses taking place. They appealed to the highest levels of government in Khartoum. They presented documented cases of violations, with no response. In at least one case, the Sudanese government warned the Darfurian representative to stop his appeals." Jan Pronk, the U.N. Secretary-General's Special Representative for Sudan stated: "Those responsible for atrocious crimes on a massive scale go unpunished. . . . The government has not stopped them." See generally, *Targeting the Fur: Mass Killings in Darfur,* A Human Rights Watch Paper, January 21, 2005, http://hrw.org/backgrounder/africa/darfur0105/darfur0105.pdf. (Summary: "To date, the Sudanese government has neither improved security for civilians nor ended the impunity enjoyed by its own officials and allied militia leaders.")

78. Judy Aita, "Brutal Attacks Still Occurring in Darfur, United Nations Reports," States News Service, May 12, 2005.

79. Eric Reeves, "Darfur Mortality Update: April 30, 2005," *Sudan Tribune* May 1, 2005.

80. Amnesty International *Sudan: Arms Trade Fuelling Human Rights Abuse in Darfur,* November 16, 2004, http://web.amnesty.org/library/index/engafr5414 22004. Egeland made the statement on July 1, 2004.

81. Ibid.

82. S/Res./1556, U.N. SCOR (July 30, 2004), ¶ 7, http://www.un.org/News/Press/docs/2004/sc8160.doc.htm.

83. *Sudan: Arming the Perpetrators of Grave Abuses in Darfur*. The Amnesty report additionally notes that "Oil now accounts for more than 11% of Sudan's Gross Domestic Product (GDP)." Ibid., ¶ 9.1. Furthermore, the report noted: "Sudan's oil wealth has played a major part in enabling an otherwise poor country to fund the expensive bombers, helicopters and arms supplies which have allowed the Sudanese government to launch aerial attacks on towns and villages and fund militias to fight its proxy war." Ibid., ¶ 9.2.

84. *Sudan: Arming the Perpetrators of Grave Abuses in Darfur*, ¶ 6.

85. Catherine Flew and Angus Urquhart, *Strengthening Small Arms Controls: An Audit of Small Arms Control In the Great Lakes Region and the Horn of Africa*, Safer Africa and Safer World, February 2004, http://www.saferworld.co.uk/publications/Horn%20narrative%20report.pdf.

86. U.S. State Dept. Pub. 11182 (September 2004), http://www.state.gov/g/drl/rls/36028.htm.

    Peter Verney, editor of London-based Sudan Update, describes "the government policy of selectively arming tribesmen while removing the weapons of the farmers, the Fur, Masalit and Zaghawa." Moreover, "Since 2001, Darfur has been governed under central government decree, with special courts to try people suspected of illegal possession or smuggling of weapons, murder and armed robbery. The security forces have misused these powers for arbitrary and indefinite detention." Peter Verney, "Darfur's Manmade Disaster," *Middle East Report Online*, July 22, 2004, http://www.merip.org/mero/mero072204.html. See also *Sudan: Arming the Perpetrators of Grave Abuses in Darfur*, ¶ 2, http://web.amnesty.org/library/index/engafr541392004. "Special Courts set up under a state of emergency declared in Darfur in 2001 . . . have been handing down summary justice after flagrantly unfair trials.")

87. See generally, *Sudan: Arming the Perpetrators*. See also *Armed Conflicts Report 2004*, Project Ploughshares, Sudan-Darfur, January 2004, http://www.ploughshares.ca/content/ACR/ACR00/ACR00-SudanDarfur.html. "The Jajaweed and other Arab militias are alleged to have been armed by the Sudanese government, previously in order to fight against the Sudan People's Liberation Army (SPLA), and recently to engage non-Arab populations in Darfur"; Verney: "One directive from February 2004, evoking the authority of President Omar Bashir, calls upon Darfur security heads to step up 'the process of mobilizing loyalist tribes and providing them with sufficient armory to secure the areas.'"

88. *Targeting the Fur: Mass Killings in Darfur*, A Human Rights Watch Paper, January 21, 2005, http://hrw.org/backgrounder/africa/darfur0105/darfur0105.pdf, 22. Among the recommendations of Human Rights Watch was that the Government of Sudan, "Clearly and unequivocally state that no one is entitled to retain or use any land illegally acquired during the conflict. A temporary measure interdicting any permanent land transfers should also be put in place." See generally, Amnesty International, *Sudan: Darfur: Rape as a Weapon of War: Sexual Violence and its Consequences*, AI Index: AFR 54/076/2004, July 19, 2004, http://web.amnesty.org/library/index/engafr540762004.

89. *Sudan: Arming the Perpetrators*, ¶ 6.

90. Ibid., ¶ 6.2.

91. Ibid.

92. *Targeting the Fur*, 8.

93. Dimitri Vassilaros, "Gun Control's Best Friend," *Pittsburgh Tribune-Review*, April 1, 2005. The official was Bill Garvelink, Acting Assistant Administrator of the Bureau for Democracy, Conflict, and Humanitarian Development, which is part of the U.S. Agency for International Development.

94. The official was Trish Katyoka, director of Africa Advocacy for Amnesty International. Unlike many other human rights groups, Amnesty International has never officially used the word *genocide* to describe the Darfur situation.

95. Reeves, "Darfur Mortality Update," whole article.

96. Ibid., 37.

97. Ibid., 46.

98. Ibid., 45.

99. Eric Reeves, "Khartoum Triumphant: Managing the Costs of Genocide in Darfur," December 17, 2005, http://www.sudanreeves.org/index.php?name=News&file=article&sid=81.

100. "A Working Formula for Arms Management and Reduction," in *Small Arms and Lights Weapons: Legal Aspects of National and International Regulations*; vol. 4 *Arms Control and Disarmament Law*. eds. Erwin Dahinden, Julie Dahlitz, and Nadia Fischer (Geneva: United Nations, 2002) (Sales no. G.V.E.02.0.4), 145 (emphasis added).

CHAPTER NINE: More Gun Control for Genocide Victims

1. Nairobi Secretariat on Small Arms, The Nairobi Protocol for the Prevention, Control and Reduction of Small Arms and Light Weapons in the Great Lakes Region and the Horn of Africa (Nairobi, Kenya). See also Ramazani Baya, Minister of Foreign Affairs and International Cooperation Democratic Republic of the Congo, "Editorial," *Progress,* June 2005, 1 (newsletter of the Nairobi Secretariat, Saferworld, and the Security Research and Information Centre).

2. Nairobi Protocol, art. 23.

3. Nairobi Protocol, art. 3(c).

4. Nairobi Protocol, arts. 5(b)(i), 9, 12, 13.

5. Protocol on the Control of Firearms, Ammunition and Other Related Materials in the Southern African Development Community (SADC) Region.

6. The nations are Angola, Botswana, Congo, Lesotho, Malawi, Mauritius, Mozambique, Namibia, Seychelles, South Africa, Swaziland, Tanzania, Zambia, and Zimbabwe. One measure of corruption is the Corruption Perception Index compiled every year by Transparency International. Using objective criteria, nations are rated on a scale from 1 to 10, with 10 being the least corrupt. In the 2005 CPI, Iceland scored at the top, with a 9.7 rating; the United States was 17th, with a 7.6. In sub-Saharan Africa, the target of the U.N. antigun regional treaties, the highest scores were Botswana (5.9), South Africa (4.5), Namibia (4.3), Mauritius (4.0), and Seychelles (4.0). Every other country in sub-Saharan Africa was below 4.0, indicating extreme and pervasive corruption. The 2005 survey is available at http://www.transparency.org/.

7. David B. Kopel, Paul Gallant, and Joanne D. Eisen, "Microdisarmament: The Consequences for Public Safety and Human Rights," *UMKC Law Review*, vol. 73 (2005), 1003–09, (Mali), http://www.davekopel.com/2A/Foreign/Micro Disarmament.pdf; David B. Kopel, "U.N. Gives Tyranny a Hand," *National*

Notes

Review Online, August 6, 2001, (Niger), http://www.nationalreview.com/kopel/kopel080601.shtml.

8. Gregory H. Stanton, "Eight Stages of Genocide" (speech, Yale University Center for International and Area Studies, 1998), http://www.genocidewatch.org/8stages.htm. Written in 1996 while at the Department of State.

9. http://www.genocidewatch.org/CotedIvoireGenocideWatch.htm.

10. Genocide Watch, "Crisis in Côte d'Ivoire,"
http://www.guinea-forum.org/Analyses/index.asp?ana=26&Lang=A

11. Mark Huband, "Liberia," Crimes of War, http://www.crimesofwar.org/thebook/liberia.html.

12. Haruna Bahago, "Don't Turn Other Cheek, says Nigerian Archbishop," *The Independent* (London), November 29, 2002.

13. Dennis C. Jett, *Why Peacekeeping Fails* (New York: Palgrave Macmillan, 2001), xii.

14. Kenneth Roth, *International Injustice: The Tragedy of Sierra Leone*, Human Rights Watch, http://www.hrw.org/editorials/2000/ken-sl-aug.htm.

15. The report is available at http://www.freedomhouse.org/. Free: Benin, Botswana, Cape Verde, Ghana, Lesotho, Mali, Mauritius, Namibia, Senegal, South Africa.

    Partly free: Congo (Brazzaville), Djibouti, Ethiopia, Gabon, The Gambia, Guinea-Bissau, Kenya, Liberia, Madagascar, Malawi, Mozambique, Niger, Nigeria, Seychelles, Sierre Leone, Tanzania, Uganda, Zambia.

    Not Free: Angola, Brunei, Burkina Faso, Burundi, Cameroon, Central African Republic, Chad, Congo (Kinshasa), Cote d'Ivoire, Equatorial Guinea, Eritrea, Guinea, Mauritania, Rwanda, Somalia, Sudan, Swaziland, Togo, Zimbabwe.

16. The Convention on the Prevention and Punishment of the Crime of Genocide, 78 U.N.T.S. 277, 102 Stat. 3045, October 9, 1948, adopted by U.N. General Assembly 1948, entered into force 1951, ratified by United States 1981.

17. Genocide Convention, art. I (emphasis added). The affirmative duty is consistent with the long-established duty in Jewish law and in Napoleonic Codes for an individual to act to rescue another person in danger. *E.g.,* Code Pén., art. 434–1 (France); David B. Kopel. "The Torah and Self-Defense," 109 *Penn State Law Review* 17 (2004), http://www.davekopel.com/2A/LawRev/The-Torah-and-Self-defense.pdf.

18. *Application of the Convention on the Prevention and Punishment of the Crime of Genocide (Bosnia and Hercegovina v. Yugoslavia (Serbia and Montenegro), Further Requests for the Indication of Provisional Measures,* ICJ Reports 325, 443–44, September 13, 1993.

19. *Prosecutor v. Akayesu,* case no. ICTR-96-4-T, Judgment September 2, 1998, ¶ 731.

20. William A. Schabas, *Genocide In International Law* (Cambridge University Press: 2000), 170–71, citing *United States of America v. von Weizaecker at al.* ("Ministeries Case"), 14 T.W.C. 314, 557-58 (United States Military Tribunal, 1948). Government cuts in special food rations applied only to Jews, and not to general German population, but cuts were not a form of genocide, because they were not so severe as to cause sickness or death.

21. Notably, the Genocide Convention abrogates the Head of State immunity, which applies in most other applications of international law. Genocide Convention, art. IV; *A-G Israel v. Eichmann,* 36 I.L.R. 18, para. 28 (Dist. Ct., Jerusalem, 1968); *A-G Israel v. Eichmann,* 36 I.L.R. 277, ¶ 14 (S. Ct. 1968); *Prosecutor v. Blaskic* (Case No. IT-95-14-AR108*bis*), *Judgment on the Request of the Republic of Croatia for Review of the Decision of Trial Chamber II of July 18, 1997,* ¶ 41

NOTES

(October 29, 1997); Schabas, 316. Given that the Genocide Convention explicitly abrogates one of the most well-established principles of general international law, it would hardly be surprising that the Convention also abrogates, by implication, some forms of ordinary internal state authority, such as the power to set standards for food rations, medical rations, or arms possession.

22. Universal Declaration of Human Rights, G.A. Res. 217 A (III), U.N. Doc A/810, art. 3.

23. Universal Declaration of Human Rights, G.A. Res. 217 A (III), U.N. Doc A/810, art. 3; International Covenant on Civil and Political Rights, 999 U.N.T.S. 171, 1976, art. 6; Convention for the Protection of Human Rights and Fundamental Freedoms, 213 U.N.T.S. 221, E.T.S. 5, 1955, art. 2; American Convention on Human Rights, 1144 U.N.T.S. 123; O.A.S.T.S. 36, 1979, art. 4.

24. Universal Declaration, art. 3.

25. Convention for the Protection of Human Rights and Fundamental Freedoms, 213 U.N.T.S. 221, E.T.S. 5, 1955), art. 2 (2); Gilbert Guillaume, "Article 2," in Louis-Edmond Pettiti, Emmanuel Decaux & Pierre-Henri Imbert, *La Convention Européenne des Droits de l'Homme: Commentaire Article par Article 152* (Paris: Economica, 2d ed. 1999). *See also* M. Cherif Bassiouni, *A Draft International Criminal Code and Draft Statute for an International Criminal Tribunal* (Boston: Martinus Nijhoff, 1987), 109-10 (right to self-defense recognized in model code written by leading scholar of international criminal and human rights law, who serves as President of the International Human Rights Law Institute, as President of the International Institute of Higher Studies in Criminal Sciences, and as President of the International Association of Penal Law).

26. Rome Statute of the International Criminal Court, U.N. Doc. A/CONF.183/9, art. 31.

27. Universal Declaration of Human Rights.

28. Johannes Morsink, *The Universal Declaration of Human Rights: Origins, Drafting & Intent* (Philadelphia: University of Pennsylvania Press: 1999), 307–12.

29. Ibid.

30. *Cf. Bivens v. Six Unknown Named Agents of the Federal Bureau of Narcotics*, 403 U.S. 388 (1971) ("where federally protected rights have been invaded, it has been the rule from the beginning that courts would be alert to adjust their remedies so as to grant the necessary relief.").

31. The rights in the Universal Declaration's Articles 1-3, including the right to armed self-defense as a last-resort defense of other rights, clearly belong to individuals:

Article 1. All human beings are born free and equal in dignity and rights. They are endowed with reason and conscience and should act toward one another in a spirit of brotherhood.

Article 2. Everyone is entitled to all the rights and freedoms set forth in this Declaration, without distinction of any kind, such as race, colour, sex, language, religion, political or other opinion, national or social origin, property, birth or other status. Furthermore, no distinction shall be made on the basis of the political, jurisdictional or international status of the country or territory to which a person belongs, whether it be independent, trust, non-self-governing, or under any other limitation of sovereignty.

Article 3. Everyone has the right to life, liberty, and security of person.

32. *United States v. Cruikshank*, 92 U.S. 542, 551-53 (1875) (quoting *Gibbons v.*

Ogden (22 U.S., 9 Wheat., 1824). The "civilized man" quote comes from the court's discussion of the right to assemble; the right to arms discussion follows immediately, and adopts the same reasoning as the right to assembly analysis. For a more detailed analysis of *Cruikshank*, see David B. Kopel, "The Supreme Court's Thirty-five Other Second Amendment Cases." 18 *St. Louis Univ. Public Law Review* 99, 177 (1999), http://www.davekopel.com/2A/LawRev/35FinalPart One.htm.

33. William Blackstone, *Commentaries*, vol. 1 (1765), 143–44.
34. Abram L. Sachar, *The Redemption of the Unwanted* (New York: St. Martin's/Marek, 1983).
35. V. V. Stanciu, "Reflections on the Congress for the Prevention of Genocide," in ed. Livia Rothkirchen, *Yad Vashem Studies on the European Jewish Catastrophe and Resistance*, vol. 7 (Jerusalem: Yad Vashem, 1968), 187.
36. Samuel C. Wheeler, III, "Arms as Insurance," *Public Affairs Quarterly*, vol. 13, no. 1 (April 1999), 121.
37. E-mail from anonymous U.S. Soldier to Dave Kopel (January 2003) (on file with author).

CHAPTER TEN: The U.N. and Terrorism

1. U.S. Department of State, "State Sponsors of Terrorism," www.state.gov/s/ct/ c14151.htm. The dates on which government was designated a state sponsor of terrorism are: Cuba, March 1, 1982; Iran, January 19, 1984; Libya, December 29, 1979; North Korea, January 20, 1988; Sudan, August 12, 1993; Syria, December 29, 1979. For an in-depth report on Syria's sponsorship of terrorism, see Reuven Ehrlich, *Terrorism as a Preferred Instrument of Syrian Policy*, Institute for Counter-Terrorism, www.ict.org.il/inter_ter/st_terror/syrian_terror.htm.
2. Terrorist states on the Security Council include: Cuba (1990–91), Libya (1976–77), and Syria (2002–03).
3. "Bin Laden 'Received U.N. Cash,'" *BBC*, October 20, 2001, news.bbc.co.uk/ 1/hi/world/middle_east/1610214.stm.
4. "Muwafaq" is Arabic for "blessed relief." "Bin Laden 'Received U.N. Cash.'" The BBC reported that the U.N. had delivered $1.4 million to a consortium of Sudanese "charities." The article did not specify how much was delivered to Muwafaq.
5. "Bin Laden 'Received U.N. cash.'"
6. Rachel Ehrenfeld, "The Saudi Buck Stops Here," *FrontPageMagazine.com*, March 3, 2005, www.frontpagemag.com/Articles/authors.asp?ID=579. Note the editors' addendum at the end of Ehrenfeld's article. She is the author of a well-known book on terrorist money laundering: "Since this was written in October 2004, Khalid bin Mahfouz [a Saudi was a ringleader in terrorist funding] was handed a [libel] judgment by default against Dr. Ehrenfeld by the same British judge that awarded him many similar judgments. Advised by her lawyers, rather than litigate with KBM (who is a defendant in most of the 9/11 lawsuits) in an unfavorable forum with libel laws antithetical to the First Amendment, Dr. Ehrenfeld has counter-sued KBM in New York's Federal Court, in what is an important legal precedent. She seeks, through innovative and novel legal procedure, to establish a precedent for all journalists and writers against libel forum shopping in British courts. The Saudi's actions deprive us of our First Amendment right to publicize their activities in support of terrorism and, in fact, constitute a new form of

terrorism in itself. In addition to winning the freedom of the American press to investigate and report fairly and responsibly on one of the most important public issues of our time–the funding of international terrorism—Dr. Ehrenfeld's lawsuit will make KBM's support of Al-Qaeda and HAMAS a matter of public record and will help all the 9/11 victims' families who are suing him.—The Editors."

7. "Bin Laden 'Received U.N. Cash.'"

8. Ibid.

9. Eric Shawn, "Did Terrorists Benefit From Oil-for-Food?" *Fox News,* September 23, 200), www.foxnews.com/story/0,2933,133212,00.html.

10. Stephen Hayes, "Saddam's Terror Training Camps," *Weekly Standard,* January 6, 2006, weeklystandard.com/Content/Public/Articles/000/000/006/550kmbzd.asp.

11. Claudia Rossett, "The Buck Still Hasn't Stopped," *Weekly Standard,* October 3, 2005, www.weeklystandard.com/Content/Public/Articles/000/000/006/118nzmcw.asp ?pg=1

12. "Excerpts: Annan Interview," *BBC News,* September 16, 2004.

13. E.g, Allan H. Meltzer, "New Mandates for the IMF and World Bank," *Cato Journal,* vol. 25, no. 1 (Winter 2005), 13–16, www.cato.org/pubs/journal/ cj25n1/cj25n1-2.pdf; Ana I. Eiras, *Time for the International Monetary Fund and World Bank to Reconsider the Strategy for Millennium Development Goals,* Heritage Foundation Backgrounder, no. 1880 (Washington, D.C., September 16, 2005), www.heritage.org/Research/TradeandForeignAid/bg1880.cfm; Ana Isabel Eiras and Brett D. Schaefer, *A Blueprint for Paul Wolfowitz at the World Bank,* Heritage Foundation Backgrounder, no. 1856 (Washington, D.C., June 2, 2005), www.heritage.org/Research/TradeandForeignAid/bg1856.cfm; Ana I. Eiras, *IMF and World Bank Intervention: A Problem, Not a Solution,* Heritage Foundation Backgrounder, no. 1689 (Washington, D.C., September 17, 2003), www.her-itage.org/Research/InternationalOrganizations/bg1689.cfm. President George W. Bush nominated Paul Wolfowitz, a strong opponent of terrorism, to be President of the World Bank, and he was unanimously approved by that body's Board of Executive Directors on March 31, 2005. I hope that Mr. Wolfowitz manages to turn the World Bank around, but he faces enormous powers of iner-tia and bureaucracy.

14. Brett D. Schaefer, *Stop Subsidizing Terrorism,* Heritage Foundation Backgrounder, no. 1485 (October 4, 2001), www.heritage.org/Research/ NationalSecurity/ BG1485.cfm.

15. Schaefer, *Stop Subsidizing Terrorism.*

16. Itamar Marcus, "World Bank Indirect Funding of Suicide Terror," *Palestinian Media Watch Bulletin,* April 2, 2004, www.pmw.org.il/Latest%20bulletin.html# worldbank. Among the terrorists who came straight from a Palestinian college or university are:

Bir Zeit University:

Mahmud Shuraytakh: Chairman of the campus chapter of Hamas of the Student Council. Organized the September 19, 2002, terror attack on Tel Aviv bus which killed six and injured 71 victims.

Ihab Abdul-Qadir Mahmud Abu Salim: Member of the Hamas student chapter. Murdered 8 people and injured 20 in a terrorist attack Zerifin on September 9, 2003.

Daya Muhammad Hussein Al-Tawil: Member of the Hamas student chap-ter. Injured 29 people in a terrorist attack in Jerusalem on March 27, 2001, in which 29 Israelis were injured.

Ramiz Ubaid: Member of the Islamic Jihad student chapter. Perpetrated a terrorist attack killing 13 and injuring 118 in Tel Aviv on March 3, 1996.

Al-Najah University:

Hamid Abu Hajlah: Member of the Hamas student chapter. Injured three victims in a terrorist attack in Netanya on January 1, 2001.

Muhammad Al-Rul: Hamas activist. Murdered 19 and injured 42 in a Jerusalem terrorist attack on June 18, 2002.

Al-Quds Open University:

Ramiz Abu Salim: Hamas student activist. Murdered seven Israelis and injured about 20 in a terrorist attack on Jerusalem on September 9, 2003.

17. Marcus, "World Bank Indirect Funding of Suicide Terror."
18. Ibid.
19. Ibid.
20. David B. Kopel, "Tragedy in Africa Gets Scant Notice," *Rocky Mountain News/Denver Post,* June 18, 2005; David B. Kopel, "Dailies Ignoring Zimbabwe Crisis," *Rocky Mountain News/Denver Post,* September 1, 2002); David B. Kopel, Paul Gallant, and Joanne D. Eisen, "Ripe for Genocide: Disarmament endangers Zimbabwe," *National Review Online,* February 13, 2001, www.davekopel.com/NRO/2001/Ripe-for-Genocide.htm.
21. United Nations Watch, *Jean Ziegler's Campaign Against America: A Study of the Anti-American Bias of the U.N. Special Rapporteur on the Right to Food* (Geneva: October 2005), www.unwatch.org/pdf_files/Jean_Ziegler's_Campaign_Against_America.pdf.
22. With respect to Sudan, by contrast, Darfur is merely a cause for grave concern; the Khartoum regime has only "allegedly" perpetrated atrocities. "Eight U.N. Human Rights Experts Gravely Concerned About Reported Widespread Abuses In Darfur, Sudan," U.N. Press Release, AFR/873, HR/CN/1065, March 29, 2004.
23. "Jean Ziegler s'attaque aux Etats-Unis, au FMI et a l'OMC," *SDA,* January 27, 2003, cited in *Jean Ziegler's Campaign Against America.*
24. Swiss Radio International, "U.N. Swiss Envoy Warns of Apocalyptic Consequences of U.S. Strikes on Afghanistan," *Swissinfo,* September 22, 2001, cited in *Jean Ziegler's Campaign Against America.*
25. In February 2003, Mr. Ziegler publicly stated that war in Iraq should be avoided at all costs, and even proposed that Switzerland offer exile to Saddam Hussein. "Swiss rights campaigner urges Swiss exile for Saddam," *Agence France Presse—English,* February 5, 2003. By April 2003, he was accusing Coalition forces of violating the rights to food and water in Iraq. "U.N. expert de l'ONU denonce les violations du droit a l'alimentation en Irak," *Agence France Presse,* April 3, 2003; "U.N. Rights Expert Demands Aid Agencies Get Access to Feed Iraqis," *Agence France Presse—English,* April 3, 2003, cited in *Jean Ziegler's Campaign Against America.* Also, "Nearly Twice as Many Iraqi Children Going Hungry Since Saddam's Ouster, U.N. Expert Says," *Associated Press,* March 30, 2005, cited in *Jean Ziegler's Campaign Against America* (condemning coalition forces, but not insurgents, for causing malnutrition in Iraq, while only expressing "concern" about hunger in other countries, including Sudan and North Korea).
26. Nat Hentoff, "U.N. Hypocrisy on Human Rights," *Washington Times,* February 13, 2006.
27. *Jean Ziegler's Campaign Against America.*

28. Ibid

29. Ibid. Magazine's website is www.empire-americain.com *and* www.unwatch.org/pdf_files/Lempire2004.pdf.

30. Aaron Goldstein, "Kofi Annan's Double Talk On Terrorism," *American Daily,* March 14, 2005, www.americandaily.com/article/7101.

31. United Nations Security Council, *Security Council,* Resolution 1559, S/RES/1559, September 2, 2004, cited on www.eyeontheun.org/documents-item.asp?d=269&id=418.

32. Aaron Goldstein, "Kofi Annan's Double Talk On Terrorism," *American Daily* (March 14, 2005), www.americandaily.com/article/7101.

33. "U.N. Delays Disarming Of Hizbullah," *The Media Line* (April 07, 2005), www.themedialine.org/news/news_detail.asp?NewsID=9649.

34. Goldstein, "Kofi Annan's Double Talk On Terrorism" Kofi Annan, "A Global Strategy for Fighting Terrorism," Keynote Address to the Closing Plenary of the International Summit on Democracy, Terrorism and Security (Madrid, Spain: March 10, 2005), www.eyeontheun.org/assets/attachments/documents/a_global_strategy_for_fighting_terrorism—annan—madrid.doc.

35. Benny Avni, "Annan Envoy Visits Hezbollah Leader," *New York Sun,* February 18, 2005.

36. Aluf Benn, "Israel Accuses U.N. of Collaborating with Hezbollah," *Haaretz,* September 11, 2005.

37. Ibid.

38. Ibid.

39. Ibid.

40. Koret, "U.N. Soldiers Reportedly Helped Hizbullah Kidnap Israelis."

41. Ibid.

42. Ibid.

43. Ibid.

44. "Investigation onto U.N. Handling of Video Launched," *ICEJ News,* July 23, 2001, (International Christian Embassy Jerusalem).

45. Ibid.

46. Ibid.

47. House Resolution 191, Cong. Rec. H4814.

48. "U.N to Release Mideast Kidnap Tape," CNN, July 7, 2001, archives.cnn.com/2001/WORLD/meast/07/07/mideast.unvid/.

49. Michelle Malkin, "The Ambulances-for-Terrorists Scandal," Townhall.com, June 2, 2004, www.townhall.com/opinion/columns/michellemalkin/2004/06/02/11886.html; *Terrorist Organizations Exploit UNRWA Vehicles,* Intelligence and Terrorism Information Center at the Center for Special Studies, May 2004, www.eyeontheun.org/assets/attachments/articles/444_terrorist_organizations_exploit_unrwa_vehicles.doc

50. Arlene Kushner, "U.N. Dollars for Terror," FrontPageMagazine.com, August 18, 2004.

51. Kushner, "U.N. Dollars for Terror"; Malkin, "Ambulances."

52. Malkin, "Ambulances."

53. David R. Sands, "Annan Aide Defends Rental from Bush Foe Soros," *Washington Times,* June 22, 2005; "Annan Staffer Defends Soros Role in U.N. Housing Fuss," Newsmax, June 24, 2005, www.newsmax.com/archives/ic/2005/6/24/85625.shtml.

54. Schaefer, *Stop Subsidizing Terrorism.*
55. Dore Gold, "The U.N. at Work: The World body Gives Financial Support to Hamas," OpinionJournal (*Wall Street Journal*), January 22, 2005, www.opinion-journal.com/extra/?id=110006194; "U.N. Funds Palestinian Campaign," Fox News, August 17, 2005, www.foxnews.com/story/0,2933,165893,00.html; Benny Avni, "Despite Israeli Alerts, U.N. Transfers Thousands to Hamas Affiliates," *New York Sun,* January 28, 2005.
56. Ibid.
57. Edith M. Lederer, "Palestinian Banners Fuel U.N. Dispute," *Washington Post,* August 17, 2005; Jacob Gershman, "United Nations Bankrolled Latest Anti-israel Propaganda," *New York Sun,* August 17, 2005; James Bennet, "The Gaza Withdrawal: The Residents," *New York Times,* August 15, 2005, A1, A8; "U.N. Funds 'Palestinian' Victory Banners," *Jerusalem Newswire,* August 17, 2005, www.jnewswire.com/library/article.php?articleid=632.
58. "U.N. funds 'Palestinian' Victory Banners."
59. Gershman, "United Nations Bankrolled Latest Anti-israel Propaganda" (quoting Amy Goldstein of B'nai Brith).
60. An FTO is designated by the State Department's Coordinator for Counterterrorism, pursuant to section 219 of the Immigration and Naturalization Act. A designated FTO must meet three conditions: It must be a foreign organization; it must engage in terrorism or terrorist activity; and it must threaten U.S. citizens or U.S. national defense, foreign policy, or economic interests. U.S. Dept. of State, Office of Counterterrorism, Foreign Terrorist Organizations (FTOs), Fact Sheet (Wash., D.C., October 11, 2005) www.state.gov/s/ct/rls/fs/37191.htm. According to United States law (8 U.S. Code sect 1182(a)(3)(B)(iii)) the definition of "terrorist activity" is: "any activity which is unlawful under the laws of the place where it is committed (or which, if committed in the United States, would be unlawful under the laws of the United States or any State) and which involves any of the following:

    (I) The highjacking or sabotage of any conveyance (including an aircraft, vessel, or vehicle).

    (II) The seizing or detaining, and threatening to kill, injure, or continue to detain, another individual in order to compel a third person (including a governmental organization) to do or abstain from doing any act as an explicit or implicit condition for the release of the individual seized or detained.

    (III) A violent attack upon an internationally protected person (as defined in section 1116(b)(4) of title 18, United States Code) or upon the liberty of such a person.

    (IV) An assassination.

    (V) The use of any—

        (b) explosive, firearm, or other weapon or dangerous device (other than for mere personal monetary gain), with intent to endanger, directly or indirectly, the safety of one or more individuals or to cause substantial damage to property.

    (VI) A threat, attempt, or conspiracy to do any of the foregoing."

    To "engage in terrorist activity" includes not just to perform the terrorist act itself, but also assisting in the planning and fund-raising for the terrorist act (8 U.S. Code sect 1182(a)(3)(B)(iv):

    "Engage in Terrorist Activity" Defined

NOTES

As used in this chapter, the term 'engage in terrorist activity' means in an individual capacity or as a member of an organization–

(I) to commit or to incite to commit, under circumstances indicating an intention to cause death or serious bodily injury, a terrorist activity;

(II) to prepare or plan a terrorist activity;

(III) to gather information on potential targets for terrorist activity;

(IV) to solicit funds or other things of value for–

(aa) a terrorist activity;

(bb) a terrorist organization described in clause (vi)(I) or (vi)(II); or

(cc) a terrorist organization described in clause (vi)(III), unless the solicitor can demonstrate that he did not know, and should not reasonably have known, that the solicitation would further the organization's terrorist activity;

(V) to solicit any individual–

(aa) to engage in conduce otherwise described in this clause;

(bb) for membership in terrorist organization described in clause (vi)(I) or (vi)(II); or

(cc) for membership in a terrorist organization described in clause (vi)(III), unless the solicitor can demonstrate that he did not know, and should not reasonably have known, that the solicitation would further the organization's terrorist activity; or

(VI) *to commit an act that the actor knows, or reasonably should know, affords material support, including a safe house, transportation, communications, funds, transfer of funds or other material financial benefit,* false documentation or identification, weapons (including chemical, biological, or radiological weapons), explosives, or training–

(aa) for the commission of a terrorist activity;

(bb) to any individual who the actor knows, or reasonably should know, has committed or plans to commit a terrorist activity;

(cc) to a terrorist organization described in clause (vi)(I) or (vi)(II); or

(dd) to a terrorist organization described in clause (vi)(III), unless the actor can demonstrate that he did not know, and should not reasonably have known, that the act would further the organization's terrorist activity (emphasis added).

An alternative or a supplement to the Foreign Terrorist Organization designation is naming an organization or an individual as a Specially Designated Global Terrorist. The U.S. Department of the Treasury is in charge of naming a SDGT.

61. U.S. Department of State, Office of Counterterrorism, *Foreign Terrorist Organizations.*

62. James Tisch, "UNRWA's Hamas Problem," *Jerusalem Post,* December 18, 2004. The money comes from the United States Agency for International Development and from the U.S. State Department.

63. Malkin, "Ambulances."

64. Dov B. Fischer, "The Overseers of Jenin: What Exactly is the U.N. Doing in Its Refugee Camps (With Our Money)?" *Weekly Standard,* May 13, 2002, www.weeklystandard.com/content/public/articles/000/000/001/213cgjov.asp; David Meir-Levi, "Terrorism: The Root Causes," *FrontPageMagazine.com,* November 9, 2005, www.frontpagemag.com/Articles/ReadArticle.asp?ID=20117.

65. Yaakov Lappin, "UNRWA's shady donors," *Jerusalem Post*, November 23, 2004.

66. Ibid.

67. Ibid.

68. Ibid.

69. United Nations General Assembly, *Assistance to Palestine Refugees,* Resolution 302 (IV). A/RES/302(IV), December 8, 1949, www.eyeontheun.org/assets/attachments/documents/un_resolution_establishing_unrwa.doc.

70. Arlene Kushner, *The United Nations Relief and Works Agency for Palestine Refugees in the Near East: A Hard Look at an Agency in Trouble* (Brookline, Mass.: Center for Near East Policy Research, March 2005), israelbehindthenews. com/pdf/UNRWAReport-Consolidation.pdf. [Hereinafter "Kushner, *UNRWA.*"]

71. Anne Bayefsky, "U.N. vs. Israel," *National Review Online*, April 20, 2004.

72. Foreign Assistance Act of 1961 (as amended), Public Law 87-195, section 301(c): "No contributions by the United States shall be made to [UNRWA] except on the condition that [UNRWA] take all possible measures to assure that no part of the United States contribution shall be used to furnish assistance to any refugee who is receiving military training as a member of the so-called Palestine Liberation Army or any other guerilla type organization or who has engaged in any act of terrorism."

73. U.S. General Accounting Office, *Department of State and United Nations Relief and Works Agency Actions to Implement Section 301(c) of the Foreign Assistance Act of 1961*, GAO-04-276R-UNRWA (November 17, 2003), www.gao.gov/new.items/d04276r.pdf; James Tisch, "UNRWA's Hamas Problem," *Jerusalem Post*, December 18, 2004.

    For UNRWA offices in Lebanon, Syria, and Jordan, UNRWA does ask the host governments about whether job applicants have terrorist connections. GAO Report (Although it is hard to believe that Syria—or what was until recently the Syrian puppet regime in Lebanon was very interested in helping keeping terrorists off the U.N. payroll.) In the West Bank and Gaza, UNRWA does not even attempt to screen out terrorist employees. General Accounting Office, *Department of State and United Nations Relief and Works Agency Actions to Implement Section 301(c) of the Foreign Assistance Act of 1961*. UNRWA refuses to ask Israel for information about whether a potential employee is a terrorist. Arlene Kushner, "U.N. Dollars for Terror," *FrontPageMagazine.com*, August 18, 2004, www.frontpagemag.com/Articles/ReadArticle.asp?ID=14703.

    GAO reports UNRWA's excuse was that it staff would be endangered (e.g., killed by terrorists) if they attempted to screen out terrorists. Even if one believes that UNRWA would genuinely prefer to screen out terrorists, and is failing to do so solely because of the danger, the excuse does not give a reason for the U.S. government to keep funding UNRWA. As long as UNRWA money goes to Hamas, existing U.S. law forbids the transfer of foreign aid to UNRWA, if UNRWA is incapable of taking *any* steps to ensure that it does employ terrorists. It is long past time for the State Department and AID to fully abide by the law, and to stop giving money to UNRWA.

    The State Department does have 14 monitors at UNRWA offices, but these monitors have obviously not been successful in preventing UNRWA from hiring Hamas employees.

    Three members of Congress have called on the State Department to cut off U.S. taxpayer UNRWA funding until UNRWA stops employing Hamas members. Office of Rep. Jerrold Nadler, "Nadler Calls on Powell to Suspend Funding for UNRWA Until Terrorists are Removed from its Staff," Press Release (October 12, 2004), www.house.gov/apps/list/press/ny08_nadler/PowellUNRWA 101204. html.

74. Jonathan S. Tobin, "At U.N., No Division Between Aid and Terror," *israelinsider,* October 12, 2004. Hansen spoke to the CBC on October 4, 2004. Hansen claimed that the Hamas employees were not necessarily terrorists (even though Canadian and American laws state that *any* member of Hamas is a member of a terrorist organization).

75. General Accounting Office, *Department of State and United Nations Relief and Works Agency Actions to Implement Section 301(c) of the Foreign Assistance Act of 1961*; Tisch, "UNRWA's Hamas problem."

76. Kushner, "U.N. Dollars for Terror" (quoting Yoni Fighel, who formerly served as military governor in disputed territories).

77. Kushner, "U.N. Dollars for Terror"; Ehrenfeld and Lappen, "The U.N. Gives Hamas a Raise."

78. David Bedein, "How Can the U.N. Address the Subject of Palestinian Refugees and Not Allow Israel to Attend the Meeting?" *Israel Behind the News,* June 12, 2004, israelbehindthenews.com/#unrwa.

79. Ehrenfeld and Lappen, "The U.N. Gives Hamas a Raise."

80. Greg Myre, "Israel Feuds with Agency Set Up to Aid Palestinians," *New York Times,* October 18, 2004.

81. General Accounting Office, U.S. Department of State and United Nations Relief and Works Agency Actions to Implement Section 301(c) of the Foreign Assistance Act of 1961.

82. Ronen Bergman, *Authority Given* (Tel Aviv: Yedi'ot Aharonot, 2002) (Hebrew), 266, quoted in Henkin, "Urban Warfare and the Lessons of Jenin."

83. Isabel Kershner, "The Refugees' Choice?" *Jerusalem Report,* August 12, 2002 (quoting Peter Hansen's attachment to a letter that Kofi Annan sent to U.S. Rep. Tom Lantos).

84. Interview conducted by Jeff Arner and Sylvia Martin, October 1991, in the UNRWA West Bank Field Office in East Jerusalem, quoted in Kushner, *The United Nations Relief and Works Agency for Palestinian Refugees in the Near East: Links to Terrorism.*

85. Kushner, "U.N. Dollars for Terror" (confession of Ala'a Muhammad Ali Hassan, a terrorist sniper who was a member of the terrorist organization Tanzim, which is one of Yassir Arafat's groups); Herb Keinon, "Shin Bet Documents Terrorists' Misuse of UNRWA Facilities," *Jerusalem Post,* December 11, 2002.

86. Kushner, "U.N. Dollars for Terror." Kushner attended the conference, and observed Hansen's finger quotes.

87. Ibid. Hansen backtracked and said, "Well, there was one case." In fact, there have been many cases.

88. Kushner, *UNRWA.*

89. United Nations Security Council, Resolution 11267, S/Res/1267, October 15, 1999.

90. Anne Bayefsky, "U.N.derwhelming Response: The U.N.'s Approach to Terrorism," *National Review Online,* September 24, 2004, www.nationalreview.com/comment/bayefsky200409240915.asp.

91. Bayefsky, "U.N.derwhelming Response."

92. Thalif Deen, "The Most Elusive Word," *Inter Press Service News Agency,* December 1, 2005, www.ipsnews.org/news.asp?idnews=31267.

93. "U.N. Gives Up on Completing Anti-terrorism Treaty by Year-end," *Haaretz* (Reuters), December 1, 2005, www.haaretzdaily.com/hasen/spages/652457.html.

94. Ibid. There are plans to re-start negotiations in February 2006.

95. Muravchik, "The U.N.'s terrorism gap."

96. Deen, "The Most Elusive Word."

97. Ibid.

98. Ibid. (noting use of "state terrorism" language against U.S. and Israel).

99. Mark Steyn, "Let's give Iran some of its own medicine," London *Daily Telegraph* (January 17, 2006), www.telegraph.co.uk/opinion/main.jhtml?xml=/opinion/2006/01/17/do1702.xml (quoting advisor Hassan Abbassi).

100. IAEA Statute, arts. III.B.4, XII.C, www.iaea.org/About/statute_text.html.

101. Anne Bayefsky, "Doing Business with Iran: Top U.N. Officials Responsible for Nuclear Nonproliferation are Facilitating Iran's Acquisition of Nuclear Weapons," *National Review Online*, January 16, 2006, nationalreview.com/bayefsky/bayefsky200601161051.asp.

102. Benny Avni, "Terror Sponsors As Decision Makers," *New York Sun*, October 3, 2005.

103. Editorial, "The U.N.'s Latest," *New York Sun*, August 26, 2005.

104. Bayefsky, "U.N. vs. Israel," www.nationalreview.com/bayefsky/bayefsky200404200848.asp.

105. Ibid.

106. Ibid.

107. "UK Freezes Assets of 5 Hamas Leaders," *Rediff India Abroad*, March 25, 2004, us.rediff.com/news/2004/mar/25hamas.htm.

108. "Secretary-General Strongly Condemns Israel's Assassination of Hamas Leader, which Resulted in Deaths of Eight Others," *United Nations Information Service*, SG/SM/9210, March 23, 2004, www.unis.unvienna.org/unis/pressrels/2004/sgsm9210.html?print.

109. Bayefsky, "U.N. vs. Israel."

110. Ibid.

111. Ibid; Office of the High Commissioner for Human Rights, "Grave Situation in the Occupied Palestinian Territory," Commission on Human Rights Resolution: 2004/1, March 24, 2004, ap.ohchr.org/documents/E/CHR/resolutions/E-CN_4-RES-2004-1.doc.

112. Bayefsky, "U.N. vs. Israel."

113. "The U.N.'s Blinkers," *Globe and Mail* (Toronto), July 22, 2004.

114. International Court of Justice, "Legal Consequences of the Construction of a Wall in the Occupied Palestinian Territory," Advisory Opinion of July 9, 2004, www.icj-cij.org/icjwww/idocket/imwp/imwpframe.htm.

115. "The U.N.'s Blinkers."

116. United Nations International Meeting on the Question of Palestine, *Theme: Implementing the ICJ Advisory Opinion on the Legal Consequence of the Construction of a Wall in the Occupied Palestinian Territory—The Role of Governments, Intergovernmental Organizations and Civil Society*, United Nations Office at Geneva (March 8–9, 2005), domino.un.org/unispal.nsf/9a798adbf322aff38525617b006d88d7/bcb37133df60c4e085256fc400757804!OpenDocument.

117. Ruth Wisse, "The U.N.'s Jewish Problem: Anti-Semitism Has Found a Comfortable Home on the East River," *Weekly Standard*, April 8, 2002, weeklystandard.com/content/protected/articles/000/000/001/076zcpic.asp.

CHAPTER ELEVEN: Don't Trust Direct Democracy

1. Rubem Fernandes, director of NGO, Viva Rio, "Lessons from the Brazilian Referendum" (remarks, forum hosted by the World Council of Churches, New York, January 17).

2. Ibid.

3. "IANSA's 2004 Review—The Year in Small Arms," http://www.iansa.org/documents/2004/iansa_2004_wrap_up_revised.doc.

4. Monte Reel, Washington Post Foreign Service, "Brazil Weighs a National Gun Ban—Country Is First To Vote on Issue,"; *Washington Post,* October 1, 2005, A01.

5. "Brazilian Gun Referendum Approaches: A Historic Opportunity to Make People Safer from Gun Violence," IANSA, www.iansa.org/regions/samerica/brazil-referendum.htm (emphasis added).

6. Terry Crawford-Browne, "Follow Brazilian Lead and Close the Arms Industry," *Cape Times & Independent,* October 13, 2005, www.capetimes.co.za.

7. Karin Goodwin, "Brazil Makes History in Vote to Ban Sale of Guns," *Sunday Morning Herald* (Scotland), October 23, 2005, www.sundayherald.com/52406.

8. James O. E. Norell, "Victory in Brazil: A Talk with Luciano Rossi," America's 1st Freedom, January 2006.

9. List of IANSA members in North America available at http://www.iansa.org/about/members/namerica.htm.

10. Anton Foek, "Shot Down: Lobby Kills Brazil Gun Ban," *CorpWatch,* October 25, 2005, www.corpwatch.org.

11. Unsigned editorial, "Of Arms and Men," *Khaleej Times Online,* October 26, 2005, www.khaleejtimes.com (emphasis added).

12. Gwenne Dyer; "Gun Control Loses Yet Again," *Japan Times,* October 30, 2005, www.japantimes.co.jp.

13. David Morton; "Gunning for the World," *Foreign Affairs* (January/February 2006).

14. "Brazil . . . Strengthening of Communication Networks and International Partnerships; International Programme for the Development of Communication"; UNESCO Headquarters, Paris (March 2005), http://portal.unesco.org/ci/en/file_download.php/53d7121e58bd595db8571998a273f592Latin+America+and+Caribbean+2005++new+projects+approved+.pdf.

15. "Projects . . . Disarmament campaigns"; Viva Rio available at vivario.org.br.

16. James O. E. Norrell, "Victory in Brazil."

17. Anton Foek, "Shot Down."

18. Brazil: Most Crime Guns Start Out Legally, Says Report; IANSA.

19. The Statute Of Disarmament, Law no. 10,826/03 (December 2003), available at www.iansa.org/regions/samerica/documents/statute-of-disarmament.pdf

20. Juan Michel (WCC media relations officer), "To Disarm, Body and Soul: Brazilian Churches Participate in National Disarmament Campaign" World Council of Churches, May 2, 2005, http://www2.wcc-coe.org/pressreleasesen.nsf/index/Feat-05-13.html.

21. "Rio's 'Flame of Peace,'" *The Ploughshares Monitor,* Autumn 2003, vol. 24, no. 3, www.ploughshares.ca.

22. "IANSA's 2004 Review—The Year in Small Arms," available at the United Nations Non-Governmental Liason Service website at http://www.un-ngls.org/cso/cso6/cso6.htm.

23. "Anti-Gun Caravan Crisscrosses Brazil," *brazillnews.com,* Tuesday, October 26, 2004, www.brazzilmag.com/content/view/513/41/.

24. World Council of Churches International Affairs, Peace & Human Security Peacebuilding and Disarmament Programme, "Summary Report on the WCC's Microdisarmament Efforts 2000–2001," September 2001, www.wcc-coe.org/wcc/ what/international/summary.html.

25. "Fight for Peace Sports Centre—Alternatives for Youth to Crime, Drug Faction Employment and Armed Violence," *Viva Rio* (Rio de Janeiro), 2004.

26. Thierry Verhelst, "A New Type of NGO in Brazil," *Journal of Cultures and Development*, South North Network Cultures and Development, May 2000, available at www.networkcultures.net.

27. Adele Kirsten, "The Role of Social Movements in Gun Control: An International Comparison Between South Africa, Brazil and Australia," Center for Civil Society Research (Durban), Report no. 21, September 2004.

28. United Nations Non-Governmental Liaison Service, "Momentum Grows to Address Problems of Small Arms," NGLS Roundup no. 45, November 1999.

29. "Women in Brazil Take a Stand against Guns," *The Wire,* available at http://web. amnesty.org/wire/February2003/brazil.

30. Laura Lumpe, "The Regulation of Civilian Ownership and Use of Small Arms" (briefing paper in advance of the International Meeting of the Center for Humanitarian Dialogue, Rio de Janeiro, February 2005).

CHAPTER TWELVE: U.N. and the Internet

1. "U.N. to control use of Internet?" *World Net Daily,* February 22, 2006; available at http://worldnetdaily.com/news/article.asp?ARTICLE_ID=42982.

2. Aoife White, "EU Wants Shared Control of Internet," Associated Press, September 30, 2005.

3. Daniel Schearf, "China Again Tightens Control of Online News and Information," *Voice of America,* September 26, 2005, http://www.clearharmony.net/ arti-cles/200509/29033.html.

4. "China Charges U.S. Monopolizes the Internet, Seeks Global Control," *World Tribune.Com,* March 2, 200), http://www.worldtribune.com/worldtribune/ 05/breaking2453432.0569444443.html.

5. "Freedom of Expression and the Internet in China: A Human Rights Watch Backgrounder," *Human Rights Watch,* 2004, available at http://www.hrw.org/ backgrounder/asia/china-bck-0701.htm.

6. Ibid.

7. Congressional Human Rights Caucus Members Briefing, *Human Rights and the Internet—The People's Republic of China,* Testimony of Tom Malinowski, Washington Advocacy Director, Human Rights Watch, http://hrw.org/english/ docs/2006/02/02/china12595.htm.

8. ACLU, 521 US 844. (1997).

9. Daniel Howden., "On the Line, the Internet's Future," *The Independent* (UK), November 16, 2005.

10. "China Charges U.S. Monopolizes the Internet."

11. "China shuts down 47 'harmful' internet cafes," *The Scotsman* (March 3, 2005).

12. Patrick Moore; "China: Beijing's Own Goals," *Radio Free Europe/Radio Liberty,* November 8, 2005.

13. Patrick Moore, "China: Acting to Keep Out 'Harmful Information,'" *Radio Free Europe/Radio Liberty,* August 14, 2005.

14. Editorial, "Beijing's New Enforcer: Microsoft," *The New York Times*, November 17, 2006.

15. Patrick Moore, "China: Bullying the Bloggers," *Radio Free Europe/Radio Liberty*, September 29, 2005.

16. Carlos Ramos-Mrosovsky and Joseph Barilli, "World Wide (Web) Takeover: The United Nations wants the Internet," *National Review*, September 28, 2005.

17. "False Freedom: Online Censorship in the Middle East and North Africa: Syria," *Human Rights Watch*, available at http://hrw.org/reports/2005/mena 1105/6 htm.

18. "The Internet Under Surveillance," *Reporters Sans Frontiers*, available at www.rsf.org.

19. Gwynne Dyer, "The Spoilers and the Web," *The Evening Standard* (Palmerston North, New Zealand), November 18, 2005.

20. Rohan Jayasekera, "Tunisia; Violence, Repression & Censorship By Hosts Mar U.N. Information Society Summit," http://indexonline.org.

21. Pete du Pont, "Cease-Fire in Tunisia," *Wall Street Journal Opinion Journal*, www.opinionjournal.com [emphasis added].

22. Robert Mugabe, (speech, World Summit on the Information Society, Geneva, Switzerland, December 10, 2003), available at http://www.itu.int/wsis/geneva/coverage/statements/zimbabwe/zw.html.

23. U.S. Senate Subcommittee on Communications, Committee on Commerce, Science and Transportation, testimony of John M. R. Kneuer, Deputy Assistant Secretary for Communications and Information, September 30, 2004.

24. Michael D. Gallagr, assistant secretary at the National Telecommunications and Information Administration (NTIA), "U.S. Principles on the Internet's Domain Name and Addressing System," www.ntia.doc.gov.

25. "World summit Agrees on Status Quo for Internet Governance," http://usinfostate.gov/gi/Archive/2005/Nov/16-609244.html.

26. Ibid.

27. Tim Receveur, "Ambassador David Gross Participates in Video Webcast December 13," www.usinfo.state.gov.

28. "U.S. Official Calls for Stable, Free, Accessible Internet," http://usinfo.state.gov/gi/Archive/2005/Nov/19-134756.html.

29. Office of U. S. Sen. Norm Coleman (R-Minn.), "Senate Unanimously Passes Coleman Resolution to Maintain U.S. Oversight Role for Internet," available at http://coleman.senate.gov/index.cfm.

30. Kevin Diaz, "Norm Coleman, Annan Now Tangle over Web Name Control: The Senator Sees an Attack on Internet Openness, the U.N. Chief Wants to Close the Digital Divide," *Star Tribune* (Minneapolis), November 21, 2005.

31. Office of U.S. Rep. John T. Doolittle (R-Calif.), "Doolittle: Don't Hand the Internet Over to U.N.," http://www.house.gov/doolittle/press/press05/pr11-16-05.html.

Index

A

ABC, 56, 112-14
Achille Lauro, 179
Adams, Brad, 211
Afghanistan, 126, 165, 172, 180, 183
Africa, xv, xix-xx, 7, 10, 12-16, 21, 26, 31, 49, 106, 109, 127, 143-48, 151-54, 158, 161, 167, 174, 188, 200
Agricola Medal, 167
Ahmadinejad, Mahmoud, 180
airgun, xxiv
AK-47, 49, 146
Akashi, Yasushi, 92, 107
Al Aqsa Fund, 174
Al-Ashtal, Abdalla Saleh, 40
al-Hussein, Zeid, 112, 115
al-Najah University, 166
al-Qaeda, 162-63, 173, 179
Al Quds, 174
al-Rantissi, Abdel Aziz, 181-82
Alabama, 80
Alatas, Ali, 139
Albania, 96-97, 141, 185
Alonso, Joseph Bruce, 57
Alpers, 14, 103
Anglo-American law, 99, 156
Animal Farm, 35
American Academy of Arts and Sciences, 20
American Revolution, 138-39
Amin, Idi, 127
ammunition, xxvii-xxviii, 33, 41-42, 45, 48, 73, 79-80, 84-86, 93, 96, 101, 142, 145, 177, 187-88, 197
Amnesty, International, 13, 46, 66, 100, 108, 144-47, 203-4

Angola, 49-50
Annan, Kofi, xxiv, 47-48, 100, 105-6, 114-15, 117-23, 128-31, 136, 140, 163-64, 167-69, 171-72, 179-80, 182
Annan, Kojo, 119
Arab, xxx, 143-46, 153, 161-62, 173-74, 183-84, 190
Arafat, Yassir, 177-78
Arifi, Avni, 64, 109
Arkansas, xii, 83
Arusha, Tanzania, 33
Asia, xv, 23, 72, 126, 136, 158, 211
Ashcroft, General John, xvi, 28
Assad, Bashar, 121, 169
Atallah, Nahd Rashid, Ahmad, 172
Atkins v. Virginia, 57
Australia, 2, 4-8, 12-14, 21, 33, 43, 98-101, 103, 136, 141-42, 198, 201
Austria, 16, 22.
automatic firearms, xvi, 3, 6-7, 28, 41, 101, 146

B

Baghdad, 117
Bakan district, 95
Balkan peninsula, 131
Bangladesh, 115, 126
Barr, Bob, xvii
BBC, 93, 134, 162-63
Beijing, 211-13
Beirut, 168
Belarus, 180
Belgium, 11-12, 14, 128-31
Bengalis, 126
Berkol, Ilhan, 14

Berlin, 45

Bermuda, 43, 51

Bhattarai, Durga P., 47

Bill of Rights, iii, xxi, xxiv, xxvi, 17, 51 61-62, 72, 80, 87-88

Bin Laden, Osama, 162-63, 174, 183

Bloomberg School of Public Health, 8

Bolton, John, xvi-xix, 27, 32, 49

Bondi, Loretta, 14

Bosnia, 106-8, 111, 122-23, 126, 131-36, 140-41, 148, 154, 162

Bougainville, 98-104

Boutros-Ghali, Boutros, 22

Bradford University, 14, 24

Brady Campaign, 1, 190, 210

Brahimi, Lakhdar, 169

Brazil, xxviii-xxix, 13, 33, 58, 167, 187-205

Breyer, Stephen, 56

Britain, xxiv, xxvii, 4, 7, 21, 117, 154, 181, 184

British American Security Information Council (BASIC), 13

Brokaw, Tom, 210

Bromley, Sandra, 41

Brown Journal of World Affairs, 31

Brown, Mark Malloch, 172

Browne, Roland, 8

Buchanan, Cate, 14

Budapest, 216

Bulgaria, 106-7, 126

Bunia, Congo, 111, 114

Bureau of Alcohol, Tobacco, and Firearms (BATF), 81-82, 89

Bush, George W., xii-xiv, xvi, xviii, 32, 53, 88, 143, 167, 217-18, 220

Buwalda, John, 97

C

Cain, Kenneth, 115

Cairo, 32-33

California, xvii, 23, 43, 99

Cambodia, 91-95, 106-7, 115, 123, 126, 185

Cambridge, 20, 24

Canada, xvii, xx, 4, 12-14, 16, 21, 26, 33, 43-44, 49, 51, 58, 197-98

Canadian Broadcasting Corporation (CBC), 175

Capitol Hill, xv

carbines, 40, 42

Castro, Fidel, 50, 167-68, 183, 214

Center for Gun Policy and Research, 8

Central African Republic, 167

Central Intelligence Agency (CIA), 168

Centre for Humanitarian Dialogue (CHD), 12-14

Chad, 167

Charter of the United Nations, 34, 132

Cheka, 76

China, xxx, 4, 35, 36, 44-47, 99, 118, 126, 161, 181-83, 185, 200, 207-9, 211-15

Christian Science Monitor, 105, 109

Christians, 127, 143, 154, 185

Churchill, Winston, xxx

Civil Rights Act of 1866, 63, 68, 70

Civil Rights Act of 1964, 56, 63

Civil Rights Bill, 63, 65, 67-70

Civil War, 62, 66, 72,

Clinton administration, xi-xii, xxvii, 23, 53, 83, 130

Clinton, Bill, 23, 53-54, 111, 122

Clinton, Hillary, 55

CNN, 2, 20

Coalition to Stop Gun Violence, 19

Coleman, Norm, 219-20

Cold War, 19-20

Columbia, 26

Columbine, 21

Commission on Human Rights, United Nations, xxix-xxx, 128, 181-82

Committee on the Rights of a child, 55

Communist Party U.S.A., 11

Confucius, 185

Congo, 106, 110-15, 120, 131, 141, 151-52, 167

Congress of the United States, xi, xvi, 10, 14, 27, 44, 54-55, 61-63, 65, 67, 70-76, 78, 81-89, 118, 164, 175, 190, 203, 207, 210-11, 219

Connor, Joseph, 171

Constitution, xii-xiii, xvii, xxii, xxiv-xxv, 16-17, 30, 50, 53, 56-57, 61-72, 76-89, 102, 191

Conte, Lansana, 153

Convention Against the Illicit Traffic in Narcotic Drugs and Psychoactive Substances, 46

Convention on Genocide, 135

Convention on the Elimination of all

Index

Forms of Discrimination Against Women, 54-55
Convention on the Rights of the Child, 55
Conzinc Riotinto, 99
Cote d'Ivoire, 167
Cotecna, 119
Counter-Terrorism Committee (CTC), 179
Crawford-Browne, Terry, 188
Croatia, 131, 132
Cuba, xxx, 4, 50, 161, 168, 180, 214
Cukier, Wendy, 14
Cyprus, 164
Czechoslovakia, 126

D
Dallaire, Romeo, 128-31
Declaration of Independence, 50-51
Delaware, 215
Deloitte Consulting, 120, 122
Democratic Republic of the Congo, 106, 110, 113, 151, 167
Democrats, 54, 75, 77, 79
Denmark, 12-13
Department for Disarmament Affairs, 11, 22-23, 27, 96
Department of Defense, xv, 84, 145
Department of State, xv, xvii, 36, 145-46, 218
Dhanapala, Jayantha, 96
Diana (Princess), 21
Domain Name and Addressing System (DNS), 218, 220
Donowaki, Mitsuro, 23-24
Doolittle, John, 220
du Pont, Pete, 215
Dunblane, Scotland, 7, 21
Dunnigan, James F., 139
Dyer, Gwynne, 215

E
East Timor, 106, 126, 136-42
Economic Community of West African States (ECOWAS), 15, 152-54, 158
Economists Allied for Arms Reduction, 188
Ecumenical Network on Small Arms (ENSA), 199
Egeland, Jan, 145
Egypt, 32, 165, 174

Eisen, Joanne, 155, 159
El Baradei, Mohammad, 165
Eliot, Thomas, 64, 68-69
Eminent Persons Group, 42, 44
Enforcement Clause (Fourteenth Amendment), 86
England, 51, 180, 182, 185, 198, 201
Eritrea, 108, 151, 167
Ethiopia, 108, 127
ethnic cleansing, 134, 137, 144
Europe, xxii, xxvii, 15, 31, 36, 41, 43, 47, 57, 72, 93, 108, 126, 134, 156, 166, 180, 212, 216
European Convention on Human Rights, 156
European Institute for Crime Prevention and Control, 41, 47
European Union (E.U.), xxvii, 15, 36, 57, 93, 166, 177, 180, 207

F
Fadlallah, Mohamed Hussein, 169
Fagan, Patrick, 54
Falintil, 138-42
Feinstein, Dianne, 39, 42
Fernandes, Rubem, 187
Finland, 12, 16
Firearm Owners' Protection Act, 82-83
Firearms Protocol, 15, 22, 32-36
First Amendment, xvi, 28, 72, 207, 210, 216
Florida, xii, 53, 56, 69, 88
Food and Agricultural Organization (FAO), 166-67
Foreign Terrorist Organization (FTO), 173, 175-76
Foundation for International Dignity, 122
Founding Fathers, xxiv, 139, 185
Fourteenth Amendment, 56, 63, 68-70, 72, 83, 86-87
Fourth Amendment, xvi, 28, 58, 82, 84
France, 12, 16, 73-74, 118, 184
Freedmen's Bureau Act, 62-71, 88
Frist, Bill, 87
Frye, Barbara 11, 58-59, 141
Funders' Collaborative for Gun Violence Prevention, 8

G
Galloway, George, 118

271

INDEX

Garauday, 168

Gaza, 166, 171-73, 177

Gbarnga, Liberia, 110

General Assembly, 23-24, 39, 85, 125, 167, 181

Geneva, Switzerland, 12, 100, 199, 214

genocide, ix-x, 2, 4, 11, 19, 46, 48-49, 59, 73, 91, 94-95, 98, 100, 122, 125, 127-31, 133-43, 145, 147-49, 151-59, 162, 166-67, 181

Germany, 13, 16, 45-46, 51, 73-74, 76, 121, 184

Gestapo, 76

Ghana, 109

Ginsburg, Ruth Bader, 56

global gun ban, xi-xii, xviii, xxvi, xxviii-xxix, 6-7, 9, 16-17, 19, 43, 149, 158, 172, 188, 202

Goebbels, Josef, 45, 73

Goff, Phil, 102

Gore, Al, xi-xii, 32, 53

Graduate Institute of International Studies, 12, 43

Gramsch, 96

Greece, 97, 185, 217

Greene, Owen, 14, 24

grenade launcher, 41, 101

Grey, Simon, xxvii

Groupe de Recherché et et d'Information sur la Paix et la Sécurite (GRIP), 13-14

Grutter v. Bollinger, 56

Guangxi High People's Court, 46

Guardian, 195

Guevara, Che, 167

Guinea, 110, 153, 167

Gulf War, 116, 181

gun-ban treaty, xvii, xxv

gun confiscation, xv, xxii-xxiii, xxv, 5-6, 21, 43-44, 81, 93, 96, 98, 142, 166, 188, 190, 198, 201, 203

Gun Control Act, 17, 44, 81-82, 85, 89

gun prohibition, ix, xix, 1, 4, 10, 19, 25, 30, 40-43, 45-48, 50-51, 55, 57-59, 63, 65, 73-75, 80-81, 83-84, 86-89, 91, 93, 95, 97, 99, 101, 103, 141, 146-47, 149, 151-52, 154-55, 158, 185, 187-88, 201

Gusmao, Kay Rala, Xanana, 137, 139

H

Habyarimana, Juvenal, 127-28

Hague, The, 135

Haiti, 111, 167

Hall, Edwin Arthur, 75

Hamas, 162, 166, 171-76, 178, 181-83

Harare, Zimbabwe, 166

Hattori, Yoshihiro, 22-23

HELP Network, 190

Herzegovina, 126, 131-32, 136

Hezbollah, 168-71, 180, 183

Higgins, William, R., 168

High Commissioner for Refugees, 110, 165

Himmler, Heinrich, 73

Hindus, 126

Hitler, Adolph, 73, 76, 79, 125, 144, 184

Hobbes, Thomas, 4

Horn of Africa, 151

House Committee on Military Affairs, 75

House International Relations Committee, 108, 117, 119

House of Representatives, 64-65, 67-70, 119, 171

Human Rights Commission, 58, 129, 182, 220

Human Rights Watch, 87, 145-46, 154, 208, 211, 214

Hurricane Katrina, xxiii, 185

Hussein, Saddam, 48, 105, 116-17, 164, 167, 178, 181, 183

Hutus, 127-31

I

IHC Services, 121

Independent, 108, 113

India, 22, 33, 56, 70, 170, 183

Indonesia, 126, 137-41, 144

Institute for Security Studies (ISS), 13

Institute for the Study of Genocide, 143, 147-48

interahamwe, 128-29

International Action Network on Small Arms (IANSA), xv, xxiv, xxvi, 1-2, 11-14, 58-59, 141, 147, 154, 185, 188-89, 197-99, 201-2, 217

International Atomic Energy Agency (IAEA), 180, 185

International Convention for the

Index

Suppression of Terrorist Bombing, 178

International Convention for the Suppression of the Financing of Terrorism, 178

International Court of Justice (I.C.J.), 133

International Criminal Court, 58, 94, 135, 148, 156

International Criminal Tribunal for the Former Yugoslavia (ICTY), 135

International Drug Control Programme report, 83

International Gun Destruction Day, 198

international law, 1, 57-58, 125, 145, 155, 158, 182-83

International Meeting on the Question of Palestine, 183

International Monetary Fund (IMF), 165

International Society for the Prevention of Crime, 157

International Telecommunications Union, United Nations (ITU), 214

International Year for Culture and Peace, 202

Internet, 20, 207-21

Internet Corporation for Assigned Names and Numbers (ICANN), 217-18, 220

Iran, 4, 48-49, 161, 165, 178, 180-81, 185

Iraq, 48, 105, 116-18, 120, 163-65, 167, 172, 180-81, 216

Islamic African Relief Agency (IARA), 174

Islamic Development Bank, 174

Islamic Jihad, 176, 183

Israel, 58, 166, 169-77, 180-85

Italy, 16, 73, 106

Ivory Coast, 153

Izetbegovic, 132

J

Jackson, Robert H., 74

Jakarta, 139-41

Jamaica, 40, 43, 56

Janjaweed, 144-48

Japan, xviii, 12-13, 16, 22-24, 26, 31-33, 62, 72-73, 81, 94, 98

Japan Times, 191

Jefferson, Thomas, 51

Jerusalem, 172-74, 177

Jett, Dennis, 154

Jews, 4, 45, 46, 73, 181, 184-85

Jiuyong, Shi, 182

John D. and Catherine T. MacArthur Foundation, 11

Johns Hopkins University, 8, 14

Johnson, Andrew, 67, 81

Jordan, 106, 112, 115

Julian, George W., 69

Justice and Equality Movement (JEM), 144

Justice Foundation, 8

K

Kampuchea, 91

Kapila, Mukesh, 147-48

Karp, Aaron, 31

Kelly, Mark, 142

Kendal, Wallis, 41

Kentucky, 65, 69, 77, 87

Kenya, 15, 151

Kerry, John, 53, 164-65

Khadaffi, Moammar, 168

Khaleej Times, 190

Khartoum, 143-48

Kheng, Sar, 93

Khmer Rouge, 91-92, 95, 126

Kilday, Paul, 75, 78-79

King's College, xxiv, 1, 6, 11

Kirsten, Adele, 7, 14, 200-4

Kok, Wim, 135

Kopel, David, vii, xviii, 20, 155, 159

Kosovo, 106, 108-9, 131, 141

Kosumi, Bajram, 109

Kurds, 48, 126

Kuwait, 116, 153

L

Lagos, 154

land mine treaty, xi, 20-21

Laogai Research Foundation, 47

Latin America, xv, xxix

Lauterpacht, Elihu, 133

Lawrence, Edward J., 23

Lawrence, William, 66

Lebanon, 121, 168-70, 174

Liberal Party (Canada), 44

Liberation, 215

Liberia, 109-10, 141, 153, 167

INDEX

Liberian Action Network on Small Arms (LANSA), 12
Libya, 161, 165, 174, 220
light weapons/arms, xi, xiii-xvii, xix, xxii, 11, 20, 27-31, 39, 41, 45, 47-48, 50, 93, 97, 131, 144, 151, 158
Liria, Yauka Aluambo, 101
Lisbon, 137
Little, Allan, 134
Ljubljana, 33
London, xxiv, 1, 11, 98, 181, 195, 211
Lula da Silva, Luiz Inácio, 167, 190-91
Lumpe, Lora, 14

M

Macedonia, 131-32
machine guns, xiii, xvi, 28, 41-42, 74, 101, 129
Malinowski, 208
Maubere, 137
May, A.J., 77
McConnell, Mitch, 87
McNamara, Robert, 42
Meddings, David, 92
Meek, Sarah, 14
Mehlis, Detlev, 121
Merimee, Jean-Bernard, 118
Mexico, 53
Michigan, 68, 81, 88
Microsoft, 211-13
Million Mom March, 190
Milosevic, Slobodan, 131-32, 135
Minnesota, 11, 58, 141
Mission of the U.N. in the Democratic Republic of the Congo (MONUC), 113
Mississippi, 67
Missouri, 88
Moisiu, Alfred, 97
Moldova, 108
Mondale, Walter, 23
Montenegro, 131-32
Monterey Institute, 14, 23
Montreal, 21
Morocco, 113, 115
Morton, David, 192
Mother's Day, 54-55
Mount Dov, 170
Mozambique, 106, 108
Mugabe, Robert, 56, 166, 216

Muslims, 132-35, 143, 153
Muwafaq, 162

N

Nairobi Small Arms Protocol, 15, 151-52
National Coalition for Gun Control, 8
National Review, xviii
National Rifle Association (NRA), xii, xxiii, 2, 16, 27, 31-33, 41, 47, 53, 55, 75, 81, 185, 189, 191, 196, 210
NATO, 132, 134, 147
Nazi, 4, 43, 46, 51, 73, 81, 138
NBC, 210
Nebraska, 107
Nepal, xxx, 47
Netherlands, 11-13
Netherlands Institute for War Documentation, 135
New Guinea, 98, 101-2
New York City, xiii, xxvi, 8, 11, 22, 43, 59, 128-30, 187
New York Evening Post, 68,
New York Sun, 113, 121
New York Times, 73, 141, 165, 213
New Zealand, 102, 115, 123, 242,
NewsMax.com, xviii, xx-xxi
Nigeria, 109, 153-54
Nigeria Action Network on Small Arms, 12
Night of the Broken Glass, 73
Nobel Peace Prize, 20-21, 122-23, 136
non-governmental organizations (NGO), xi, xiv-xv, xvii-xviii, xxiv, xxvii-xxviii, 2, 11-14, 16, 19-22, 26-27, 29, 30-32, 44-45, 47, 49-50, 58, 93, 106, 110-15, 120, 131, 141-42, 151-52, 162, 167, 187, 197-200, 203-4
North Korea, 4, 58, 126, 178, 180
Norway, 11-14
Nowak, Manfred, 181

O

Observer Group Lebanon (OGL), 170
O'Connor, Stephanie, 92
Office for Iraqi Programmes, 163
Office on Drugs and Crime, 22, 32, 46
Offices of Oversight Services (OSIS), 113-14
Oil-for-Food program (OFFP), 105, 116-20, 122, 148, 163-65, 167, 171
Ona, Francis, 100-1, 103

Onaiyekan, Olorenfemi, 154
Open Society, 8, 172
Organization for Security and Cooperation in Europe (OSCE), 15
Organization of American States (OAS), xxvii, 15, 34
Orwell, George, 35
Ottawa Treaty, 21
OXFAM, xxvii, 13

P
Pagtakhan, Rey, 40
Pakistan, 109, 115, 126, 162, 180
Palestine, 118, 166, 171-75
Pashayan, xvii-xviii, xx-xxi, 39
Patterson, Robert P., 75, 77, 79-80
Peters, Rebecca, xxiv-xxviii, 1-10, 14, 59, 147, 188-89, 191, 197, 200, 221
Philippines, 43, 162
Ploughshares, 11, 13, 198
Pol Pot, 91
Port Arthur, 6-8, 21, 201
Portugal, 50, 137
Programme of Action, xxi, xxiii, 8, 22, 25, 27, 29, 41, 44, 49, 93, 97, 163
Property Requisition Act, 72, 81
Protection of Lawful Commerce in Arms Act (PLCAA), 84, 86-88

R
Reagan, Ronald, 19, 83
Remington, 6
Revolutionary United Front (RUF), 154
Reyes, Camillo, xix
Rio de Janeiro, 13, 194-95, 201-4
Rio Tinto, 98-99
Riza, S. Iqbal, 118, 129
Robinson, Tommy, 83
Romania, 108, 126
Rossett, Claudia, 121
Rossi, Luciano, 189-90, 193, 195-96
Ruak, Taur Matan, 142
Rubin, Gail, 166
Rubin, Samuel, 11
Rufino, Santos, 49-50
Ruger, 6
Rummel, R. J., 125, 127
Russia, xxx, 73, 76, 79, 118, 134, 161, 164, 167, 181

Rwanda, 9, 100, 127-31, 133-34, 141, 147, 151, 153-54
Ryerson University, 14

S
Santorum, Rick, 87
Saudi Arabia, xxx, 162, 173-74, 183
Schwarz, Joe, 88
Second Amendment, vii, ix, xi, xiii, xvi, 1, 4, 23, 28, 32, 39, 42, 51, 53, 55-57, 59, 61-63, 65, 67, 69-89, 210, 221
Security Council (UNSC), 29-30, 115, 118, 130, 132-35, 142, 147-48, 161, 164, 168-69, 179-81
semiautomatic weapon, 3, 6-7, 20, 41, 152
Senate, xxvii-xxviii, 1, 53-55, 63, 65, 67-70, 75, 77, 82, 87, 219
Serbs (Serbia), 12, 131-36, 148
Sevan, Benon V., 117, 119, 164
Short, Dewey, 78
Silent March, xiv, 49
Slovenia, 33, 131-32
Somalia, 106, 162, 167
Soros, George, 1, 8-9, 172, 191, 221
South Africa, 10, 13-15, 21, 200
South America, 26, 198
Soviet Union, 19, 43, 51, 126, 190
Sparkman, John J., 80
Srebrenica, 131, 134-36
Straw, Jack, xxvii
Sudan, xxx, 58, 142-49, 151, 161-63, 165, 167
Sumner, Charles, 63
Supreme Court, xii, 56-57, 62, 74, 85, 156, 209, 216
Sweden, 11-14, 32, 43, 123, 200
Swing, Lacy, 67, 111, 113-15, 174
Switzerland, xvii, 12-14, 16, 214
Symms, Steve, 83

T
Taiwan, xix, 183
Taliban, 165, 167, 172, 179, 183
Tanzania, 33, 151, 167
Tehran, 180
Tennessee, xii, 53, 87
terrorism, x, 10, 19, 43-44, 91, 105, 118, 120, 139-40, 143-44, 153-54, 161-85, 188, 211, 216

INDEX

Texas, 75, 77-79, 87
Third World, 36, 44, 48, 146, 158, 165
Tiananmen Square, 99
Togo national network, 12
Transnational Organized Convention, 33
Trumbull, Lyman, 63, 65, 67, 70
Tutsi, 127-31
Tuzla, 135

U
Uganda, 127, 151, 167
U.N. Development Program (UNDP), 97, 172-73
U.N. Educational, Scientific, and Cultural Organization (UNESCO), 193, 197, 199-200, 202
U.N. Interim Force in Lebanon (UNFIL), 169-70
U.N. Relief and Works Agency (UNRWA), 171-78
U.N. Transitional Authority in Cambodia (UNTAC), 92
U.N. Transitional Authority in East Timor (UNTAET), 142
U.N. Truce Supervision Organization (UNTSO), 170
UNICEF, 106, 200
United Kingdom (U.K.), 11-14, 16, 21, 43, 197, 200, 216
Universal Declaration of Human Rights, 95, 98, 103, 116, 149, 155-56
University of Bradford, 14, 24
University of Hawaii, 125
University of Minnesota, 11, 58, 141

V
Van Leer Jerusalem Institute, 177
Verille, Elizabeth, 36
Vienna, 22, 32, 36, 55, 180
Vietnam, 11, 42, 91, 126
Viva Rio, 58, 187, 193-94, 198-203, 205
Vojvodina, 131
Volker Commission, 164
Volker, Paul, 119
Völkischer Beobachter, 45

W
Wall Street Journal, 121, 215
Warden's Court, 99

Washington D.C., xvii, 79, 139
Washington Post, 106, 110, 122, 188
Wassenaar Arrangement, 28
Weapons in Exchange for Development program (WED), 96-97
Weapons of Mass Destruction (WMD), xxv, 116-18
Weekly Standard, 164
Weiss, Cora, 11
West Africa, 106, 109, 152-53,158
West Bank, 173, 177, 183
West Pakistan, 126
West Timor, 137
West Virginia, 53
Wheeler, Samuel, 158
White House, 167, 219
Whiteman, Burchell, 40
Whittlesey, Faith, xvii, 49
Winchester, 6
Wire, 203
Working Group for Weapons Reduction in Cambodia (WGWR), 94
World Bank, 42, 137, 165, 166, 178, 183
World Council of Churches, 187, 199
World Forum on the Future of Sport Shooting Activities (WFSA), 16, 44
World Summit of Information Society (WSIS), 214-15, 219
World War I, 40
World War II, 40, 48, 62, 72-73, 81, 101, 125, 134
World Wide Web, 209, 219
World Without Zionism, 180
Wu, Harry, 47

Y
Yahoo, 212-13
Yakovlev, 120
Yassin, Ahmad, 181-82
Yemen, 40
Yugoslavia, 126, 131-135
Zhao, Houlin, 214
Zhao Jing, 213
Zhirinovsky, Vladimir, 118
Ziegler, Jean, 167-68
Zimbabwe, xxx, 56, 58, 152, 166, 216
Zionism, 180-81